CHILDREN'S CONCISE SCIENCE ENCYCLOPEDIA

General Editor: Neil Grant
House Editors: Brenda Apsley and John Malam
Consultant: Dr Norman Stein, University of Lancaster
Art Direction, Design and Layout: Bob Swan
Typesetting: Hilary Edwards-Malam
Index: Ian Horn

Artists
Andrew Calvert
Ray Hutchins
Paul Adams/Image Directory
Alan Raine

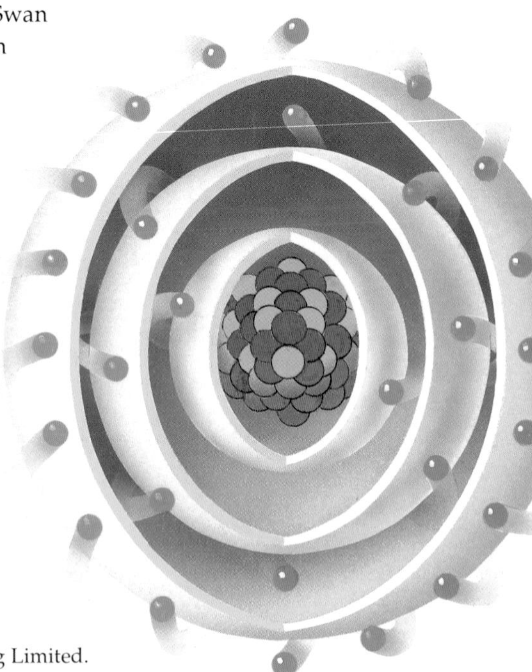

Published in Great Britain by World International Publishing Limited,
An Egmont Company, Egmont House, PO Box 111,
Great Ducie Street, Manchester M60 3BL.

ISBN 0-7498-0339-8

Printed in Singapore

World Horizons is an imprint of World International Publishing Ltd.

A catalogue record for this book is available from the British Library

CHILDREN'S CONCISE SCIENCE ENCYCLOPEDIA

LIONEL BENDER

Contents

Manufacturing Industry

Sky and the Cosmos

Measuring and Analysis

Communications

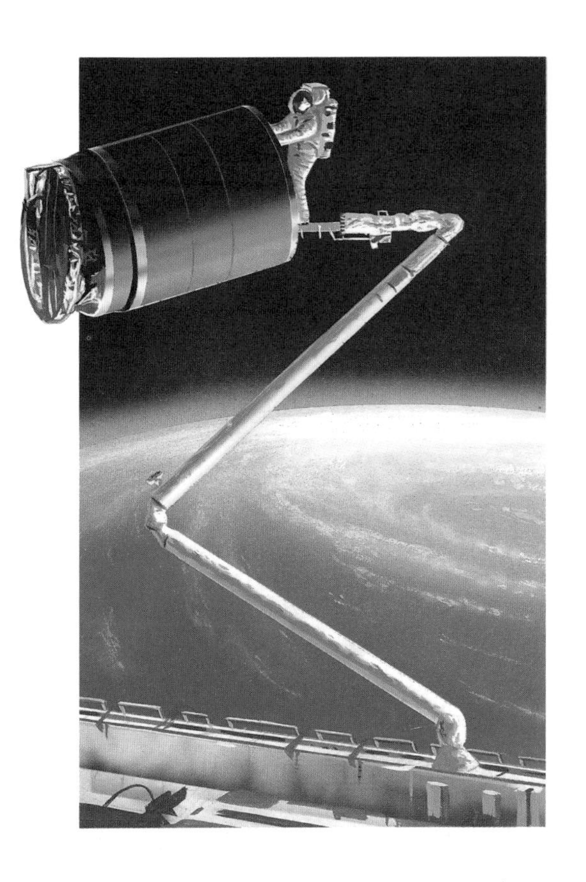

Introduction

The word science comes from a Latin word meaning 'knowledge'. Nowadays, it means only certain kinds of knowledge, but even so, scientific knowledge covers an enormous area, from the laws of maths to the life of a star. Our world today is dominated more than ever before by science and technology, which means all the practical uses to which scientific knowledge is put, whether it is making pottery from clay or producing power by nuclear fission.

Scientific knowledge and technology have been developing fast for the past 500 years, and today the speed of change is greater than ever. Take computers, for example. The first successful electronic computer was made in the 1940s. It required more than 150,000 watts of electricity to power its circuits, which contained about 18,000 valves. It filled a large room and weighed several tonnes. Today, computers can be powered from the mains or by a battery and can fit on a desk top or in a briefcase. They are no longer confined to large scientific laboratories or government offices, but appear in almost every part of everyday life, from supermarket shopping and school lessons to video games or running a small business.

This encyclopedia explains the basic laws and principles of matter and energy – the sciences of physics and chemistry – and shows how these are applied to modern technology.

The first section describes the relationships between force, energy and power. By looking at gears, levers and mechanics, for example, we understand how motor cars, aeroplanes and ships work, and there are further sections on engineering and transport. The science and technology of making such things as glass, bricks, rubber tyres or petrol – the man-made products on which our everyday lives depend – are described in a separate section.

Under Sky and the Cosmos, we find out about the planets, stars and the universe, and how this subject can teach us about the history and nature of our own planet, the Earth. Methods of scientific measurement and analysis, which are vital parts of all scientific work, receive special emphasis in this encyclopedia, along with – the final section – Communications, or the science of conveying information. This is the most rapidly developing subject in modern technology and the one that has the most impact on our daily lives.

To find out the subjects in each of the main sections of this encyclopedia, you can look at the Contents. At the end of each section you will find a page of references, which contains difficult words and ideas not explained in the main text. If you want to find out a particular fact, the first place to look is the Index, which gives the numbers of all relevant pages.

Matter and Materials

Atoms and Molecules

Everything in the universe is made up of tiny particles, or bits of matter, called atoms. Atoms are very small. If 10 million atoms were placed side by side, the whole lot would measure less than one millimetre across. In most substances atoms join together to form groups called molecules. Most molecules are made up of small numbers of atoms but some contain many hundreds or even thousands.

Inside the atom
In each atom there is a tiny but heavy central part, called the nucleus. The nucleus contains particles called protons and (except in hydrogen atoms) neutrons. Circling around the nucleus, there are much lighter particles called electrons.

Each electron has an electric charge – it carries a tiny amount of electricity. The protons in the nucleus have an electric charge too, but they carry a different kind of electricity. The protons have a positive charge, while the electrons have a negative charge. Neutrons have no electric charge.

Electron shells
The paths, or orbits, of the electrons circling around the nucleus make up a series of layers, like the layers of an onion. Each layer, or shell, can hold a certain number of electrons. The shell nearest the nucleus can hold two electrons, the second shell can hold eight electrons, and so on.

A shell that holds eight electrons is very stable (difficult to disrupt). For this reason, substances such as neon, which have atoms with eight electrons in the outer shell, do not react easily with other substances. Other atoms can achieve a stable outer shell either by sharing electrons with other atoms, or by gaining and losing electrons.

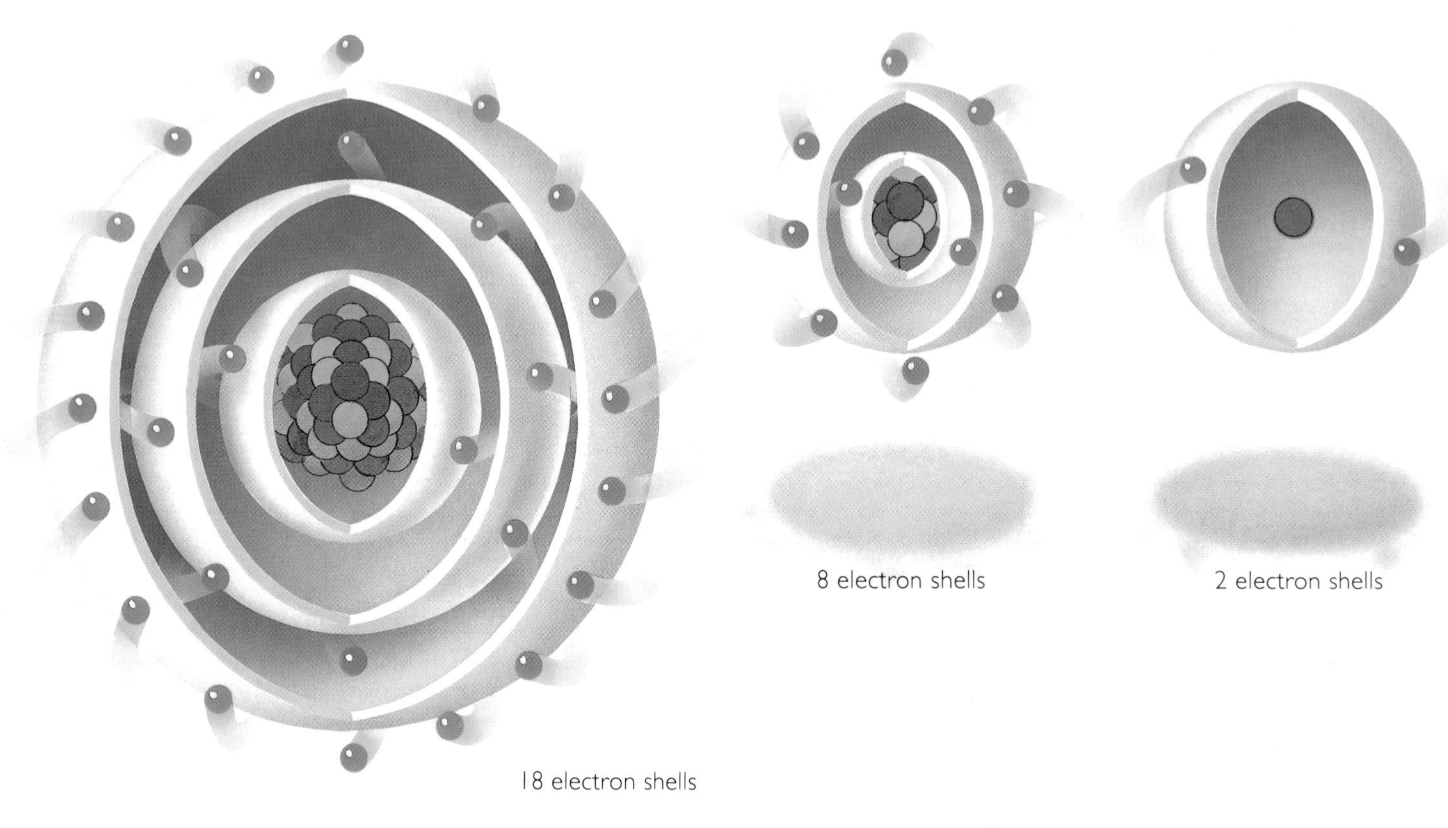

Representations of the three innermost electron shells of atoms. The first shell holds two electrons (right)*, the next shell eight* (middle) *and the third shell eighteen* (left).

QUARKS

In modern experiments, beams of high-energy particles probe inside the protons and neutrons themselves. These experiments show that protons and neutrons contain even smaller particles which are called quarks. Protons and neutrons each contain three quarks.

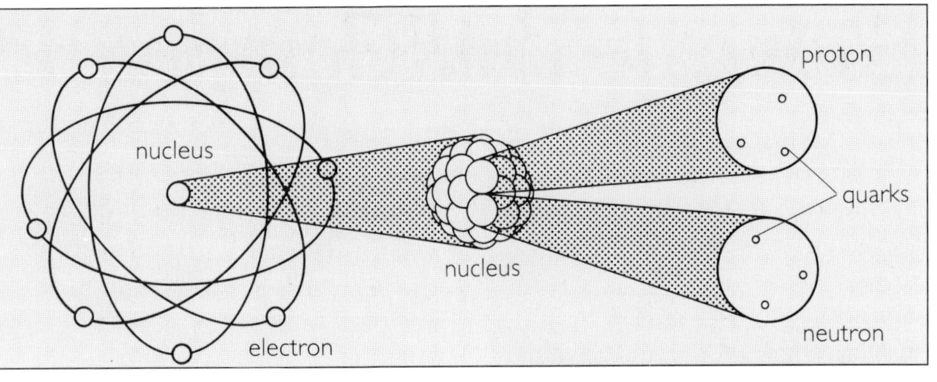

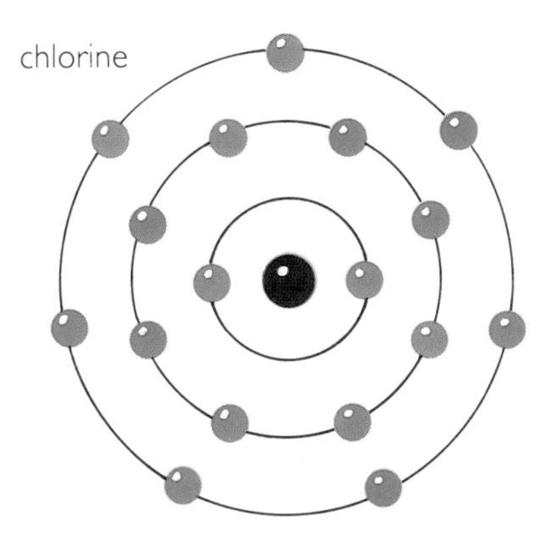

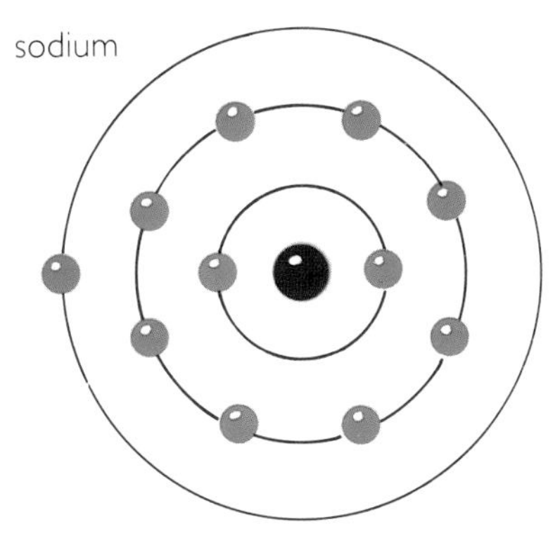

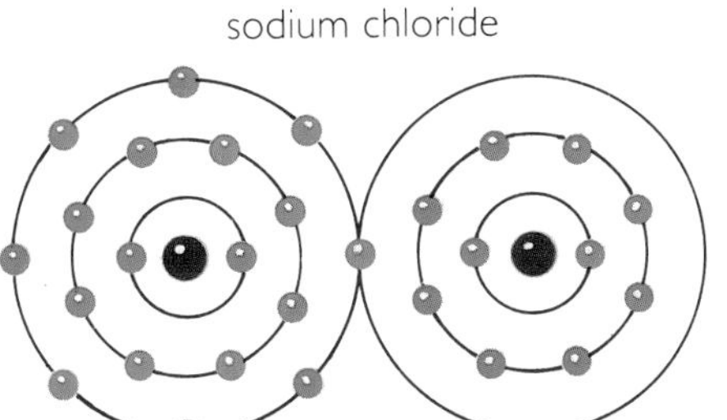

Above: *Ionic bonding, as between atoms in a molecule of common salt (sodium chloride).* Below: *Covalent bonding, as in a molecule of chlorine gas.*

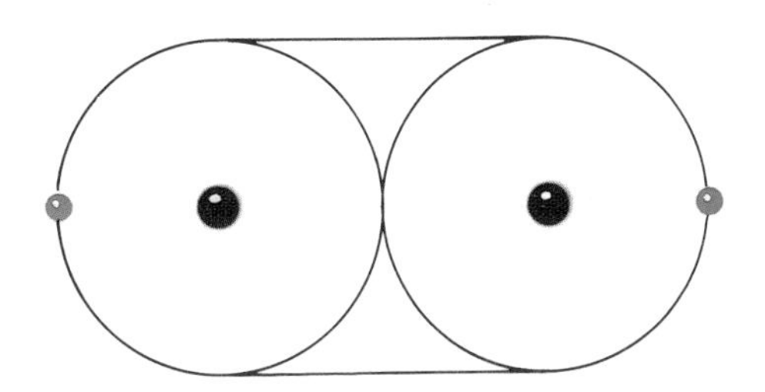

Forming molecules

Molecules are formed when atoms come together in order to share or swap electrons. A sodium atom, for example, can join with a chlorine atom by swapping an electron: an electron from the sodium atom transfers to the chlorine atom. The transfer produces an outer shell of eight electrons on both atoms. But the transfer also produces electric charges on the atoms, which bond the atoms together. This kind of bond is called an ionic bond.

Another kind of bond, the covalent bond, forms between atoms of chlorine. Chlorine atoms normally have seven electrons in their outer shell. However, if two chlorine atoms come together, a pair of electrons, one from each atom, can be shared. This arrangement completes the outer shell of each atom and forms a stable molecule of two chlorine atoms.

ATOMIC NUMBER

The number of protons in the nucleus usually equals the number of electrons circling the nucleus, so that the atom has no overall electric charge. The number of protons in the nucleus of an atom is called the atomic number.

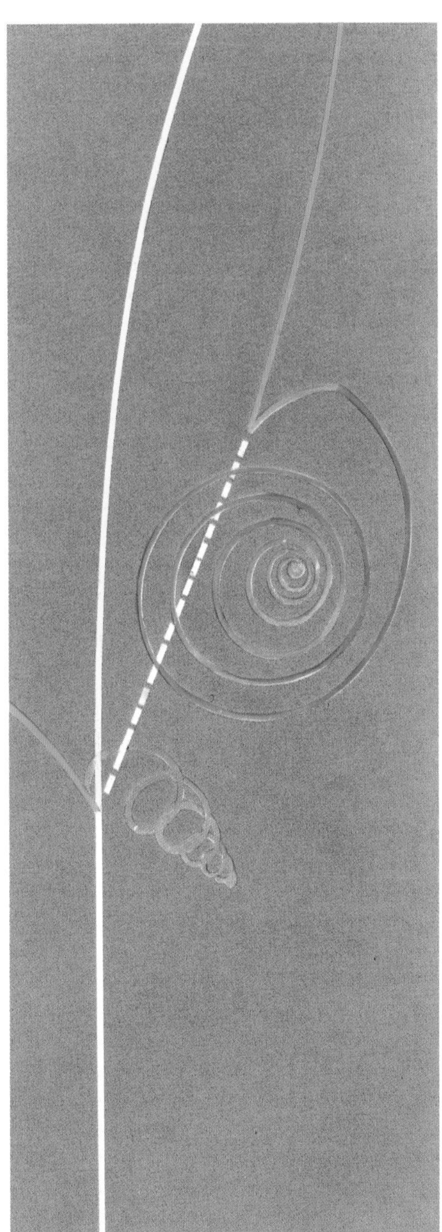

Above: *Beams of electrons bombarding an atomic nucleus reveal its component particles. As each negatively-charged electron passes through the nucleus, it leaves a trail of electricity which indicates the type of particle in its way.*

Elements and Compounds

Every substance in the universe is either an element or a compound. An element is a substance that is made up of one kind of atom. There are just over 100 known elements. When two or more elements combine as the result of a chemical reaction, atoms of the elements join together to form molecules, and a compound is produced. A compound is a substance made up of different kinds of atoms joined together into molecules.

Compounds have very different properties from those of the elements that make them up. For example, sodium is a metal which burns when it touches water, and chlorine is a poisonous yellow gas. Yet these two elements are combined in a compound that is much less startling – common salt.

The Periodic Table

When the elements are listed in order of their atomic number, elements with similar properties are found at definite points in the list. It is possible to draw a table or diagram, called the Periodic Table, which shows these similarities.

In the Periodic Table elements with similar properties are found in the vertical columns. For example, helium, neon, argon, krypton, xenon and radon are found in the column on the right. All these gases are rather alike. They are called the noble gases because they are very unreactive. The elements in each column gradually become more reactive moving down the table. The most reactive elements are in the lithium and fluorine columns.

The position of an element in the Periodic Table is related to the way its electrons are arranged around the nucleus. The unreactive noble gases have a stable outer shell of electrons. The reactive elements on the left have an unstable outer shell of electrons, with only a single electron in their outer shell.

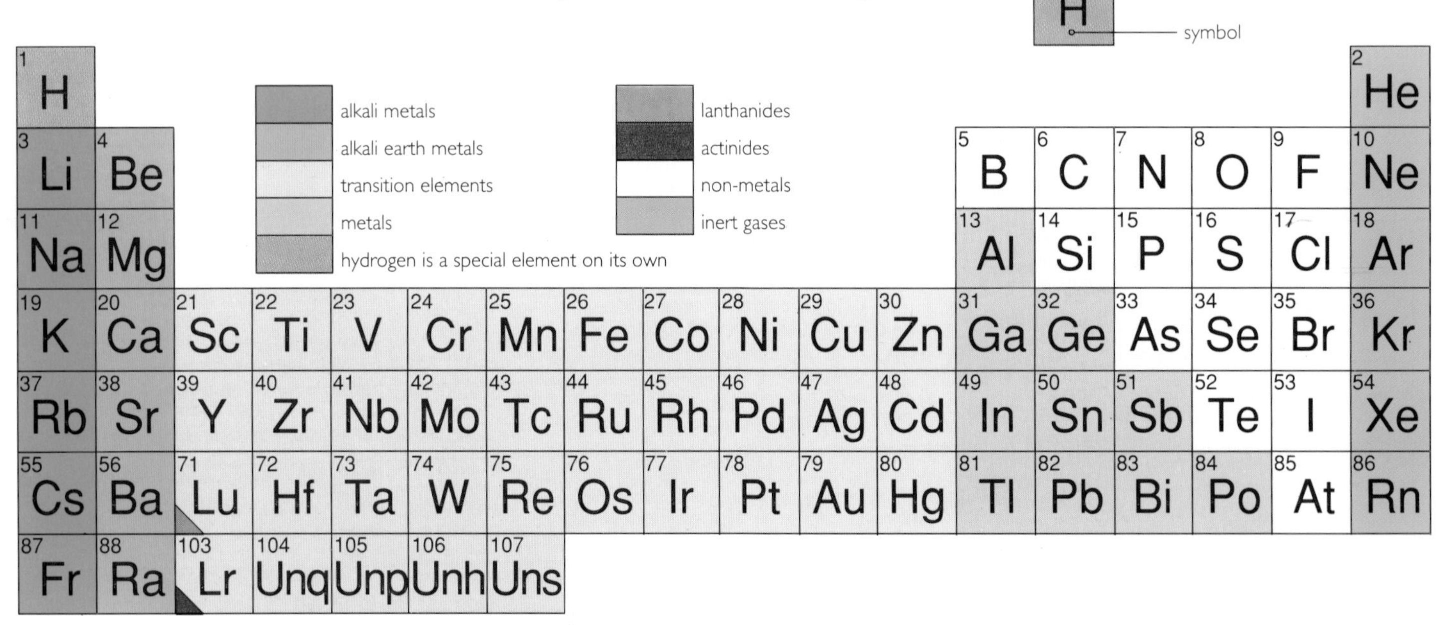

Element	Symbol	Atomic No.	Element	Symbol	Atomic No.	Element	Symbol	Atomic No.	Element	Symbol	Atomic No.	Element	Symbol	Atomic No.
Actinium	Ac	89	Copper	Cu	29	Lanthanum	La	57	Plutonium	Pu	94	Tellurium	Te	52
Aluminium	Al	13	Curium	Cm	96	Lawrencium	Lr	103	Polonium	Po	84	Terbium	Tb	65
Americium	Am	95	Dysprosium	Dy	66	Lead	Pb	82	Potassium	K	19	Thallium	Tl	81
Antimony	Sb	51	Einsteinium	Es	99	Lithium	Li	3	Praseodynium	Pr	59	Thorium	Th	90
Argon	Ar	18	Erbium	Er	68	Lutetium	Lu	71	Promethium	Pm	61	Thulium	Tm	69
Arsenic	As	33	Europium	Eu	3	Magnesium	Mg	12	Protactinium	Pa	91	Tin	Sn	50
Astatine	At	85	Fermium	Fm	100	Manganese	Mn	25	Radium	Ra	88	Titanium	Ti	22
Barium	Ba	56	Fluorine	F	9	Mendelevium	Md	101	Radon	Rn	86	Tungsten	W	74
Berkelium	Bk	97	Francium	Fr	87	Mercury	Hg	80	Rhenium	Re	75	Unnilhexium	Unh	106
Beryllium	Be	4	Gadolinium	Gd	64	Molybdenum	Mo	42	Rhodium	Rh	45	Unnilpentium	Unp	105
Bismuth	Bi	83	Gallium	Ga	31	Neodymium	Nd	60	Rubidium	Rb	37	Unnilquadium	Unq	104
Boron	B	5	Germanium	Ge	32	Neon	Ne	10	Ruthenium	Ru	44	Unnilseptium	Uns	107
Bromium	Br	35	Gold	Au	79	Neptunium	Np	93	Samarium	Sm	62	Uranium	U	92
Cadmium	Cd	48	Hafnium	Hf	72	Nickel	Ni	28	Scandium	Sc	21	Vanadium	V	23
Calcium	Ca	20	Helium	He	2	Niobium	Nb	41	Selenium	Se	34	Xenon	Xe	54
Californium	Cf	98	Holmium	Ho	67	Nitrogen	N	7	Silicon	Si	14	Ytterbium	Yb	70
Carbon	C	6	Hydrogen	H	1	Nobelium	No	102	Silver	Ag	47	Yttrium	Y	39
Cerium	Ce	58	Indium	In	49	Osmium	Os	76	Sodium	Na	11	Zinc	Zn	30
Cesium	Cs	55	Iodine	!	53	Oxygen	O	8	Strontium	Sr	38	Zirconium	Zr	40
Chlorine	Cl	17	Iridium	Ir	77	Palladium	Pd	46	Sulphur	S	16			
Chromium	Cr	24	Iron	Fe	26	Phosphorus	P	15	Tantalum	Ta	73			
Cobalt	Co	27	Krypton	Kr	36	Platinum	Pt	78	Technetium	Tc	43			

Chemical symbols

Scientists use symbols made up of one or two letters to represent the elements. The symbol for hydrogen is H, for oxygen, O. The same symbols are used to show the make-up of elements in a compound. Water, for example, is a compound with molecules made up of two atoms of hydrogen and one atom of oxygen. A molecule of water is therefore written as H_2O.

Chemical changes can be shown using the same symbols. When hydrogen combines with oxygen to produce water, the reaction is written $2H_2 + O_2 \longrightarrow 2H_2O$. This shows that two molecules of hydrogen, each consisting of two atoms of hydrogen, combine with one molecule of oxygen, consisting of two atoms of oxygen, and the result is two molecules of water.

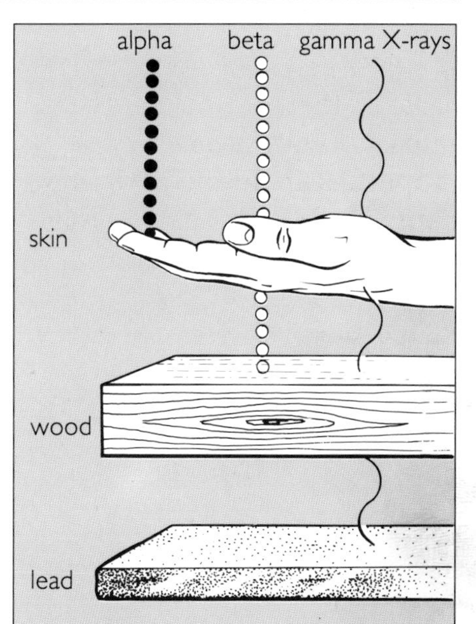

ISOTOPES

Scientists have found that although the atoms of an element always have the same number of protons in their nucleus, the number of neutrons varies. Atoms which have the same number of protons but a varying number of neutrons are called isotopes. Every element has several isotopes. Hydrogen, for example, has three. The most common isotope of hydrogen has one proton but no neutron in its nucleus. The isotope known as deuterium has one neutron. The isotope tritium has two.

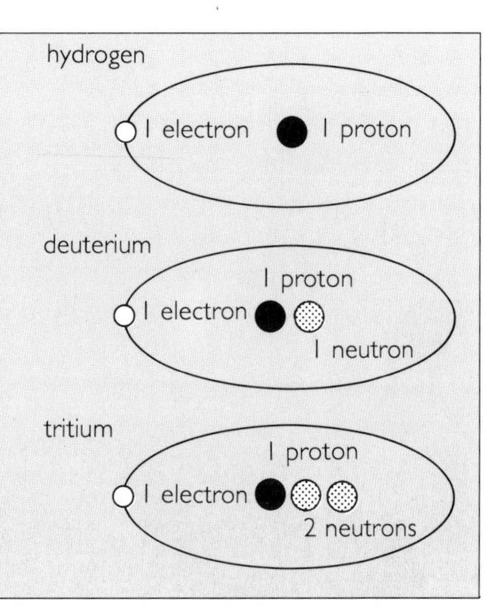

RADIOACTIVITY

The nuclei of many isotopes are stable and unchanging. But some isotopes are unstable. They give out energy in the form of radiation to become more stable, and are said to be radioactive. Three types of radiation are given out by radioactive isotopes.

Alpha radiation consists of tiny particles called alpha particles, in which two protons and two neutrons are bound together. Second is beta radiation consisting of high-energy electrons. Third is gamma radiation, or high-energy X-rays.

Solids, Liquids and Gases

Atoms and molecules are never still. Even in solids such as a copper coin or a block of concrete they are vibrating slightly. In liquids, the atoms or molecules move more vigorously, and in gases still more.

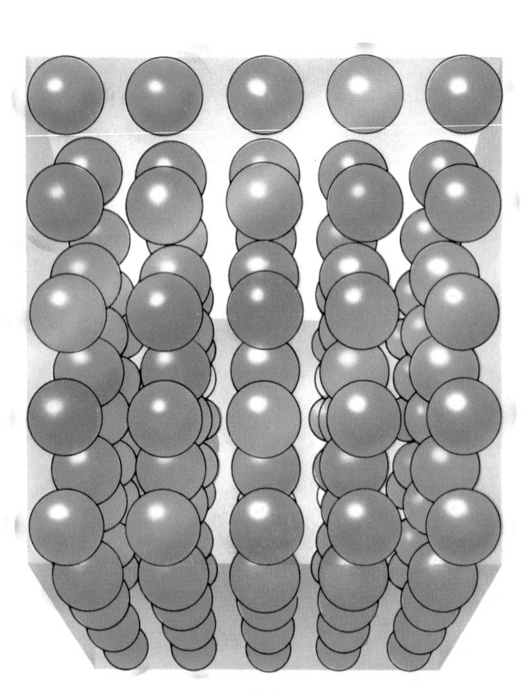

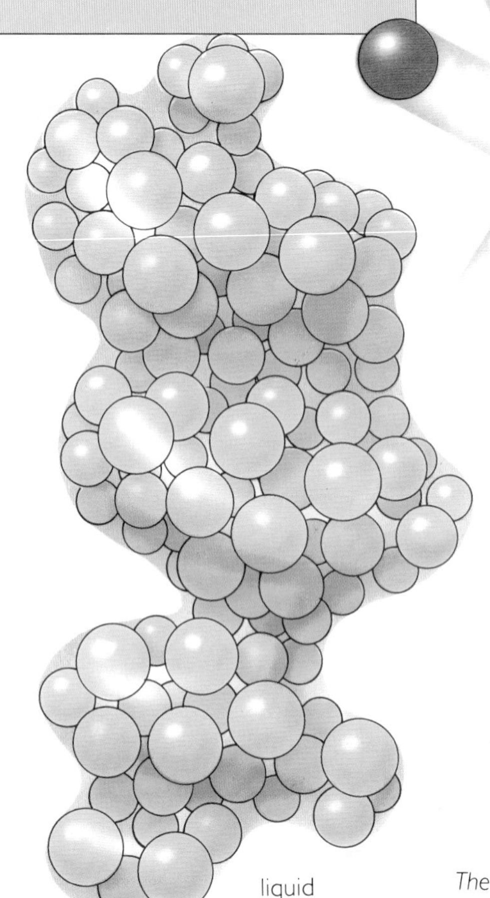

gas

The atoms in solids, liquids and gases can be thought of as tiny balls which move about with varying degrees of freedom.

Solids
The atoms or molecules in a solid are close together. Though able to vibrate slightly, they stay roughly in the same position. As a solid is heated, the atoms or molecules start to move faster. The higher the temperature, the faster they move. Eventually they vibrate so swiftly that they are able to move from their position. When this happens the solid melts and becomes a liquid.

Liquids
In a liquid the atoms or molecules are able to move around, although loose groups can be bound together for short periods. The key difference between liquids and solids is that, in a liquid, atoms or molecules are not associated with a particular localized region or place. They are free to move about. The liquid can thus flow easily and take up the shape of its container.

Gases
When a liquid is heated, some of the atoms or molecules may gain enough energy to escape through the surface and form a gas. In a gas the atoms or molecules are able to move with complete freedom. Their speed increases as the gas is heated and expands. Also, because there are large spaces between the atoms or molecules, a gas can be compressed easily.

In geysers, water is heated beneath the surface of the ground under great pressure. As the water is forced to the surface and the pressure is released, it turns to steam of its own accord.

INSIDE THE STARS

At very high temperatures the fast-moving atoms of a gas collide and are broken into electrons and electrically charged atoms called ions. The gas of electrons and ions that is formed is called a plasma. Plasmas are found inside stars, where the temperature is very high. (At the surface of the Sun, for example, the temperature is 6,000°C and at the centre it reaches 14,000,000°C.) Plasmas also form inside the ball of fire produced by a nuclear explosion, where the temperature reaches 100,000,000°C, high enough to rip any atom apart.

Laws of gases

One of the first scientists to study how a gas can be compressed was Robert Boyle. As long ago as 1662 he showed that if the pressure on a gas is doubled, its volume is halved. In general, the product of the pressure and the volume is constant for a given mass of gas at constant temperature. This became known as Boyle's Law.

Another important law is Charles's Law (1787), which describes how a gas expands when it is heated. It states that if the volume of a gas is known at 0°C, the volume increases or decreases by $\frac{1}{273}$ of this value for every 1°C of rise or fall in temperature. At a temperature of -273°C, a gas will have zero pressure, so this must be the lowest possible temperature, called absolute zero. At that temperature atoms and molecules are completely still and therefore will not collide with one another.

Electricity and Magnetism

When you press the button of an electric bell, electricity flows from a battery to the bell. It makes a coil of wire into a magnet and this attracts an arm that strikes the bell. Clearly, electricity and magnetism are closely linked.

In most materials the electrons stay inside the atoms or molecules, but in metals some electrons can move about freely. Normally the free electrons in a metal wire do not move in any particular direction. But if a battery is connected to the ends of the wire, the electrical pressure of the battery makes the electrons all move in the same direction along the wire towards the positive terminal of the battery, producing an electric current.

However, not all free electrons flow. Sometimes they remain still. This produces static electricity. You can see static electricity in action when you comb your hair. Some electrons are rubbed off the hair on to the comb. The comb becomes negatively charged, while your hair becomes positively charged because it has lost electrons. Opposite charges attract each other, so your hair rises towards the comb.

Electromagnets

When electrons flow along a wire they produce magnetic effects. A small magnet or a compass needle is affected if an electric current flows in a nearby wire. The compass needle will turn when the current starts to flow. This shows that the electric current is producing a magnetic field in the space around the wire.

A coil of wire with a strong magnetic effect is called an electromagnet. The magnetic power of an electromagnet (or any other magnet) is greatest at two points called the poles, which are usually near the ends of the magnet. If the magnet is allowed to swing freely (as in a compass) the North Pole turns to point north. Opposite poles attract; similar poles repel, or push apart.

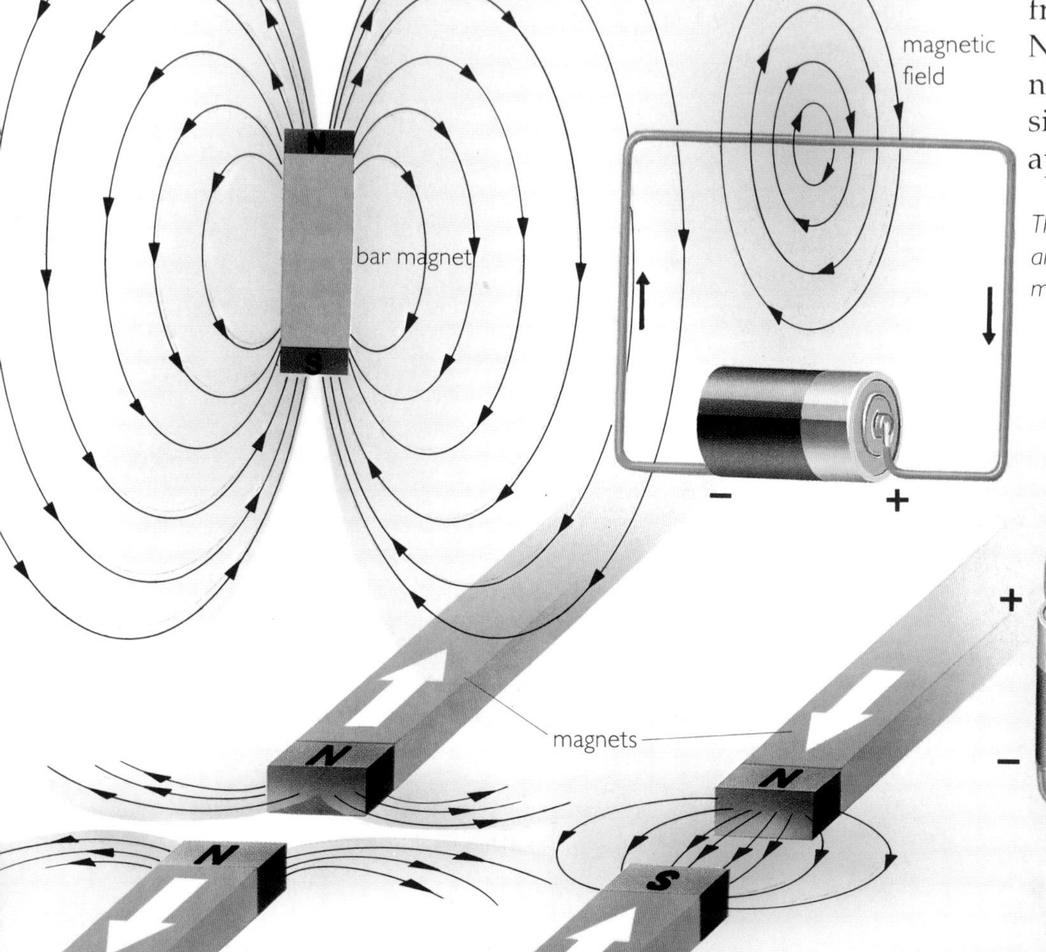

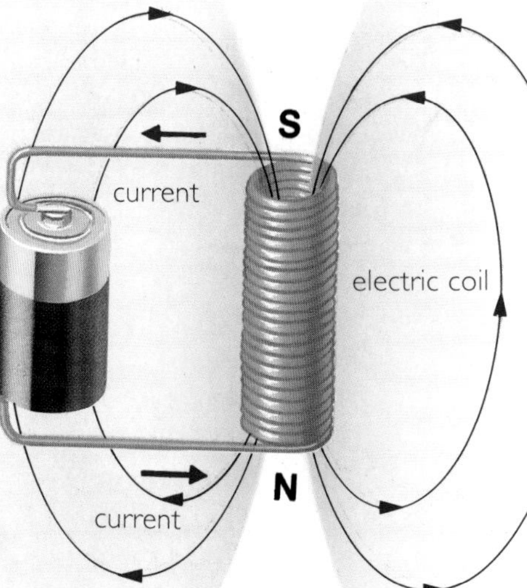

The magnetic fields and lines of force around a bar magnet, between the poles of magnets, and around an electric coil.

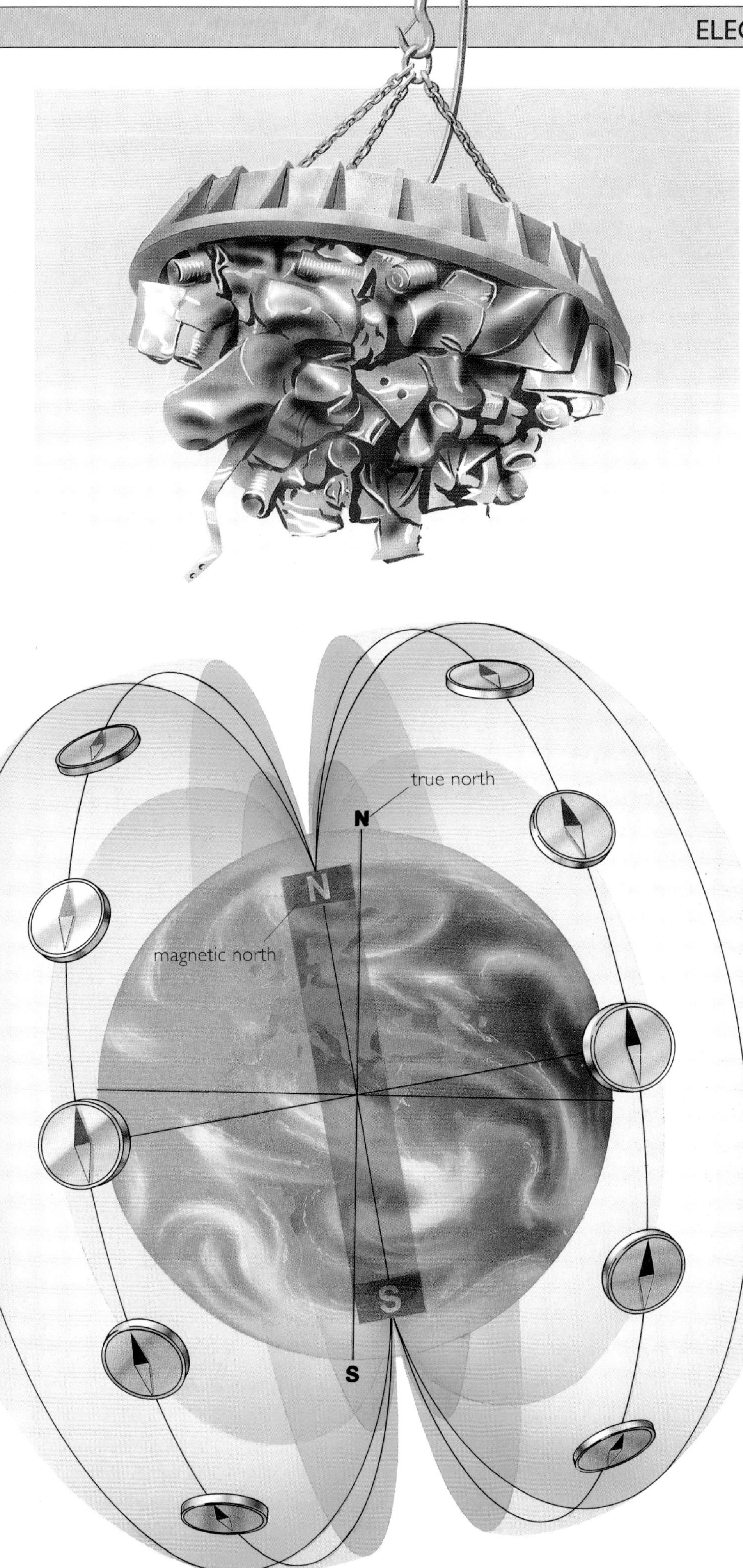

Atomic magnets

In a material such as iron or steel, the electrons circling around the nucleus of each atom make the atoms act like small electromagnets. When the metal is demagnetized, these mini-magnets are pointing in all different directions, cancelling each other out. When a rod or bar of the metal is placed in a coil of wire carrying electricity, or stroked with a magnet, the mini-magnets line up so that they all point in the same direction. Their magnetism then combines to turn the rod into a strong magnet.

Above left: *When switched on, an electromagnet can be used to extract iron-containing (ferrous) metals from non-ferrous*

Left: *The Earth's magnetic field radiates from the North and South Poles, causing a compass needle to follow its lines of force.*

THE EARTH'S MAGNETISM

We live on a huge magnet! Like an ordinary bar magnet, the Earth has two magnetic poles, which are near (though not at) the geographical North and South Poles. It is the magnetism of these poles which makes a compass needle point north and south. The Earth's magnetism is produced by molten metal which lies deep within the Earth's core. As the Earth spins, electric currents are created in the molten metal, producing the magnetic effect.

Light

When light enters our eyes, we see the object that the light has come from. If the light has come from a glowing light bulb we see the bulb. If the light has bounced off a table or chair we see the table or chair.

The path of a light beam is defined by straight lines called rays. When light rays bounce or are reflected from a flat mirror, they leave the mirror at the same angle as they hit it.

THE RAINBOW

You see a rainbow when sunlight shining from behind you falls on water droplets (rain, usually) in front of you. Often you see a fainter secondary rainbow outside the primary rainbow. The colours in the secondary bow are the reverse of those in the primary. The primary rainbow is caused by light from the Sun being first refracted as it enters a rain drop, then reflected from the back of the drop. When it emerges, it is spread into a band of colours. The secondary bow is caused by light which is reflected twice within the rain drop before it emerges. The additional reflection reverses the order of the colours.

Bending light

When a beam of light shines on to a transparent material, such as a pool of clear water, some of it enters the water. However, the direction of the beam changes as it does so. The change of direction, called refraction, produces some interesting effects. When you look at a fish in a pond the fish is closer than it seems to be because light rays from the fish are bent as they leave the water.

What is light?

The electrons circling the nucleus of an atom can sometimes move from one shell, or electron layer, to another. When the electron jumps to a shell closer to the nucleus, it can be thought of as a small electric current. This current produces a pulse of magnetism and electricity in the space around the atom, which we see as a flash of light. Light is therefore a type of electromagnetic wave, a ripple or pulse of electricity and magnetism that spreads through space like the ripples of water on a lake.

Rays of light from a fish beneath water are refracted at the water surface such that, to the observer, the fish appears to be closer than it really is.

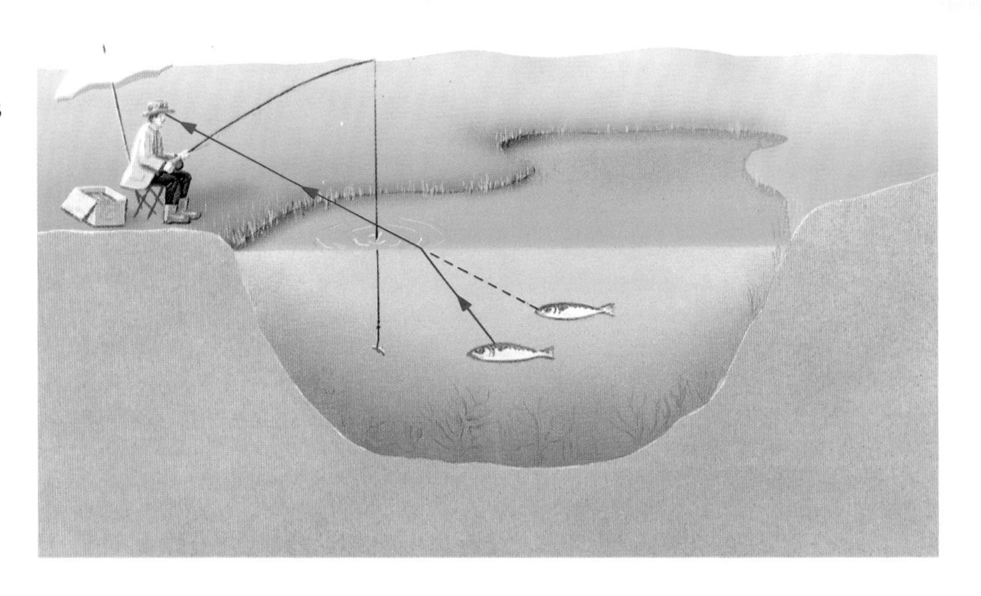

ECLIPSES

Because light travels in straight lines, when the Moon comes out in front of the Sun it blocks out sunlight to Earth. This is a solar eclipse. Depending on the Earth–Moon distance, there is a total or annular eclipse of the Sun in the area of deepest shadow. Light travels at 300,000km (186,000 miles) a second and takes 8 minutes to travel from the Sun to the Earth.

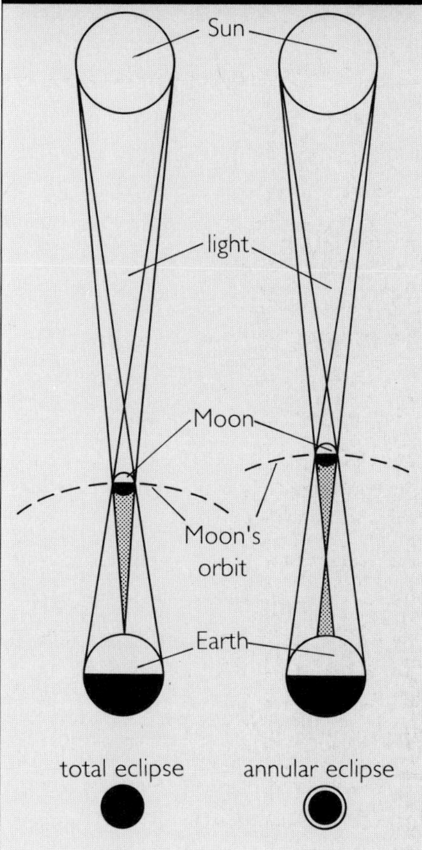

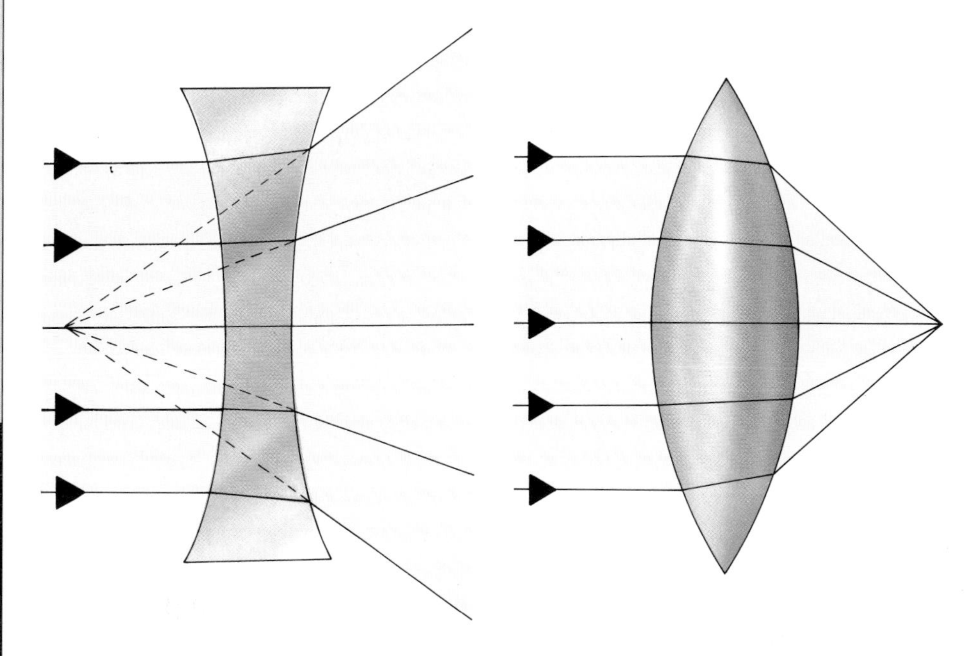

Parallel rays of light entering a convex lens (right) are brought to a point behind the lens but those entering a concave lens (above) are spread out as if they came from a point in front of the lens.

Lenses and curved mirrors

Optical instruments, such as small telescopes, cameras and microscopes, make use of refraction in their lenses, which are pieces of glass with curved surfaces. It is possible to understand how lenses work by tracing the light rays that pass through them.

Convex lenses, with surfaces that bulge outwards, bend light rays from distant objects towards a point called the focus. Concave lenses, which have surfaces curved inwards, bend light rays away from the focus. By bending light rays, lenses in optical instruments are able to produce larger images of distant or small objects.

Curved mirrors work in the same way. Concave mirrors produce magnified images. Convex mirrors produce smaller images. Concave mirrors are used in large astronomical telescopes, shaving mirrors and car headlamps. Convex mirrors are found in cars' rear-view mirrors and sometimes in supermarkets, to give a reflection of a large area.

The speed of light

Light, like all electromagnetic waves, travels at very high speed, 300,000km (over 186,000 miles) per second. At this speed, light takes 0.1 seconds to travel from New York to London, 8 minutes to reach the Earth from the Sun, and 4.3 years to reach Earth from the nearest star. In 1905 Albert Einstein proved that the speed of light is the greatest speed possible. Nothing in the universe can travel faster.

Colours

A beam of ordinary white light is actually made up of all the colours of the rainbow. This can be seen with the help of a prism (a piece of glass shaped like a pyramid). When a beam of white light passes through a prism, it separates into the colours that make it up.

Seeing colours

Coloured objects or paints absorb certain colours from white light and reflect the rest. Our eyes see the reflected light only, and the object appears to be the colour of the reflected light. For example, red paint absorbs the green and blue colours in white light, and reflects only the red light.

Mixing colours

Mixing different-coloured paints together produces new colours. Any colour can be made by mixing combinations of red, blue and yellow in different ways. These are called the primary colours. However, if you mix red, blue and yellow together, you get black, because all light falling on the mixture is absorbed.

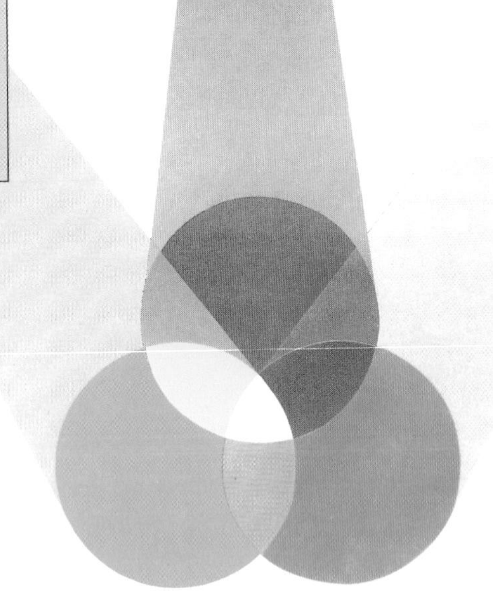

Mixing of coloured light beams (above) *and paints* (below).

Below: *When a beam of white light is split by a prism, violet light gets refracted, or bent, the most and red light the least, producing a complete spectrum of colours.*

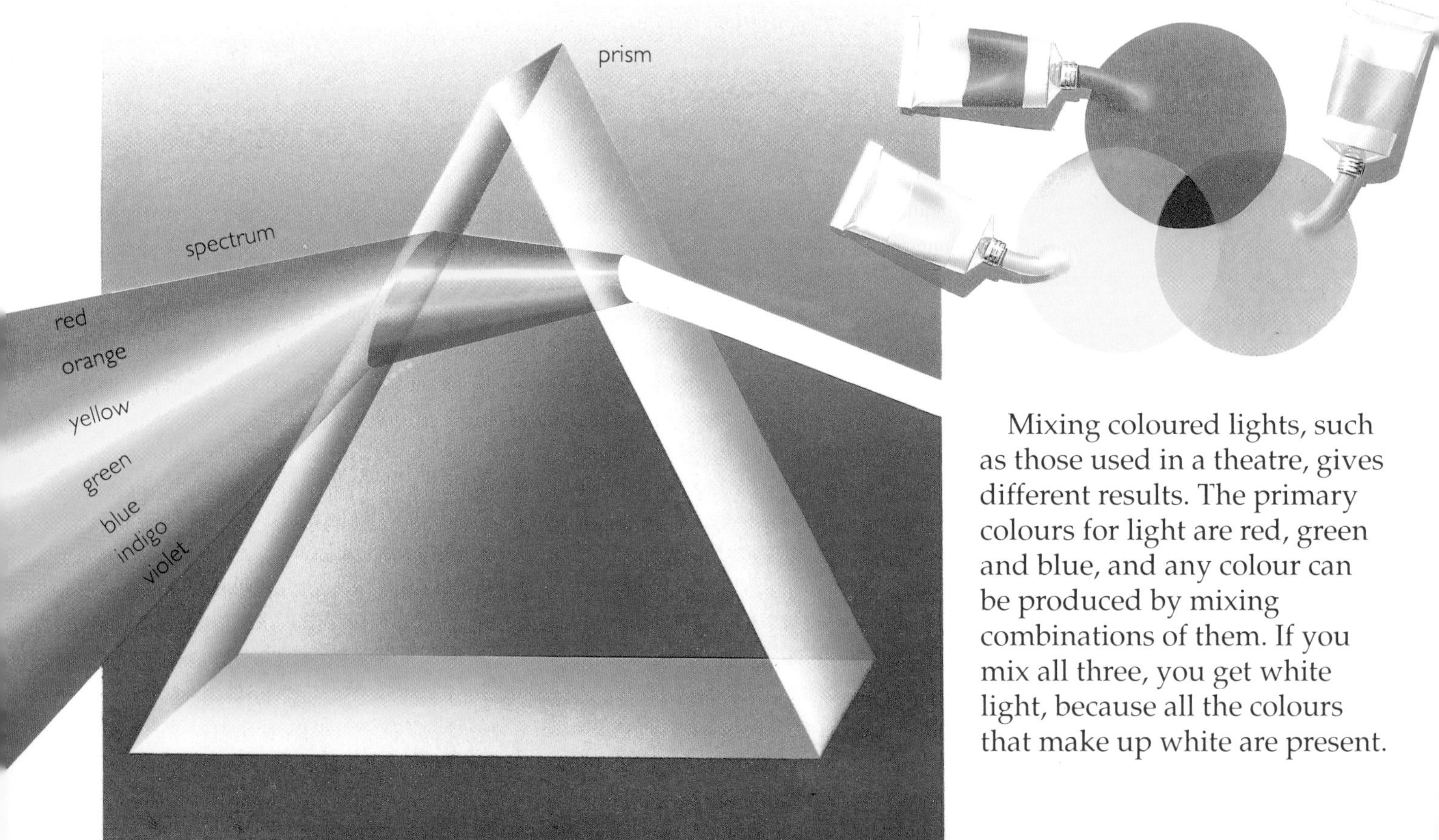

Mixing coloured lights, such as those used in a theatre, gives different results. The primary colours for light are red, green and blue, and any colour can be produced by mixing combinations of them. If you mix all three, you get white light, because all the colours that make up white are present.

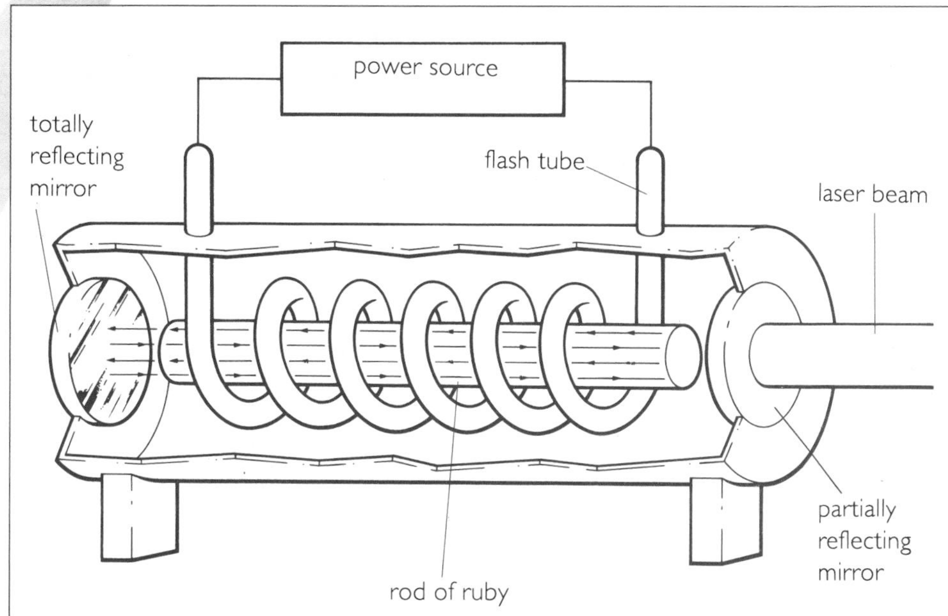

LASERS

A laser is a device that can produce a thin, very powerful beam of light. A common type of laser uses a small rod of ruby to produce the light. A powerful flash tube is wrapped around the ruby rod. At each end of the ruby is a mirror. One of the mirrors has a small hole in the centre. When the flash tube is turned on, the ruby is bathed in light. The atoms in the ruby absorb the light, but after a short time they can no longer hold it. They release it again as a pulse of light. Because all the atoms release the light at the same instant, a powerful beam is produced which shines through the hole in the mirror.

Electromagnetic waves

Light is not the only form of energy that travels as electromagnetic waves. Radio waves, X-rays, infra-red waves, ultraviolet and microwaves are all electromagnetic waves. They differ from light only because they have a different wavelength or frequency.

The wavelength is the distance between two crests of the wave. The frequency of a wave is the number of crests which go past a fixed point per second. Frequency is measured in units called hertz. One hertz equals one wave per second.

Different colours of light have different wavelengths. Red has a wavelength of about 800 nanometres (one nanometre is one thousand-millionth of a metre). Violet has a wavelength of about 400 nanometres. Yellow, green and blue light have wavelengths between 400 and 800 nanometres.

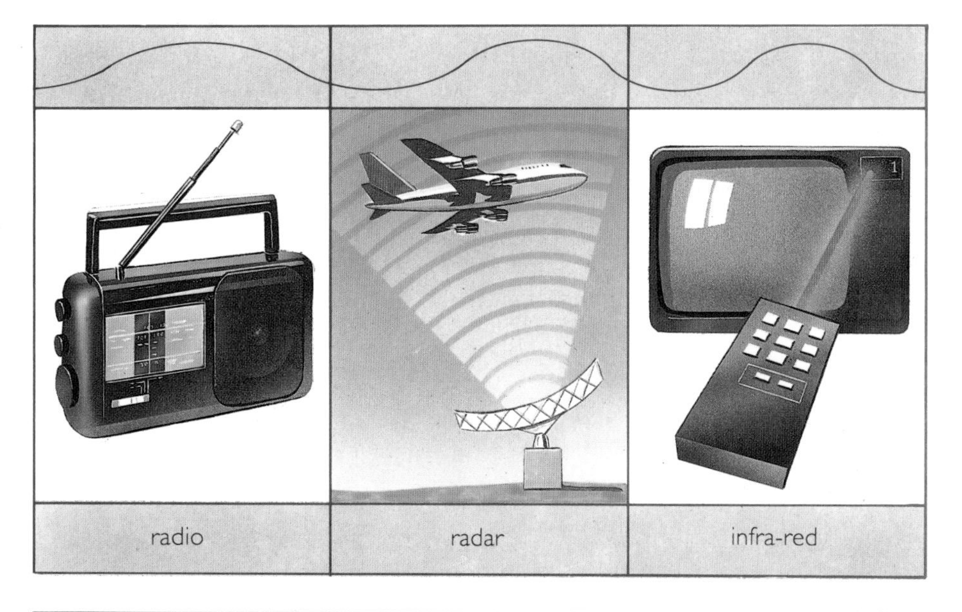

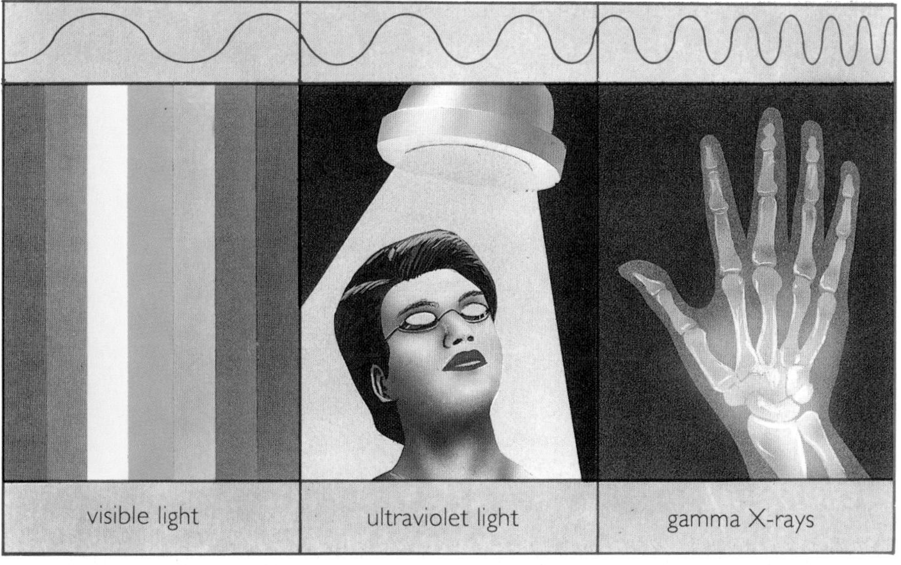

Right: *The electromagnetic spectrum.*

Heat

Heat is a form of energy produced by the movement of molecules in a hot object. The higher the temperature of an object, the faster its molecules move. (Heat is not the same as temperature. Temperature measures the degree of hotness of an object, while heat is the total amount of molecular energy in the object.)

Measuring temperature
Thermometers are used to measure temperatures accurately. Simple thermometers work because liquids expand when heated. The liquid, usually mercury or coloured alcohol, expands up a thin tube marked with a scale.

In the Celsius or centigrade scale, the temperature at which water freezes is 0°. The temperature of boiling water is 100°. On the Fahrenheit scale, the freezing point of water is 32°, and the temperature of boiling water is 212°.

Another temperature scale, the absolute or Kelvin scale, starts from the coldest possible temperature, absolute zero, which is -273°C. Absolute zero is 0°K (Kelvin). One degree Kelvin is equal to one degree Celsius, so 0°C becomes 273°K, and 100°C is 373°K.

Effects of heat
The liquid in a thermometer shows one effect of heat: expansion. Heat can also cause chemical changes. For example, burning is a chemical change which is started by heat. Heat can also melt a solid object or turn a liquid into a gas. These changes are called physical changes because, unlike chemical changes, they can easily be reversed.

As this dragster races along, friction heats up the tyres, sometimes melting the rubber.

A comparison of the degree scales in the main temperature measuring systems.

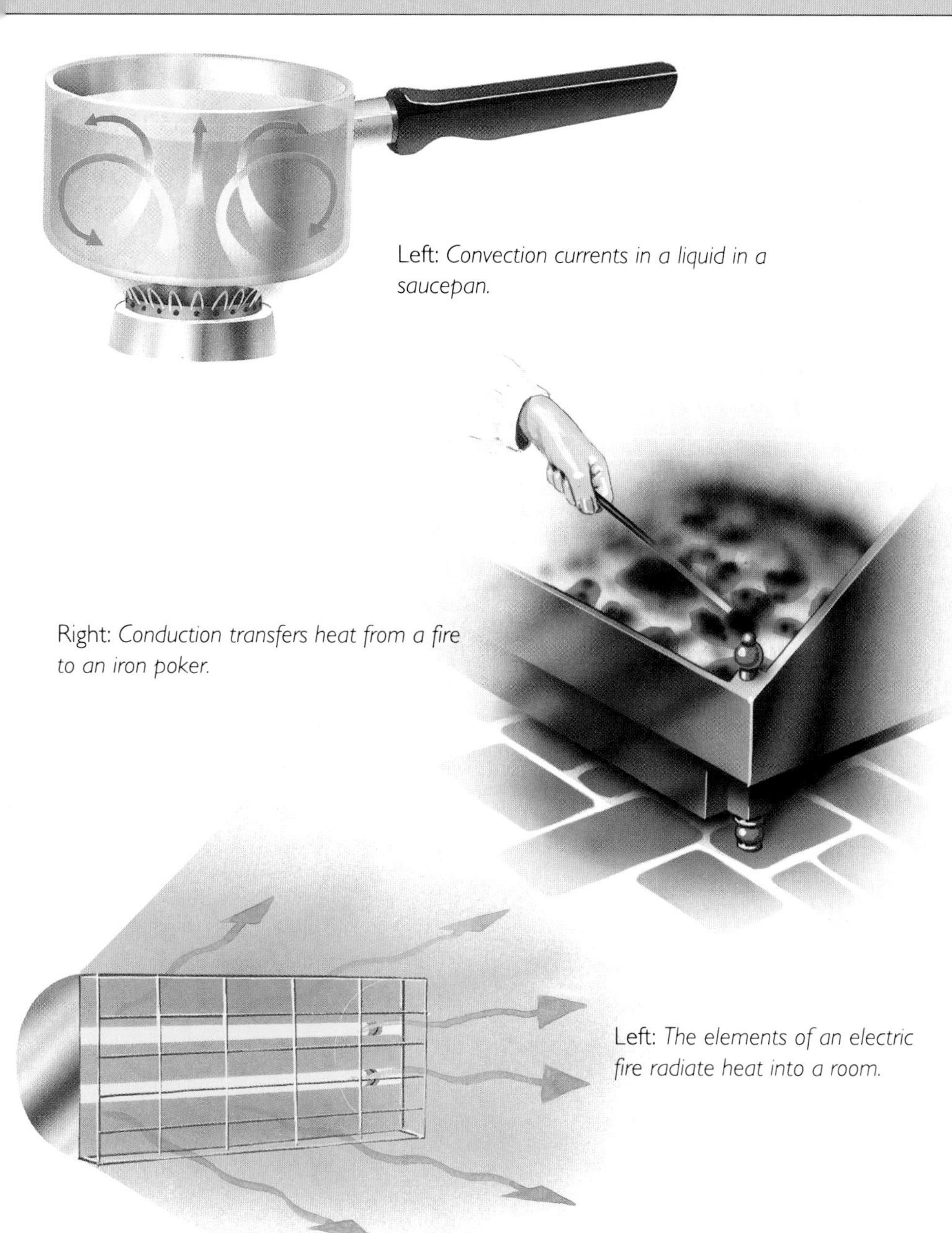

Left: *Convection currents in a liquid in a saucepan.*

Right: *Conduction transfers heat from a fire to an iron poker.*

Left: *The elements of an electric fire radiate heat into a room.*

How heat travels
Expansion causes currents of heated material to flow in liquids and gases. If a gas is heated, it expands and becomes less dense. The heated gas is forced upwards by the unheated gas around it. This creates a current of heated gas called a convection current. Convection currents in the atmosphere carry heat from hot regions to cold ones, causing winds and breezes. In the home, convection currents carry heat from heaters, and fires to all parts of the room and around the house.

In solids heat travels by conduction. This is a process in which vibrating molecules jostle against their neighbours and cause them to move more swiftly. The energy of the vibrating molecules is spread throughout the object. If you poke the end of a metal poker in a fire, the handle will soon get hot too, because of the process of conduction.

Heat can travel through empty space by radiation, as electromagnetic waves. This is how heat reaches the Earth from the Sun. Heat rays, called infra-red rays, are similar to red light rays although they have a slightly longer wavelength. A sunbather feels warm because of the infra-red rays flowing from the Sun.

Keeping the house warm
A quarter of all heat lost from a house flows through the roof. Another quarter is lost through the walls. The windows leak about one-fifth of the heat lost. The rest goes through the floors and draughty doors. The lesson is clear. To save heat, insulate the roof and walls, double-glaze the windows, use thick carpets and stop all draughts.

SUPERFLUIDS AND SUPERCONDUCTORS

At very low temperatures strange things happen. Helium, a gas at normal temperatures, turns into a liquid at -270°C. Liquid helium is called a superfluid because of its strange properties. It can flow uphill! If an empty cup is placed in liquid helium, the helium flows up the side and into the cup. If the cup is then placed on a table, the liquid helium flows over the sides on to the table.

Some materials, such as mercury, become superconductors at temperatures near absolute zero. This means that an electric current will flow for ever in the mercury once it is started. With superconductors, very strong electromagnets can be made for use in medicine and certain scientific experiments.

Sound

All sounds are caused by objects vibrating. Each forward movement of a vibrating object creates a region of high pressure where the air molecules are compressed together. When the object moves backwards, it creates a region of low pressure where the molecules are farther apart than normal. These high and low pressure regions travel out from the vibrating object as sound waves, like ripples on a pond. When the sound waves enter a human ear, they make the eardrum vibrate and the sound is heard.

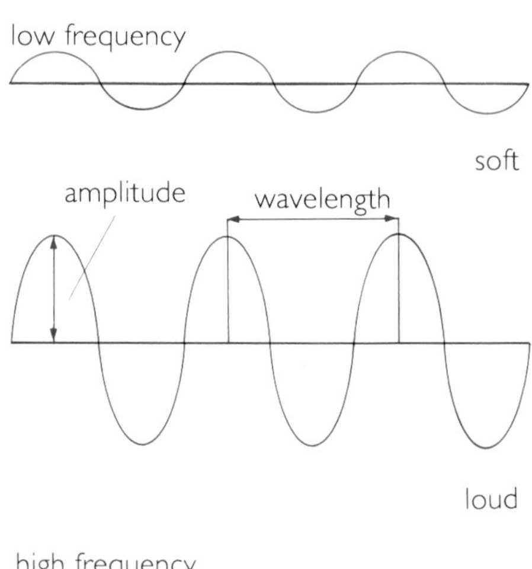

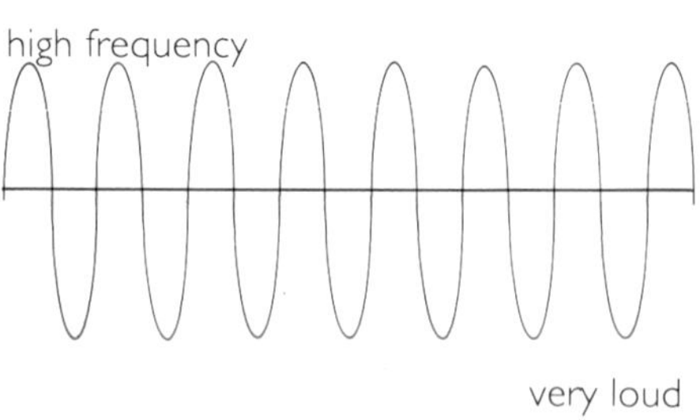

The height of a sound wave is a measure of loudness, and the number of waves in a second is a measure of the frequency.

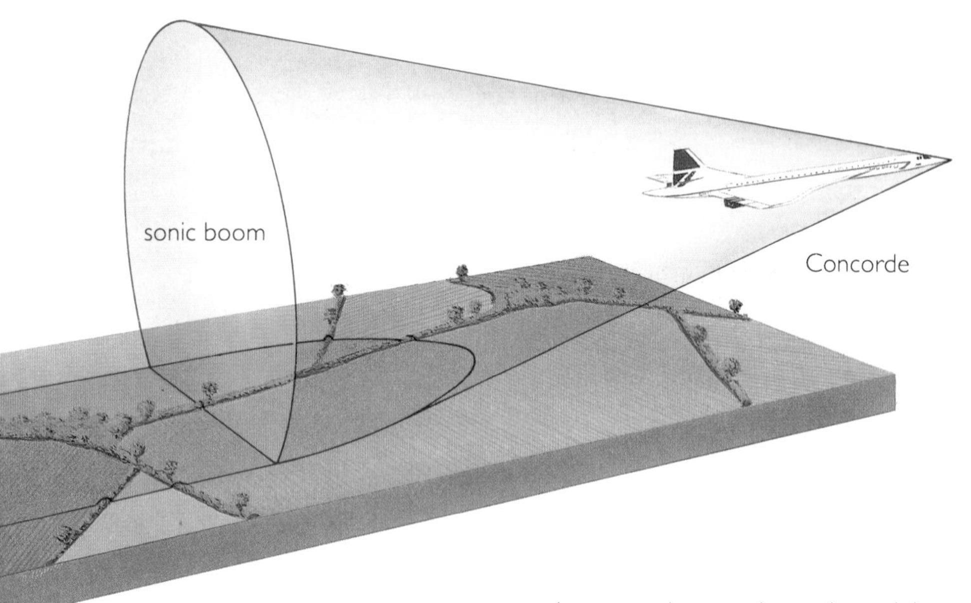

As an aeroplane accelerates beyond the speed of sound – 1,190kph (730mph) – it creates a sonic boom as air pressure and sound waves interact.

Loudness and pitch

The size of a vibration or sound wave is called its amplitude. The greater the amplitude of a wave, the louder the sound we hear. The unit used to measure loudness is the decibel. The softest sound we can hear, such as leaves rustling, has a value of 0 decibels. Ordinary speech is between 50 and 70 decibels. A jet aircraft can be in the range of 120 to 140 decibels. Beyond 120 decibels, sound can cause pain to human ears.

The number of complete vibrations or waves entering the ear per second is called the frequency. The greater the frequency of a sound wave, the higher the pitch of the sound we hear. Frequency is measured in hertz, or vibrations per second. A person with good hearing can hear sounds with frequencies between 20 and 20,000 hertz.

'Silent' sounds

Infrasonic sounds, or infrasounds, have frequencies below 20 hertz. They cannot be heard by a human ear. They are produced by slow movements of the Earth's crust, by waterfalls and seaside waves, and by wind passing over mountains. Birds can hear these sounds and may use them to navigate. Elephants and whales use infrasound to communicate over long distances.

A sound with a frequency above 20,000 hertz is called an ultrasonic sound, or ultrasound. Ultrasounds are common in nature although we cannot hear them. Cats and dogs can hear sounds with frequencies up to 35,000 hertz.

Rats, mice, shrews and hamsters make sounds with frequencies up to 100,000 hertz. Insect-eating bats are able to locate flying insects in the dark using ultrasound. They send out rapid bursts of ultrasound as they fly around, and by listening to the reflections, or echoes, of the sounds bouncing back, they can work out the position of a flying insect. Radar, as used to locate aircraft, is a similar system, although radar uses electromagnetic waves, not sound waves.

Ultrasound is used in industry to detect faults in metal sheets. When a beam of ultrasound is directed at the metal any faults cause echoes. Shoals of fish are also tracked by ultrasound, and in medicine, pregnant women are given an ultrasound scan which shows how their unborn baby is developing.

Echolocation. Bats (left) *locate moths in flight and ships* (above) *locate shoals of fish and sunken wrecks by detecting the sound waves that bounce back from them.*

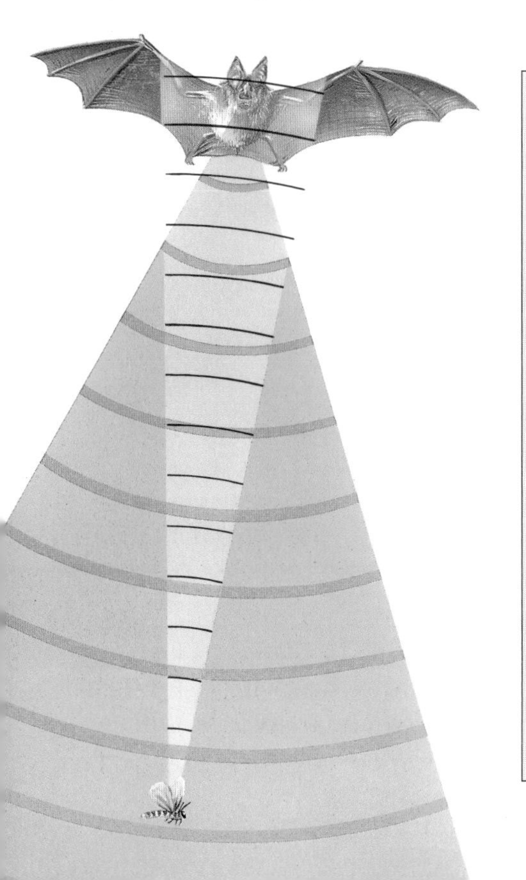

MUSICAL SOUNDS

Musical sounds are pleasant because they are made up mostly of a single frequency. Unpleasant noises are made up of a jumble of frequencies. The main note in a musical sound is called the fundamental frequency. Other notes, called harmonics, may also be present, but they are much softer than the fundamental note. The flute has a sound wave that is rounded and smooth, producing a sound that is gentle and soothing. The wave of a clarinet is more jagged, producing a rougher sound.

THE DOPPLER EFFECT

The sound made by the siren of an ambulance as it approaches, rises in pitch. As the ambulance passes by, the sound drops in pitch. This change is called the Doppler effect, after the Austrian scientist who first explained the principle in 1842. When the ambulance is approaching, the sound waves from the siren are bunched together by the movement of the vehicle. More waves per second reach a bystander's ear (higher frequency) and so a high pitch is heard. When the ambulance recedes, the sound waves are drawn apart by the movement of the ambulance. Fewer waves per second reach the bystander's ear (lower frequency) and a lower-pitched sound is heard.

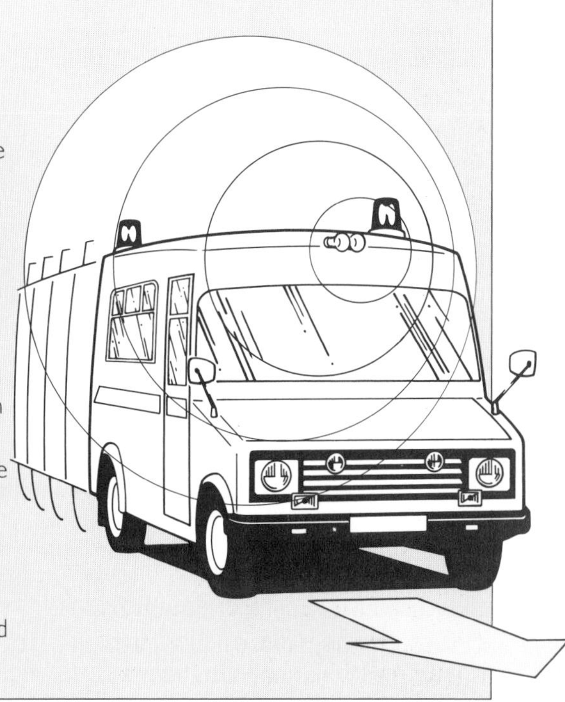

References

Absolute zero The lowest possible temperature, -273°C.
Amplitude The strength of a wave, or the distance from the top of a wave crest to the trough.
Atom The smallest part of a chemical element that can exist; *see* **Molecule**.
Atomic number The number of protons in an atom's nucleus.
Boyle, Robert (1627–91) Irish scientist who studied how pressure affects gases.
Celsius, Anders (1701–44) Swedish astronomer who invented the centigrade, or Celsius, temperature scale.
Charles, Jacques (1746–1823) French scientist who studied how heat affects gases.
Compound A substance which is made up of molecules consisting of two or more elements chemically joined.
Concave mirror or **lens** A mirror or lens whose surface is curved inwards (like a cave).
Conduction The way heat and electricity travel through a solid.
Conductor Any substance, including all metals, which allows electricity to travel through it.
Convection The way heat travels through a gas or liquid as currents of heated material.
Convex mirror or **lens** A mirror or lens that is curved outwards.
Covalent bond A bond between two atoms caused when the atoms share electrons.
Decibel A unit for measuring the loudness of sounds.
Doppler, Christian (1803–53) Austrian physicist who studied the sounds produced by moving objects.
Doppler effect The way the pitch or frequency of waves seems to change if the source of the waves is moving.
Electromagnet An iron bar with wire coiled around it, which acts as a magnet when an electric current flows through the wire.
Electromagnetic wave Waves of electricity and magnetism that can carry energy through empty space.
Electron A tiny particle that circles the central nucleus of an atom and has a negative electric charge.
Element A substance made up of one type of atom; *see* **Compound**.
Fahrenheit, Gabriel (1686–1736) German scientist who invented the Fahrenheit temperature scale.
Frequency The number of vibrations per second of radio or other waves.
Hertz A unit for measuring the frequency of a wave or vibration. One hertz is one vibration per second.
Hertz, Heinrich (1857–95) German scientist who discovered radio waves.
Infra-red ray A type of electromagnetic wave with a wavelength slightly longer than that of red light.
Infrasound Low frequency sound which human ears cannot hear.
Ion An atom which carries an electric charge.
Isotope An atom of an element which is chemically the same as the normal atoms but has a different number of neutrons in its nucleus.
Kelvin, Lord William Thomson (1824–1907) British physicist who invented the absolute or Kelvin temperature scale.
Laser A device that produces a very intense beam of light.
Magnetic field The space around a magnet where the magnetic effects can be felt.
Magnetic pole The place on a magnet where the magnetic effect is strongest.
Molecule The smallest particle of a chemical substance, consisting of one or more atoms.
Nanometre A unit for measuring extremely small distances, equal to 0.000000001m (one thousand-millionth of a metre).
Neutron A particle in the nucleus of all atoms except hydrogen which, unlike protons and electrons, has no electrical charge.
Nucleus A positively charged region at the centre of an atom, containing protons and neutrons and circled by electrons.
Physical change A change, such as melting or boiling, that does not produce a new chemical substance.
Plasma A very hot gas made up of ions and electrons, which exists inside stars.
Proton A positively charged particle found in the nucleus of all atoms.
Radiation The transfer of energy by electromagnetic waves such as light, radio, X-rays, etc.
Radioactivity A type of radiation caused by the breaking-up of the unstable nucleus of an element such as radium.
Reflection The bouncing of light or other rays from a surface.
Refraction The bending of light rays as they pass from one material to another.
Resistance The force acting against a change in motion, as water 'resists' a ship; electrical resistance is the force acting against the flow of current through a conductor.
Rutherford, Ernest (1871–1937) New Zealand scientist who discovered the atomic nucleus and split the atom.
Spectrum A rainbow-coloured band of light produced when white light passes through a prism.
Static electricity Electric charges that are not moving.
Superconductor A substance which loses its electrical resistance at very low temperatures.
Ultrasound A sound whose frequency is too high for human ears to hear.
Wave A regular disturbance that spreads out from its source; sound waves make the molecules of the air vibrate, as ripples make the molecules of water vibrate.

Forces, Energy and Power

Force and Motion

Nothing starts to move without a push or a pull. For example, a football does not speed towards the goal until you kick it. A push or a pull that starts an object moving is called a force. Forces not only start things moving, they can also speed up or slow down moving objects, or make them change direction.

Laws of motion

Isaac Newton explained 300 years ago how forces produce movements and affect moving objects. He stated three laws of motion. The first law said that an object at rest will stay at rest unless a force acts on it, and an object moving at a constant speed in a straight line will continue at the same speed and in the same direction unless a force acts on it. The second law said that when a force acts on a moving object, the object changes its speed or direction of motion. The greater the force acting on it, the greater the change of speed or direction produced. The third law said that for every force there is an equal force acting in the opposite direction, but acting on the object which created the original force.

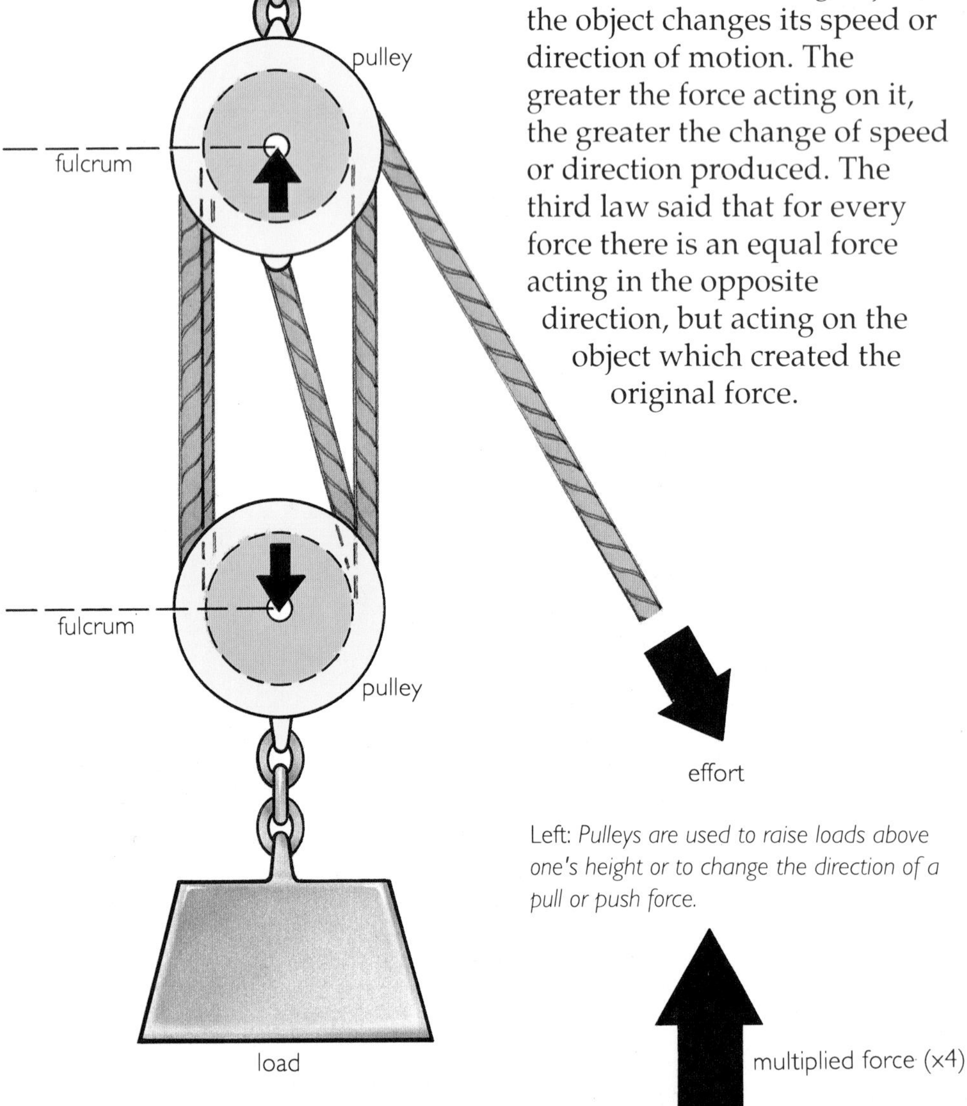

Left: *Pulleys are used to raise loads above one's height or to change the direction of a pull or push force.*

Forces and work

Forces are needed to do work, such as moving a heavy load. When you carry a heavy suitcase upstairs, you are doing hard work, or in other words you are exerting force. The amount of work you do depends upon how heavy the suitcase is and how far and how fast you lift it. The heavier the suitcase and the farther and faster you lift it, the more work you do.

Energy

Energy is needed to move objects and do work. After lifting the suitcase up the stairs you may say, *"I've used up all my energy!"* But the energy you have used has not disappeared. It has just changed into a different form, called potential energy. If you release the suitcase at the top of the stairs it will fall down. The moving suitcase gained potential energy when you carried it upstairs. This energy makes the suitcase move when you release it.

Right: *To avoid gravity pulling them back to Earth, satellites must orbit high in space and at high speeds.*

RELATIVITY

In 1905, Albert Einstein discovered that when objects move at very high speeds – near the speed of light – strange things happen. His ideas became known as the 'Theory of Relativity'. Einstein showed that if two trains set their clocks to the same time, and one train starts to move at nearly the speed of light, to the passengers on the stationary train the clock on the moving train seems to be running slow. Furthermore, the moving train seems to be shrinking as it moves away. However, to passengers on the moving train, the clock on the stationary train seems to be slow, and the stationary train seems to be shrinking.

These effects on objects relative to one another have been observed many times by scientists using very accurate clocks flown in high-speed aircraft. It seems that at high speeds our everyday sense of time, size and movement is unreliable.

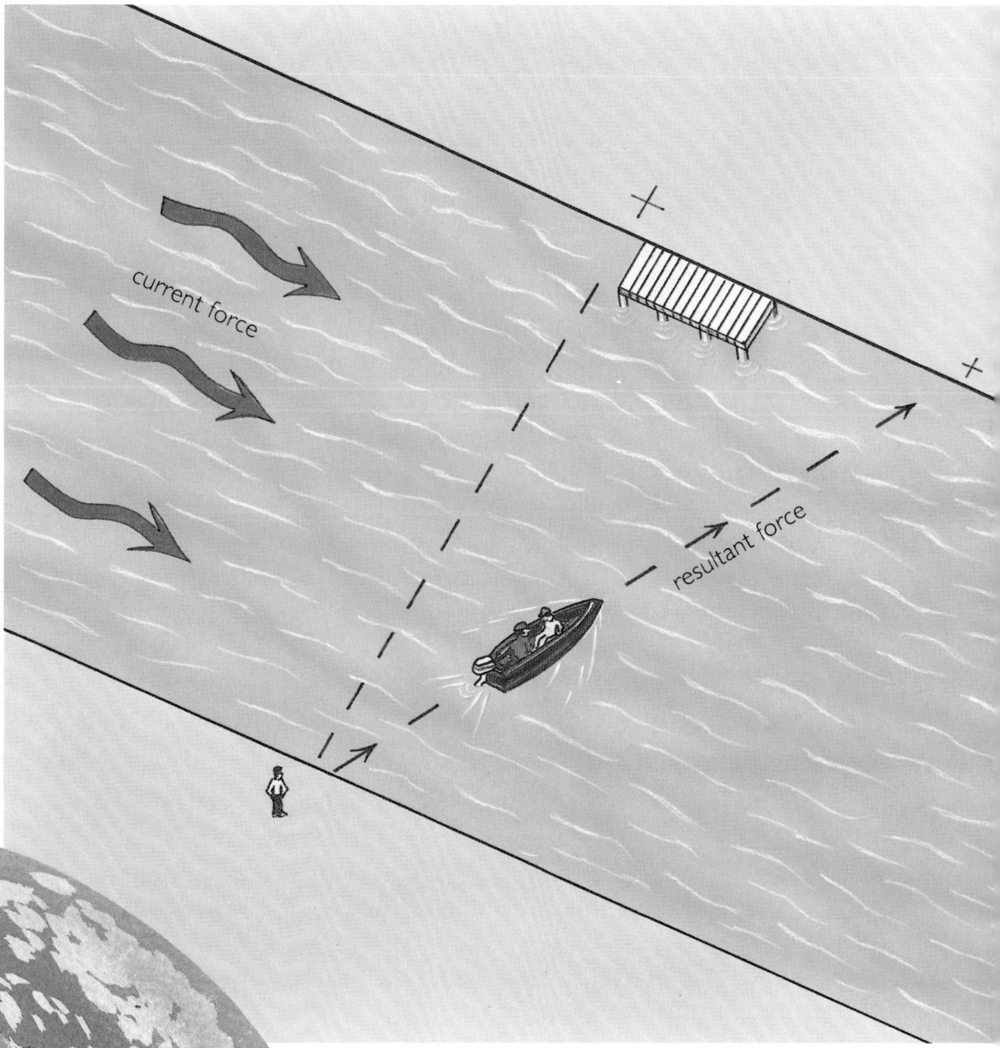

current force
resultant force

The force of river currents acting on a boat trying to cross straight from one bank of a river to the other results in the boat landing some way down river. The stronger the currents, the further the boat is shifted.

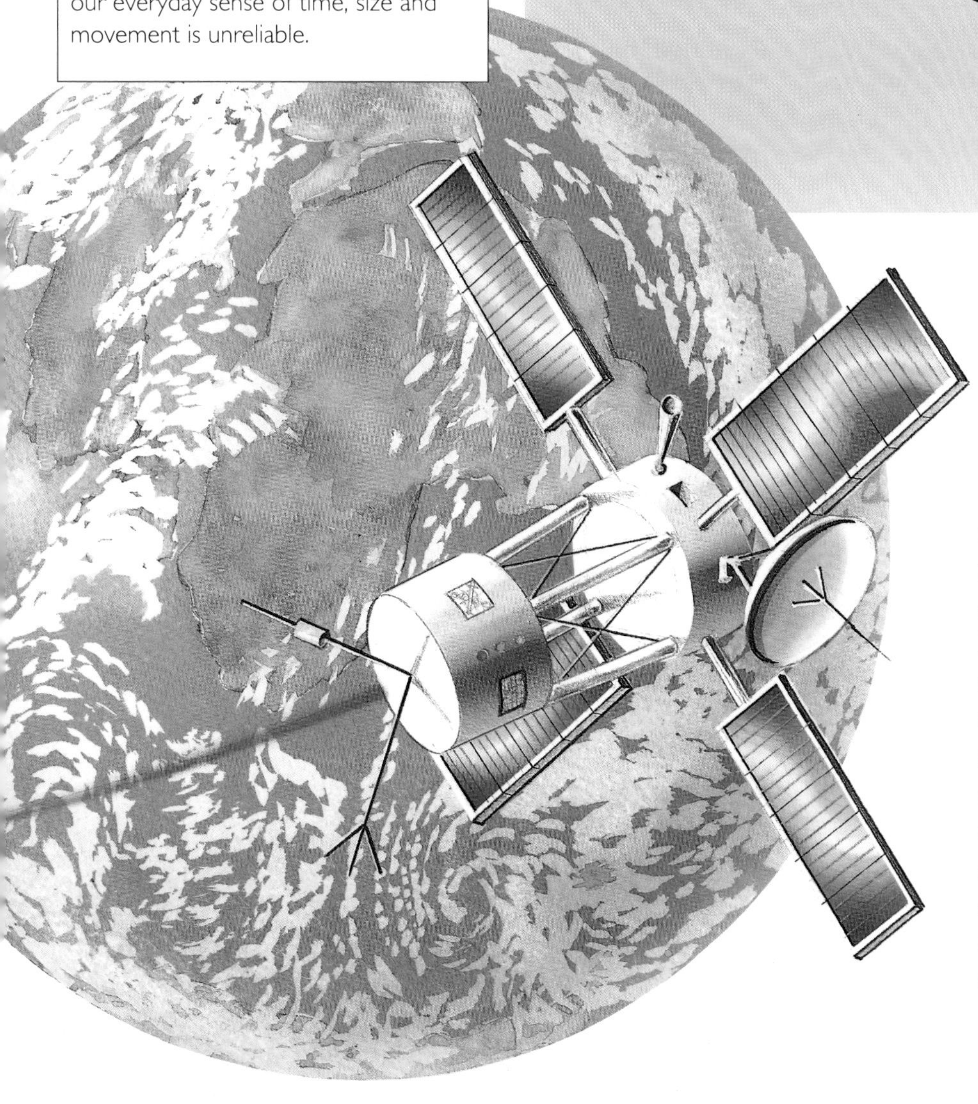

Energy takes many different forms. Your energy comes from the food you eat. This is called chemical energy. Electricity, which can make an electric motor turn, is a form of energy. Heat, sound and light are also forms of energy. The energy of moving objects is called kinetic energy. When energy changes form, the total amount of energy does not change. This is called conservation of energy.

Electrical Machines

Electricity is one of the most useful forms of energy. It is clean and silent. It is available at the flick of a switch. Most importantly, it can be changed easily into other forms of energy. An electric heater or cooker works because electric currents produce heat energy. Electricity can produce sounds in a hi-fi system, or light in a spotlamp. Many household gadgets – food mixers, washing machines, electric toothbrushes, record players, etc. – convert electricity into kinetic energy.

The electric motor
The simplest electrical machine consists of a thin wire hung loosely near a strong magnet. When the ends of the wire are connected to an electric battery, the wire feels a force which makes it move. The force is caused by the magnetic effect of the electric current pulling the wire towards, or away from, the magnet. The direction in which the wire moves depends upon which direction the current is flowing in the wire, and which pole of the magnet is nearer the wire.

If the wire is bent into a circle or coil and arranged so that the coil can rotate, the coil will twist when the battery is first connected. To allow the coil to keep turning, a device called a commutator is used. This consists of two half-circles of metal attached to the ends of the coil. The connections to the battery terminals press against the metal half-circles. As the coil rotates, the commutator ensures that the wires do not become tangled. The commutator also reverses the current flowing through the coil every half turn, and this keeps the coil turning in the same direction. This arrangement is a simple electric motor.

The electrical circuits and magnetic fields of electric motors suited for alternating and direct currents. Note the different types of commutators.

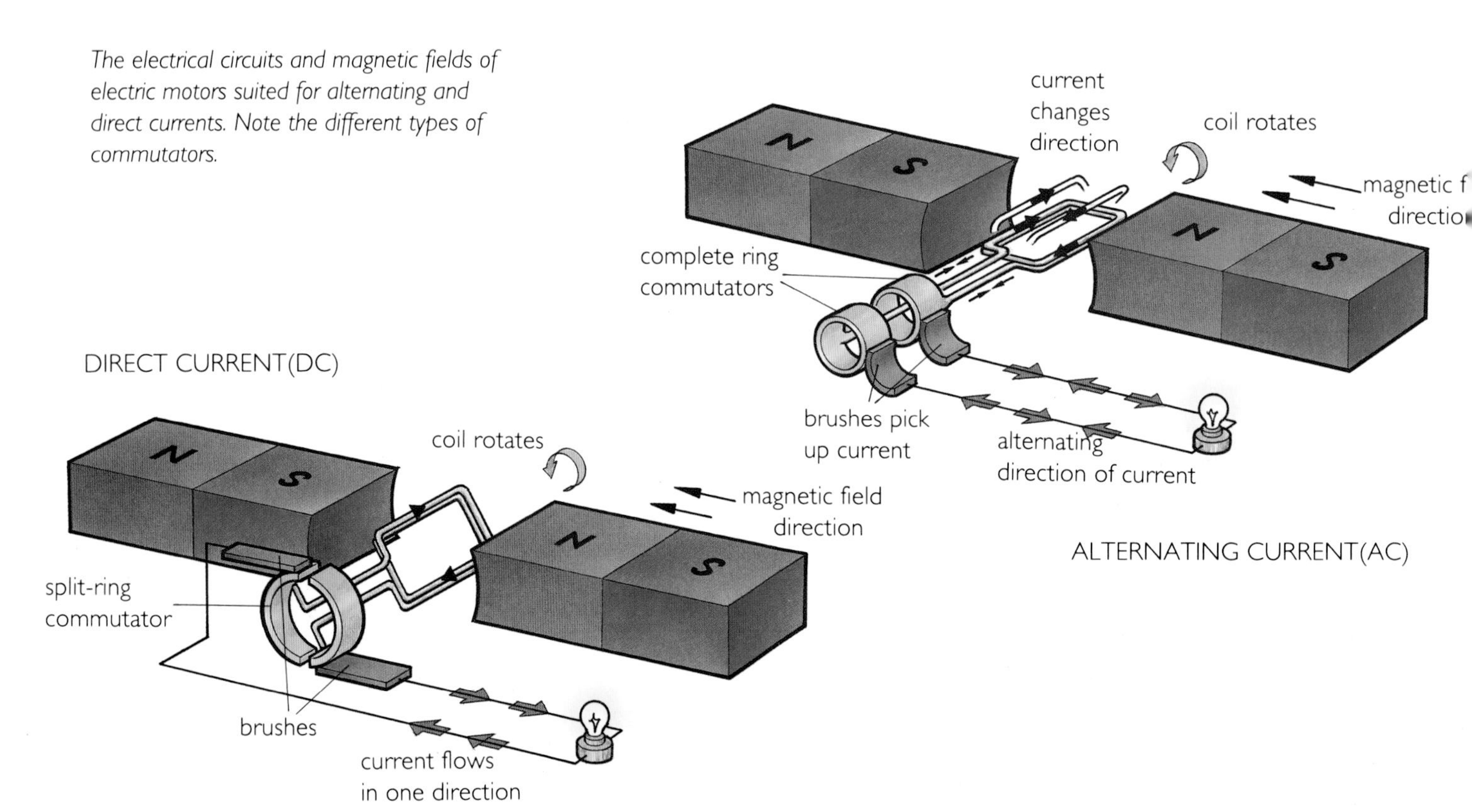

Electricity in action – providing lighting and power to machinery.

The generator

A motor, besides converting electricity into movement, can also do the reverse and convert movement into electricity. If the coil of a motor is connected to a light bulb and the coil is turned by hand, the bulb will light up. The rotating coil is producing, or generating, an electric current which is flowing through the bulb, making it glow. When it produces electricity in this way, the device is called a generator or dynamo.

If a generator has a split-ring commutator, the current produced always flows through the lamp in the same direction. This type of current is called direct current (DC). Some generators, however, have a commutator which has a complete metal ring attached to each end of the coil. This produces a current which flows back and forth, first in one direction, then in the opposite direction. This type of current is called alternating current (AC).

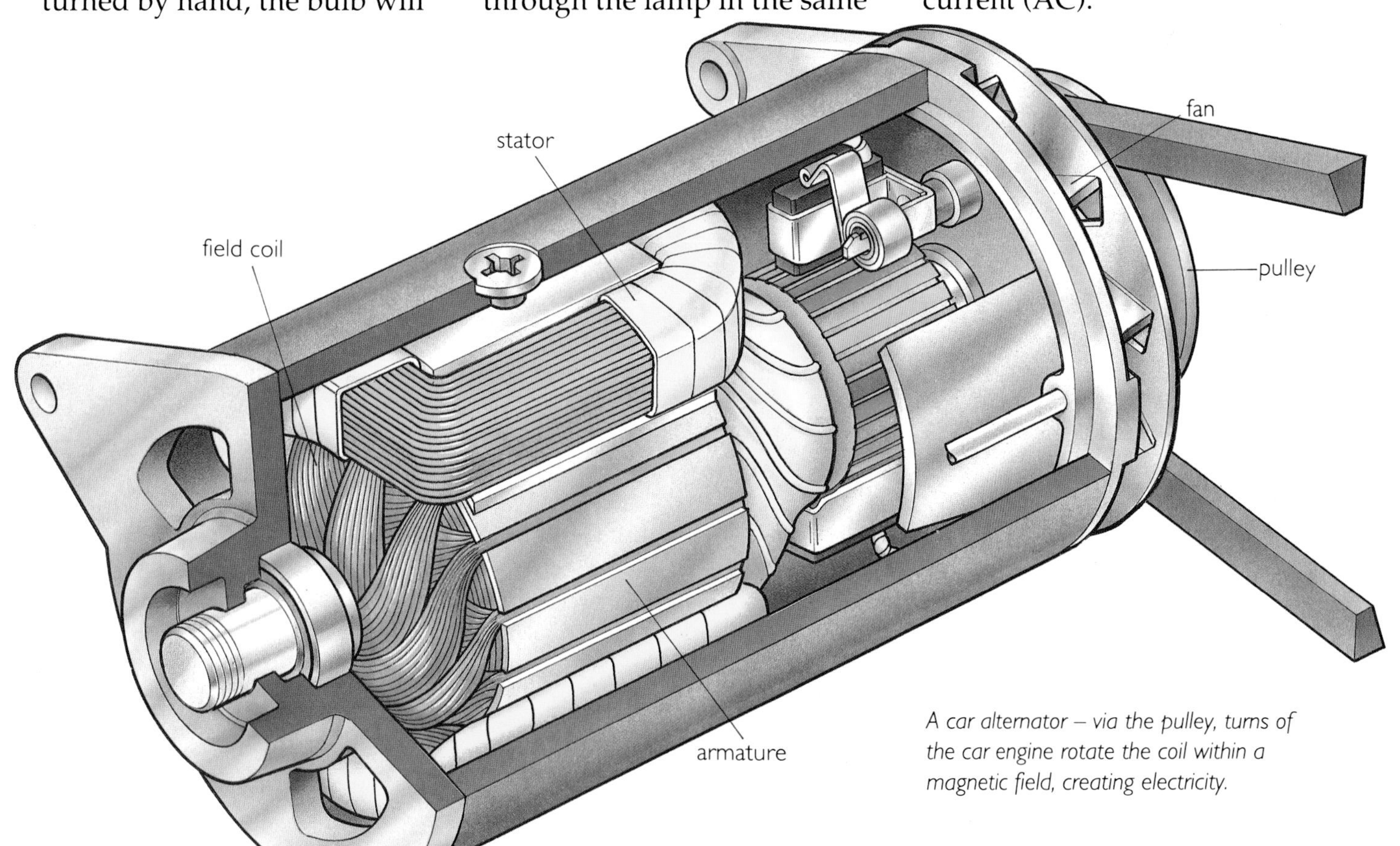

A car alternator – via the pulley, turns of the car engine rotate the coil within a magnetic field, creating electricity.

Engines and Turbines

An engine is a machine for making things move. An electric motor is one kind of engine. Other kinds are used in motor vehicles, locomotives or aircraft.

The steam engine

In a steam engine water is boiled to produce steam by burning fuel, such as coal or wood. The steam is fed into a hollow tube called a cylinder. Inside the cylinder is a thick, tight-fitting disc, called a piston, which can move up and down the cylinder. As the steam flows into the cylinder, the piston is forced to move. Steam is fed into each end of the cylinder in turn, driving the piston back and forth. If the engine is fitted into a locomotive, for example, the movement of the piston can be used to turn the wheels.

Below: *Steam entering the cylinder pushes a piston which turns a wheel to drive machinery. This is a steam engine of the late nineteenth century.*

Petrol engines

The engines used in motor cars and motorcycles are called internal combustion engines. They burn petrol fuel inside the cylinder, and the hot gases produced push the piston down the cylinder.

Car engines are called four-stroke engines because they produce their power in four movements, or strokes, of the piston. During the first stroke a mixture of fuel and air is drawn into the cylinder through a valve as the piston moves down. The piston then moves up again, compressing the fuel/air mixture.

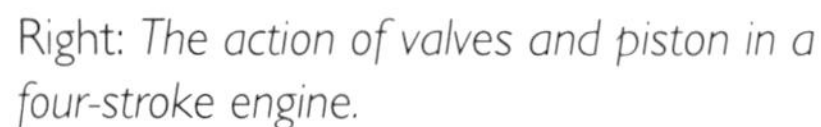

Right: *The action of valves and piston in a four-stroke engine.*

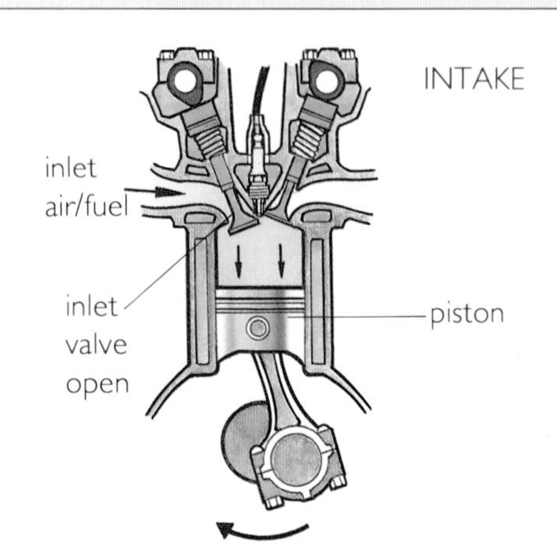

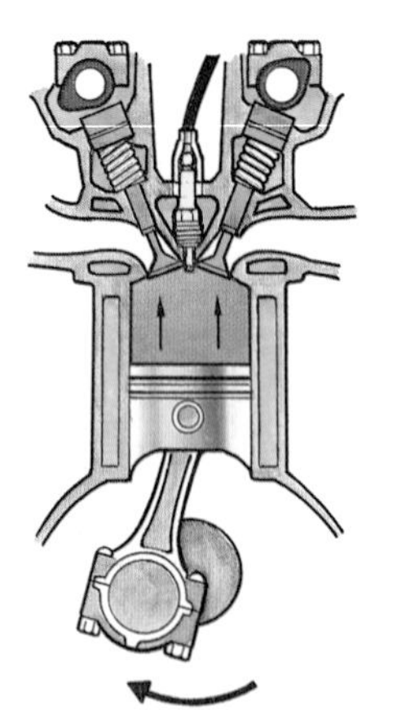

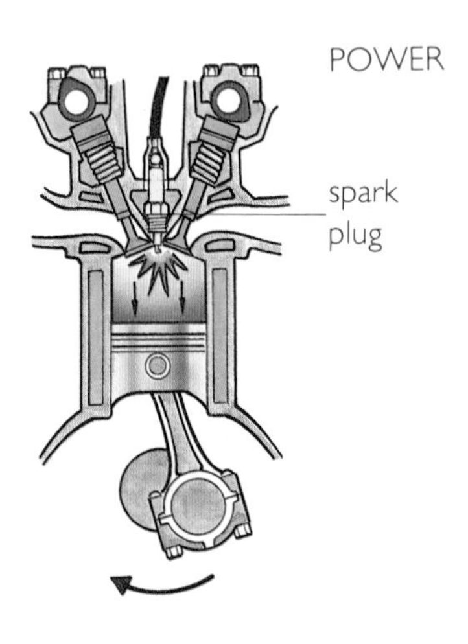

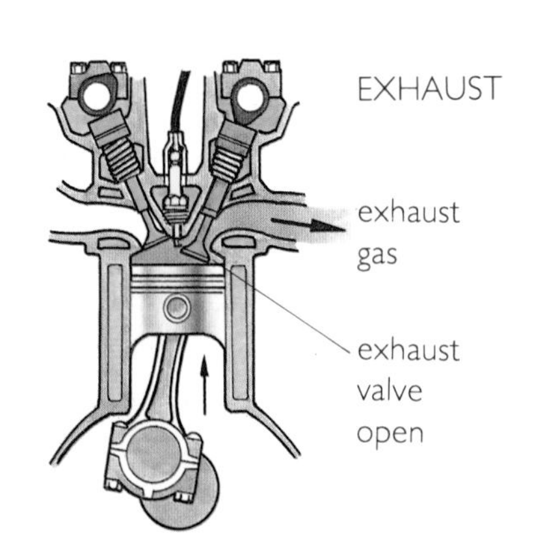

When the mixture is fully compressed, a spark plug at the top of the cylinder produces an electric spark which explodes the fuel. The hot gases produced in the explosion drive the piston down for the third stroke, called the power stroke. During the fourth stroke, the piston moves upwards, forcing the burned gases out of the cylinder through a valve.

In a diesel engine, used in many trucks and locomotives as well as some cars, no spark plug is required. The diesel fuel, which is similar to petrol (but cheaper), is squirted into the cylinder when the up stroke of the piston has compressed the air so much that it is hot enough to explode without a spark.

Motorcycles use a two-stroke engine, which is similar to a four-stroke engine but produces its power with two movements of the piston.

The jet engine

Another type of engine is called the gas turbine. The jet engine used in many aircraft is one type of gas turbine. Inside this engine hot gases are produced by burning fuel and air which is drawn in at the front of the engine. The hot gases expand, forcing their way through the blades of a small turbine which turns at high speed. The turbine is connected to a fan at the front of the engine which sucks air into the engine and compresses it. The driving power comes from the exhaust gases hurtling from the rear.

Above: A jet fighter plane capable of speeds of 2,500kph (1,500mph).

Below: A turbofan engine, with a big front fan forcing air into the jet system and also around it.

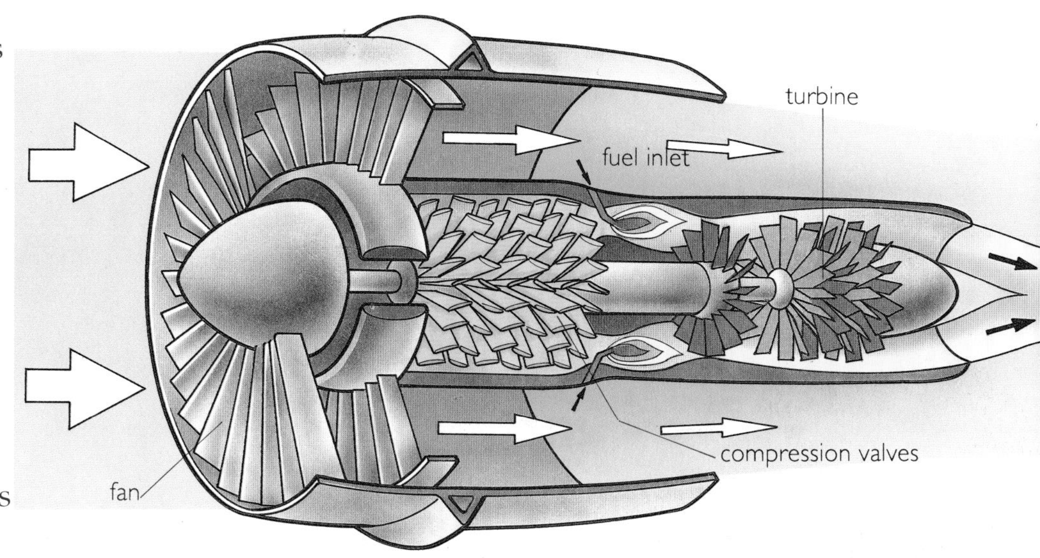

Batteries and Fuel Cells

Batteries are used where it is difficult to get electricity from the mains supply. They are used, for example, in torches, portable radios and hearing aids. Batteries convert chemical energy into electrical energy. Inside a battery chemical changes take place. These changes produce an electrical pressure, or voltage, which can push electrons along a wire, making a complete circuit with the battery. Electrical pressure is measured in units called volts.

Simple cells

In the earliest batteries, a plate of copper and a plate of zinc were placed in a bowl of liquid, called an electrolyte. The electrolyte was weak sulphuric acid. An electric current flowed through a wire connected to the copper and zinc plates, called electrodes.

These simple devices were called cells. When many cells are connected together they make a battery. Until the electrical generator was invented in 1831 by Michael Faraday, simple cells and batteries were the only way that steady currents of electricity could be made.

The dry cell

The type of cell used in torches is called a dry cell, because it does not contain a liquid electrolyte. One electrode is a carbon rod in the centre of the cell. The casing of the cell, made of zinc, forms the other electrode. Lining the inside of the zinc casing is a layer of paste made with a chemical called ammonium chloride. This is the electrolyte. Between the carbon rod and the electrolyte layer is a black powder made up of various chemicals which help the cell last longer.

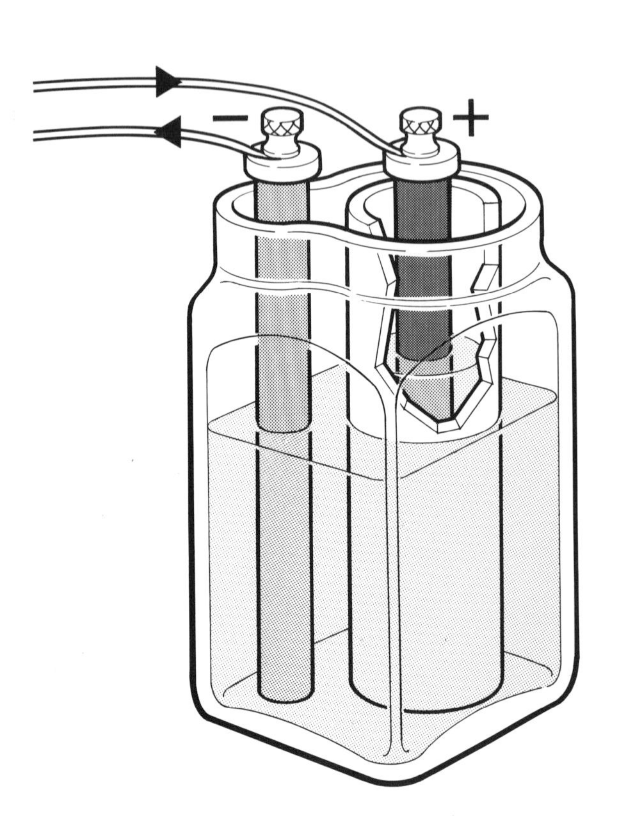

Above: *A Leclanché 'wet' cell – the electrolyte is a mixture of a liquid and a paste, or in the 'dry' version, just a paste.*

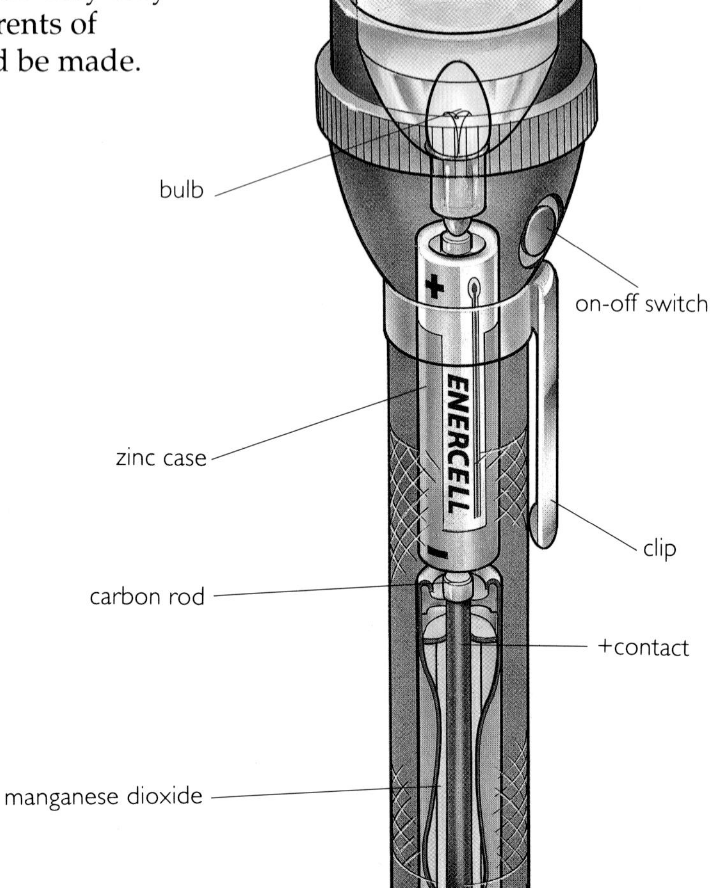

Right: *A torch with two batteries, or dry cells, the bottom one cut away to show the electrodes and electrolyte.*

THE SOLAR CELL

The solar, or photoelectric cell is a device which produces electricity from light. It is used in some calculators, in space satellites, cameras, light meters, and even to power experimental vehicles.

Inside a photoelectric cell are layers of materials called semiconductors. When light falls on to the edges of the layers, a small electric current is produced. This current is largest when the light is bright so, by measuring the size of the current produced, the brightness of the light can be calculated. That is how a light meter works. To produce a large current many photoelectric cells are connected together. In this way enough power can be produced to run a motor vehicle or even an aeroplane.

In 1987 solar-powered vehicles raced across Australia, north to south, a distance of 3,138km (1,950 miles). The winner completed the journey in six days. Solar-powered aircraft have been developed too. One flew across the English Channel in 1981.

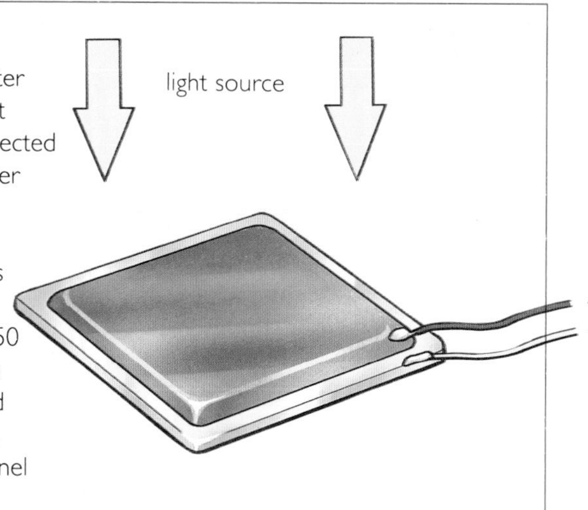

A lead accumulator or 'car battery'. Unlike simple cells or primary batteries, it can be recharged if it runs down.

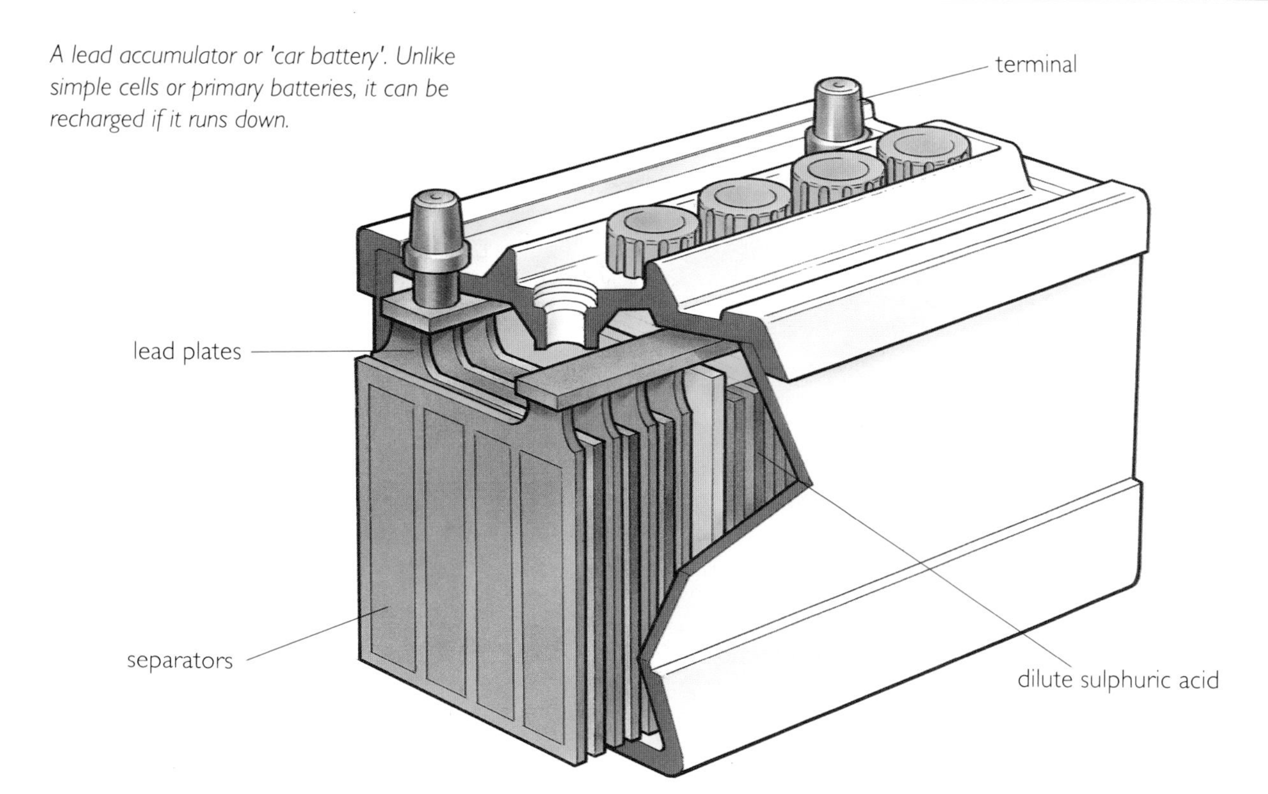

Storage batteries

Dry cells have one big disadvantage. After a time they run down and stop producing electricity, because the chemicals in the cell are used up. To overcome this, storage cells have been developed. These cells can be recharged with electricity if they run down.

A motor-car battery is a storage battery. It has lead electrodes, with sulphuric acid as the electrolyte, and is usually called a lead accumulator. When the car is moving, a generator attached to the engine produces electricity. This electricity is pumped into the battery and stored, or accumulated, there. When the car is stationary the electricity stored in the battery can be used to run the lights or start the engine.

Fuel cells

The fuel cell is similar to other batteries. Like them, it changes chemical energy to electrical energy. However, a fuel cell needs to be supplied with fuel all the time it is in use. Some fuel cells use hydrogen and oxygen as fuels. The hydrogen and oxygen gases combine inside the cell to form water, at the same time producing electricity.

Power Stations

The electricity that we use in our homes, offices and factories is produced in power stations. Most power stations run on coal, oil or natural gas. Other stations are powered by nuclear energy or by the energy of water flowing from a high dam.

A modern coal or oil-powered power station uses heat from the burning fuel to heat water in a boiler. The steam produced travels through pipes to a turbine where it flows over a series of windmill-like vanes, making the turbine revolve. The turbine drives a generator, which produces the electricity.

The boiler

The boiler consists of a tall furnace whose inside walls are lined with pipes carrying water. In a coal-powered station, the coal is brought to the boiler by conveyor belts. It is ground into a powder as fine as flour, then mixed with air and blown by fans into the furnace, where it burns.

The heat produced boils the water, producing steam. The steam is first collected and then recirculated through the hottest parts of the furnace. This produces extra-hot, or superheated, steam.

The turbine

The superheated steam passes through pipes to three turbines, connected together. After passing through the first, high-pressure turbine, the steam is taken back to the boiler where it is reheated. It then passes through the other two turbines, gradually giving up its energy. Finally, the steam is changed back to water in a condenser, a large container cooled by pipes carrying cold water from a nearby river. The cooling water takes the last of the heat from the steam, which condenses as hot water and goes back to the boiler to start all over again.

Below: *The major parts of a coal-fired power station. The generator produces electricity which is fed into the national grid.*

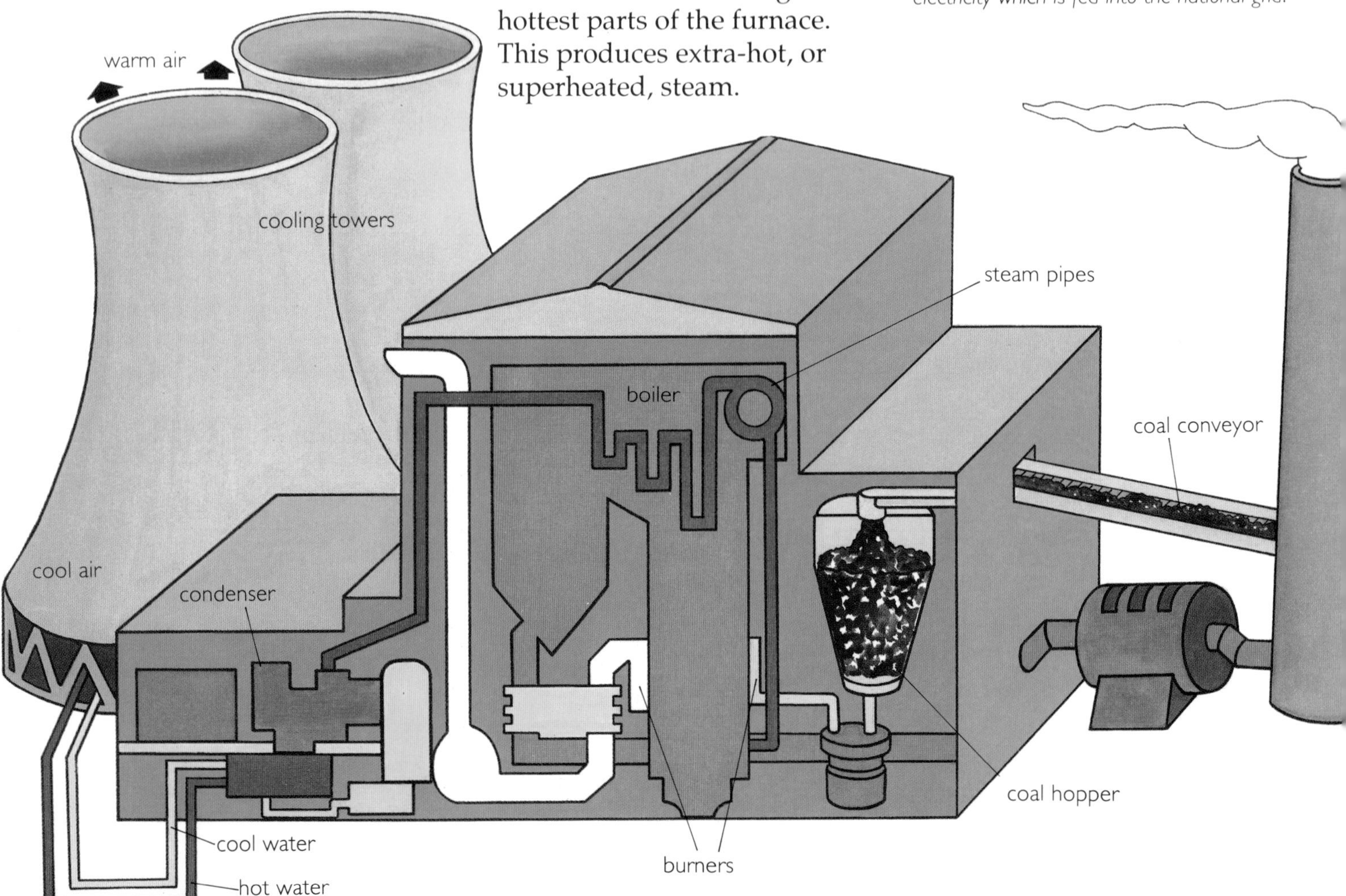

The generator

The rotating turbines turn the generators, which consist basically of two coils of wire. One, called the rotor, is turned by the turbine. The other, called the stator, is wound around an iron core and fixed to the floor. The iron core is weakly magnetic at all times, so that when the generator first starts up a small electric current starts to flow in the rotating coil. Some of the current is fed into the stationary coil, which becomes a strong electromagnet. As this happens, the strength of the electric current increases steadily until full power is reached.

Right: *A dam built across a river to use the force of falling water from the reservoir behind it. The falling water turns turbines built into the wall of the dam. This is a form of hydroelectric power.*

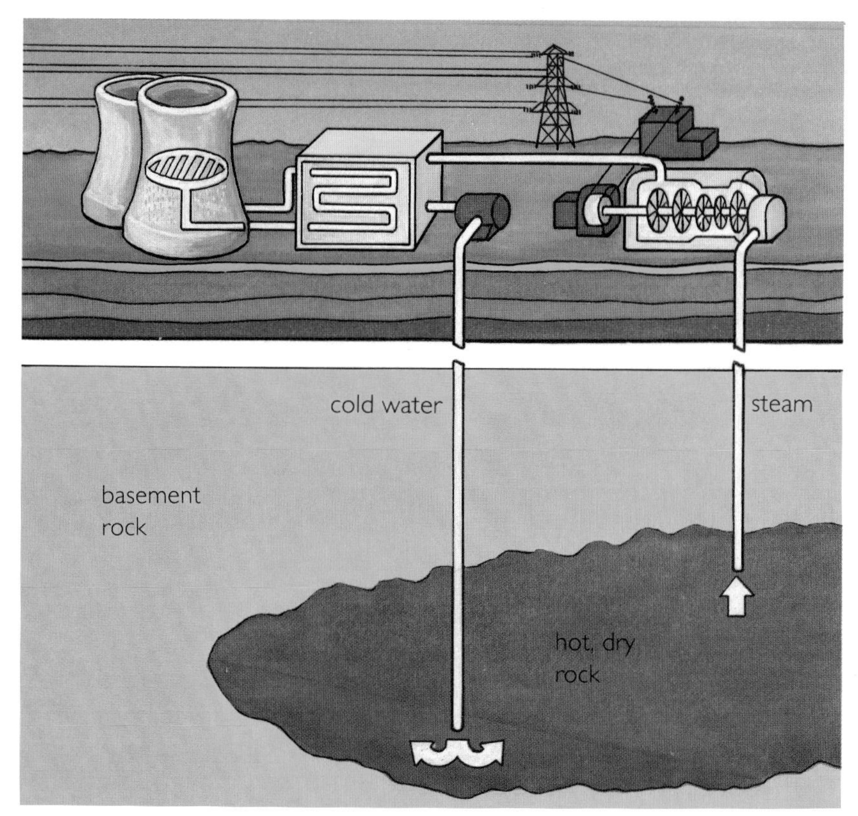

HOT ROCK

The Earth is a vast storehouse of geothermal ('Earth-heat') energy. Heat from the layers of hot rock near the centre of the Earth sometimes flows to the surface and can be used as a source of energy.

The most successful use of geothermal energy has been in regions of natural hot springs and geysers, such as those in Yellowstone National Park in the United States, Wairakei in New Zealand and Larderello in Italy. Boreholes are drilled into the ground near a hot spring or geyser. High-pressure, hot steam flows out of the hole and is pumped directly into nearby power stations to produce electricity. Where the underground rocks are hot but dry, water is pumped down to them and when it has been heated it is then pumped back to the surface.

Nuclear Power

A nuclear power station is very similar to a coal or oil-powered one. The only real difference is the source of heat. Inside a nuclear station, the nuclei of uranium atoms are broken apart, or split, to produce heat. This process is called nuclear fission.

Nuclear fission

Natural uranium is a mixture of two kinds of atoms or isotopes known as uranium 235 and uranium 238. The number tells how many particles exist in the nucleus of each atom. The nucleus of uranium 235 consists of 92 protons and 143 neutrons; uranium 238 has 92 protons but 146 neutrons.

The nucleus of the uranium 235 atom can break into parts if it is hit by a neutron. When a uranium 235 nucleus splits it releases energy and two or three more neutrons. If these neutrons hit more uranium atoms, further splitting can occur. A 'chain reaction' is set off, in which one nucleus after another is split, with power being released continually.

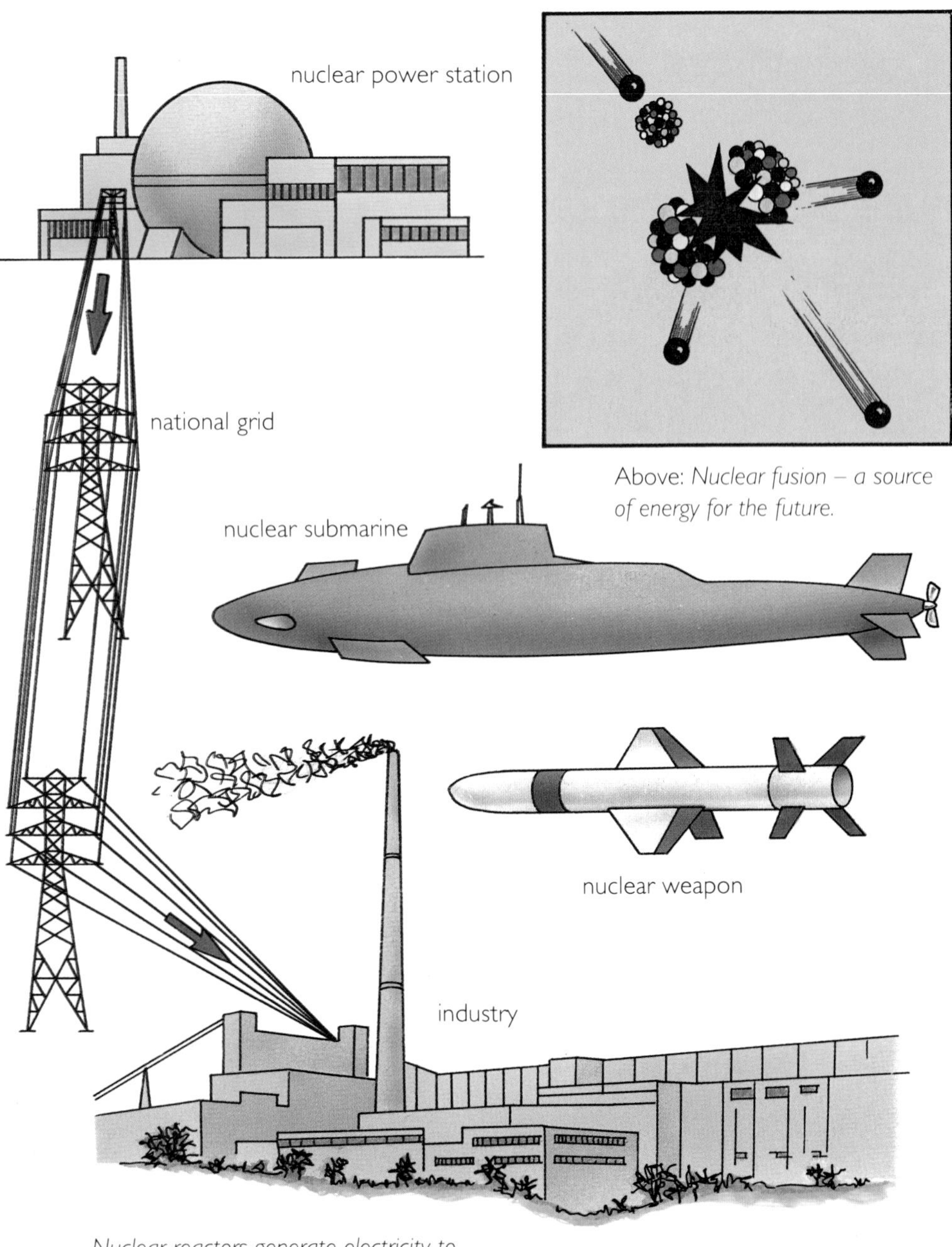

Above: *Nuclear fusion – a source of energy for the future.*

Nuclear reactors generate electricity to operate machinery in factories, engines on craft such as submarines, and to produce plutonium for nuclear weapons.

NUCLEAR FUSION

Nuclear fusion is the process which powers the Sun and stars. The nuclei of hydrogen atoms join together to form helium, which releases enormous amounts of energy. Scientists are trying to harness the power of nuclear fusion but there are many problems to be solved. The hydrogen nuclei have to be heated to very high temperatures, up to about 100,000,000°C, and kept close together for a few seconds before they join, or fuse. No ordinary container could hold this super-hot plasma. Instead, powerful magnetic fields are used. The magnetism is produced by huge electric currents flowing through coils of wire wrapped around a hollow, doughnut-shaped container, called a torus, which holds the plasma. The magnetic fields produced force the plasma away from the wall of the container. The plasma then becomes very hot and the hydrogen nuclei in the plasma fuse together.

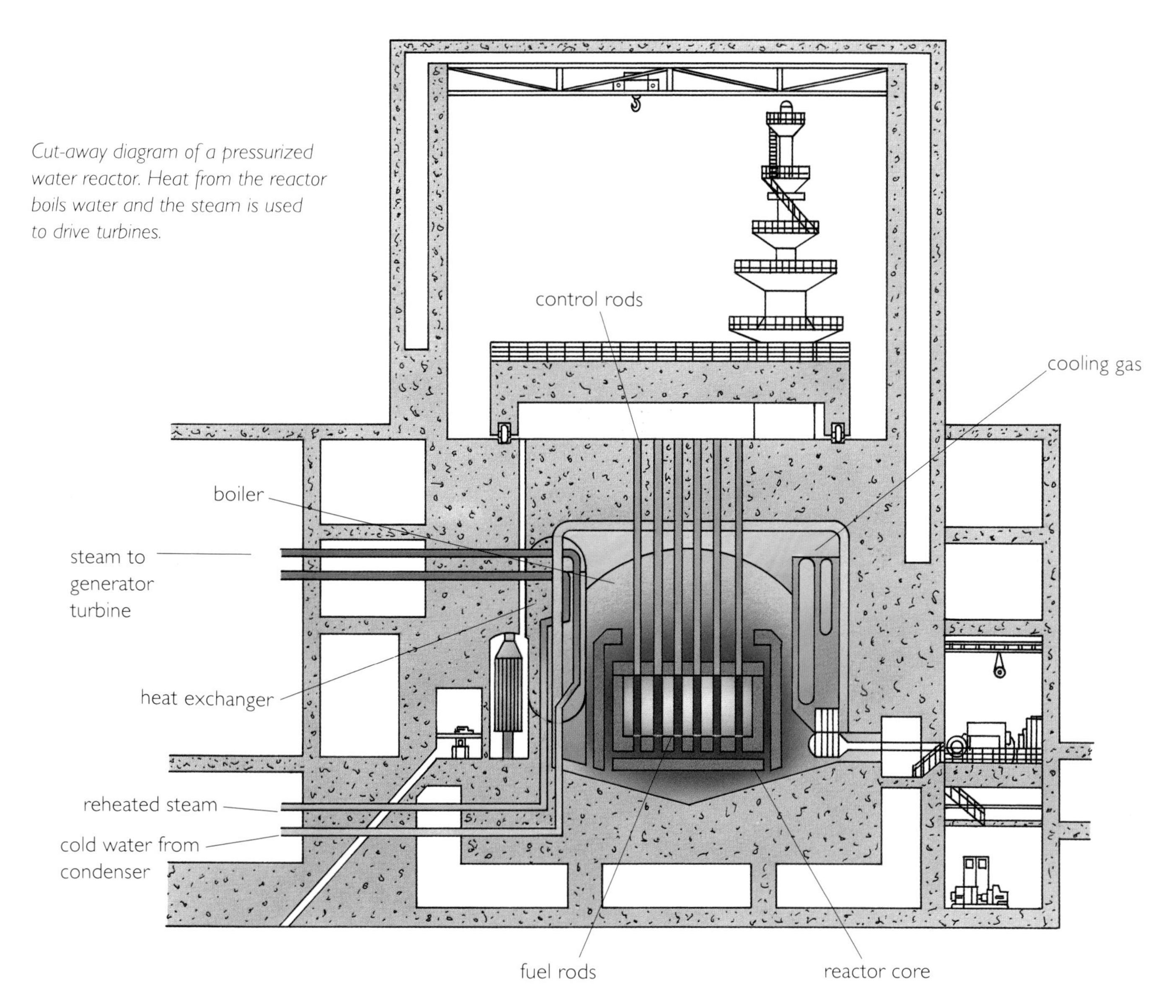

Cut-away diagram of a pressurized water reactor. Heat from the reactor boils water and the steam is used to drive turbines.

Inside a nuclear reactor
In a nuclear reactor natural uranium, or uranium oxide treated or 'enriched' to increase the amount of uranium 235, is sealed in rods. The rods are grouped in clusters called fuel elements. A liquid or gas flows around the rods to carry the heat produced to the boiler.

Other rods, called control rods, made from a material like boron which can absorb neutrons, are placed near the fuel rods. They can be raised and lowered to control the amount of heat produced by the fuel elements.

The whole collection of fuel elements and control rods is embedded in a material known as a moderator, which can be graphite or water. Its function is to slow down the neutrons produced. This makes the energy-production process much more efficient.

The reactor assembly is surrounded by a shield of concrete or steel several metres thick. This is intended to prevent any dangerous radiation escaping from the reactor.

The fast-breeder reactor
A different and important type of reactor is the fast-breeder reactor. The fuel used in the fast-breeder is highly enriched uranium 235 or plutonium, a very powerful nuclear fuel. Surrounding the fuel is a layer of uranium 238. As fission takes place in the fuel, some of the uranium 238 is changed into plutonium. This plutonium can be extracted and used as fuel. In this way the fast-breeder reactor actually produces more fuel than it uses.

Electricity Supply

Electrical power stations are usually built far from large towns so that the people in the towns are not bothered by smoke and fumes. However, this means that homes, offices and factories in the cities must be connected to power stations by a system of long cables called the electricity grid.

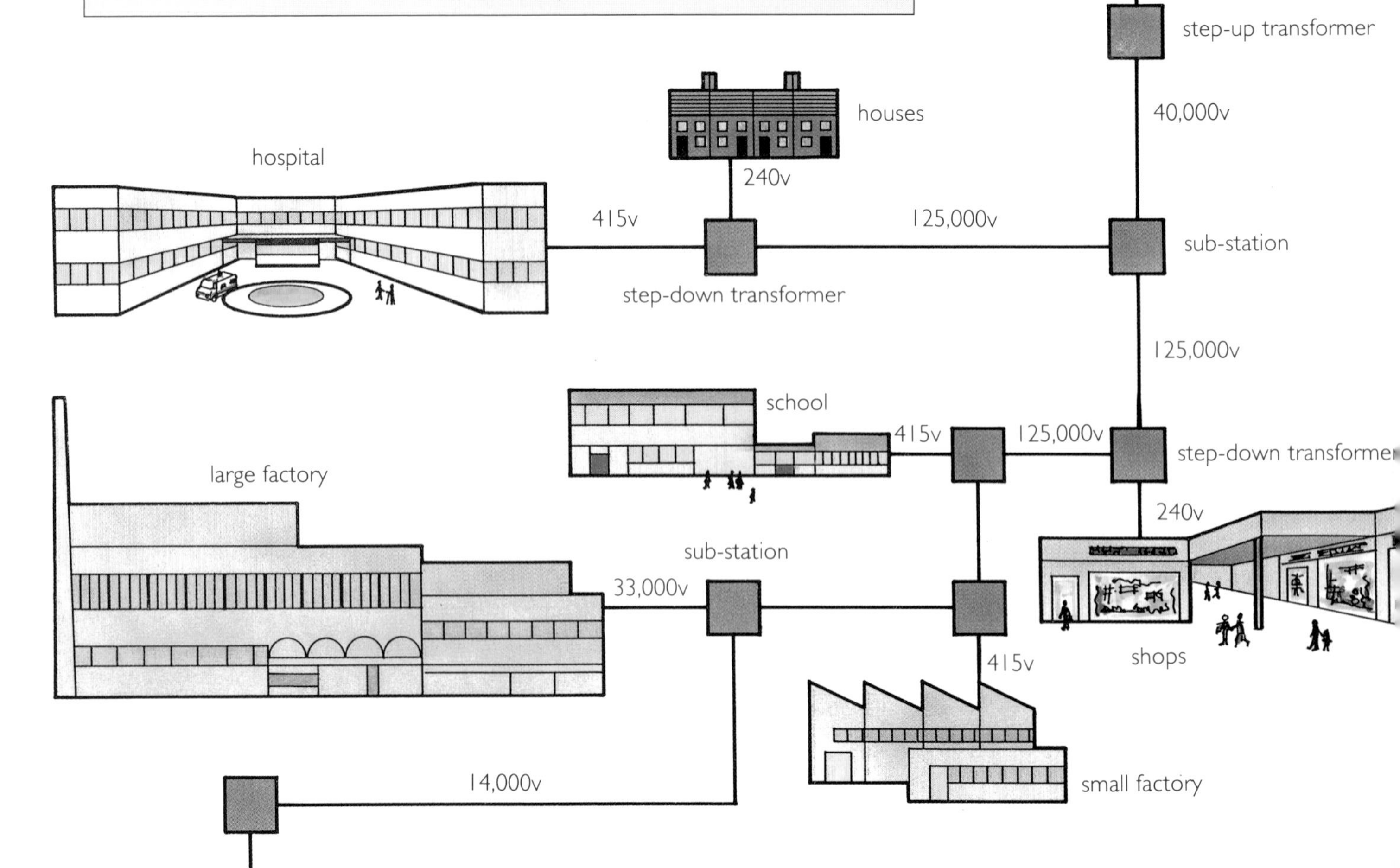

Above: *An electricity grid leading from a coal-fired power station to houses, shops, factories, schools and hospitals. All along the grid are transformer stations which control how much electricity to allow into buildings.*

The electricity grid
The most obvious parts of the electricity grid are the large towers or pylons that support cables across country. The cables on these pylons carry electricity at a very high voltage – 400,000 volts or more – because energy is wasted if electricity is conducted at low voltages. At each end of a high-voltage transmission line is a device called a transformer, which can change the voltage of an alternating electrical current. 'Step-up' transformers increase the voltage, while 'step-down' transformers reduce it.

At the power station a step-up transformer forms the link between the generator and the transmission line. At the users' end of the line, a step-down transformer creates the lower voltage that can be safely used in factories, shops, hospitals, schools and homes.

Inside the home
Inside the home electricity flows first through a meter which measures the amount of power being used.

Different kinds of electrical equipment use electricity at different rates. The rate at which the equipment uses electrical energy is called its power, which is measured in units called watts. An average light bulb uses electricity at a rate of 60 or 100 watts. An electric heater uses much more power – perhaps 3,000 watts (three kilowatts). A radio uses only about 50 watts.

Every electrical circuit has a fuse, or circuit-breaker, a thin piece of wire that melts easily when a dangerously large electric current passes through it. It is a kind of safety switch. It ensures that if too much current flows through the wires, the current is switched off before the wires heat up and start a fire.

The electric wiring in a home is made up of two separate systems. The power circuit connects the cooker and hot-water heater to the electricity supply. The lighting circuit connects the lights. The two systems are kept separate so that different fuses can be used on each circuit. The power circuit must be able to carry a much bigger current than the lighting circuit.

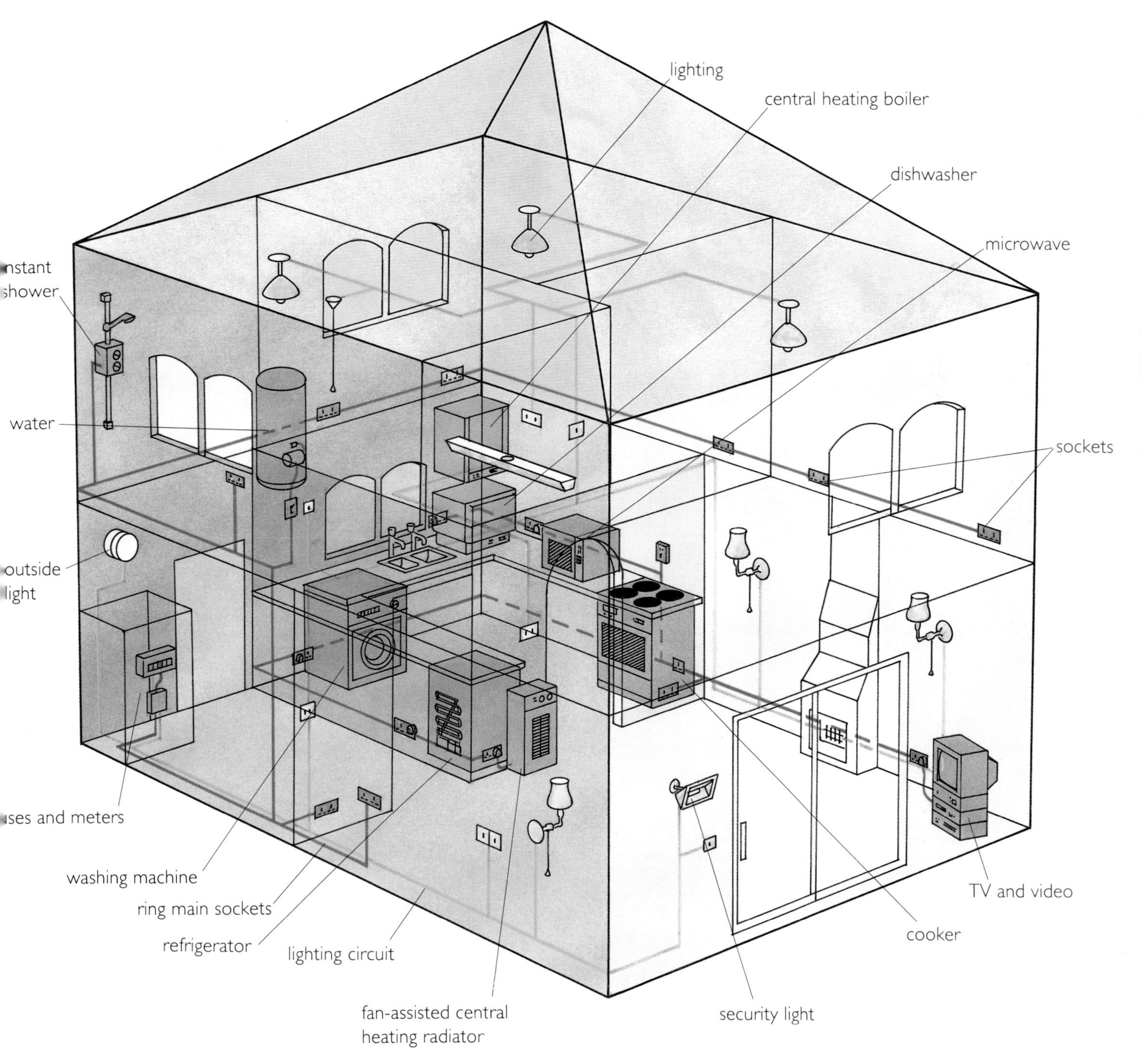

Fossil Fuels

Most of the world's energy comes from burning oil, coal and natural gas. The energy they produce in the form of heat is turned into electricity or used to drive machines. These fuels are called fossil fuels because they were formed from the remains of things that lived millions of years ago. Coal was formed from rotting, compressed trees and ferns; oil and gas from the remains of tiny sea animals and plants. As fossil fuels are found below the Earth's surface, they have to be extracted by mining or drilling.

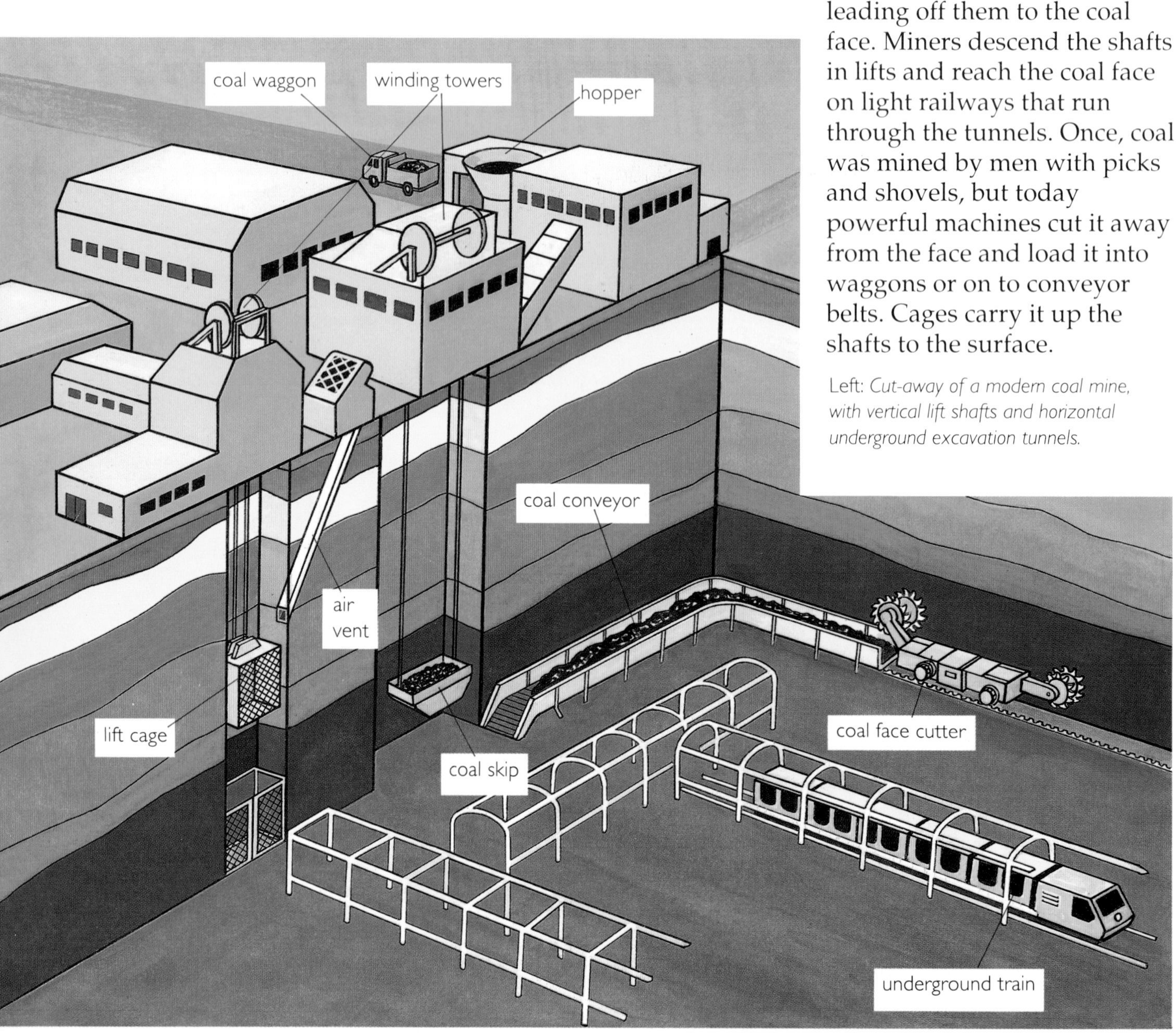

Coal

In some places, coal deposits lie near the surface. They can then be extracted by open cast mining. After the surface soil has been removed, enormous excavators (some weigh up to 12,000 tonnes) and power shovels break up the coal and load it direct into lorries.

More often, the coal lies deeper, sometimes several hundred metres below the surface. Shafts are bored downwards, with tunnels leading off them to the coal face. Miners descend the shafts in lifts and reach the coal face on light railways that run through the tunnels. Once, coal was mined by men with picks and shovels, but today powerful machines cut it away from the face and load it into waggons or on to conveyor belts. Cages carry it up the shafts to the surface.

Left: *Cut-away of a modern coal mine, with vertical lift shafts and horizontal underground excavation tunnels.*

Oil

Coal used to be much the most common fuel, but in the past 30 years it has been overtaken by oil. In 1939 world production of oil was under 300 million tonnes a year. By 1979 it was over 3,000 million tonnes. Some of the oil is used to make chemicals, from which we get plastics, drugs, explosives and other materials, but most is burned by the engines of motor vehicles.

Oil deposits first have to be located by geologists. At a spot where oil is believed to exist, a hole is drilled by a powerful cutting bit at the end of a long pipe. When the oil is reached, it gushes up to the surface. Since the 1970s, oil has also been obtained from below the sea-bed, especially in the North Sea. The extraction process is much the same, but it is more difficult and dangerous because drilling has to be done from floating oil rigs, and when oil is found, a production platform has to be built which stands on giant legs resting on the sea-bed. In a fire and explosion on a British rig in the North Sea in 1988, 167 oil workers were killed.

Below: *An offshore oil rig with drilling, accommodation and heliport facilities.*

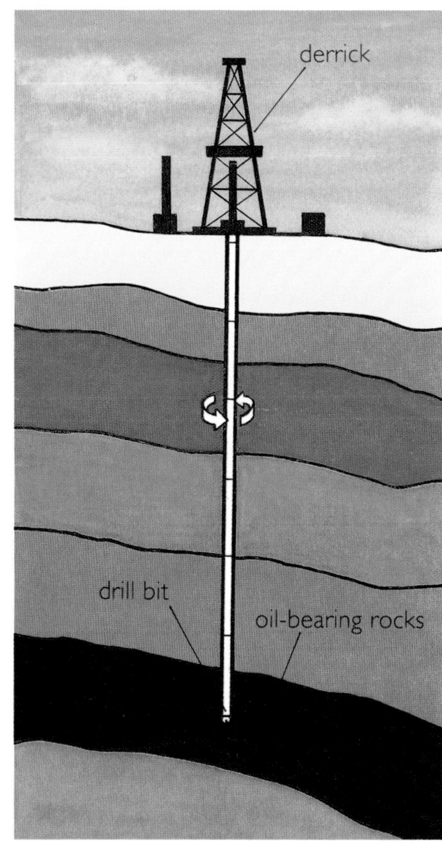

Above: *Diagram of a land-based oil drilling derrick. The drill pipe, with drill bit on the end, is extended at the derrick by adding new sections.*

The future

Fossil fuels have serious drawbacks. They cannot be replaced and they will not last for ever. At the present rate, the Earth's oil supply is likely to run out in the next century, though coal will last longer. Also, the world's largest oil-producing region is the Middle East, where political troubles, including war, occur, as in the 1991 Gulf War. Middle Eastern conflicts caused a huge and sudden rise in world oil prices in the 1970s – about 600 per cent in six years. That created severe economic problems throughout the world, especially for poorer countries which could no longer afford to buy the oil they needed.

Sun and Sea Power

Coal and oil-fired power stations have one serious disadvantage. They produce pollution in the form of waste gases and fumes. Some of the gases create acid rain. Others are believed to be causing a change in the Earth's climate. Nuclear power stations do not cause this kind of pollution, but they produce radioactive materials that are harmful to all living things.

Because of these disadvantages, scientists are seeking new, safer ways of producing energy. In particular they are interested in the unlimited power of the sea and the Sun which, unlike coal or oil, are 'renewable' resources: they will not run out.

Solar power

Every year energy from the Sun equal to 500,000 billion barrels of oil reaches the Earth. Some of it is absorbed by clouds, but a vast amount of it reaches the ground. One way to capture this energy is with solar panels, which are made up of many photoelectric cells connected together to produce electricity. Solar panels are used to run water pumps in dry, sunny climates, but they are expensive.

A cheaper way of collecting the Sun's energy is to use mirrors. In California in the United States, there is a power station that has 1,800 mirrors to reflect sunlight on to a tank of liquid at the top of a tower. The heated liquid is used to produce steam to turn a turbine and electricity generator. But solar power stations are difficult to make because the mirrors have to be controlled by computers so that they always face the Sun.

Above: *Solar dishes at the electric power station at Themis, France.* Below: *In California, 1,800 mirrors direct solar radiation to a heat collector.*

Energy from the sea

The endless motion of the sea can also be used to provide energy. One method makes use of special buoys. As they bob up and down their movement can be harnessed to generate electricity. The lights on some navigation buoys are powered in this way.

In another method, a tall column is fixed to the sea-bed, open at the bottom so that water can flow into it. When that happens, air inside the column is squeezed through a turbine at the top. There are generators like this in Scotland, Ireland and Norway.

A new kind of hydroelectric power station on the River Rance in France makes use of tidal power. As the tide flows up the river it passes through gates in a dam. At high tide the gates are closed, trapping the water above the dam. It is allowed to flow back to the sea through turbines.

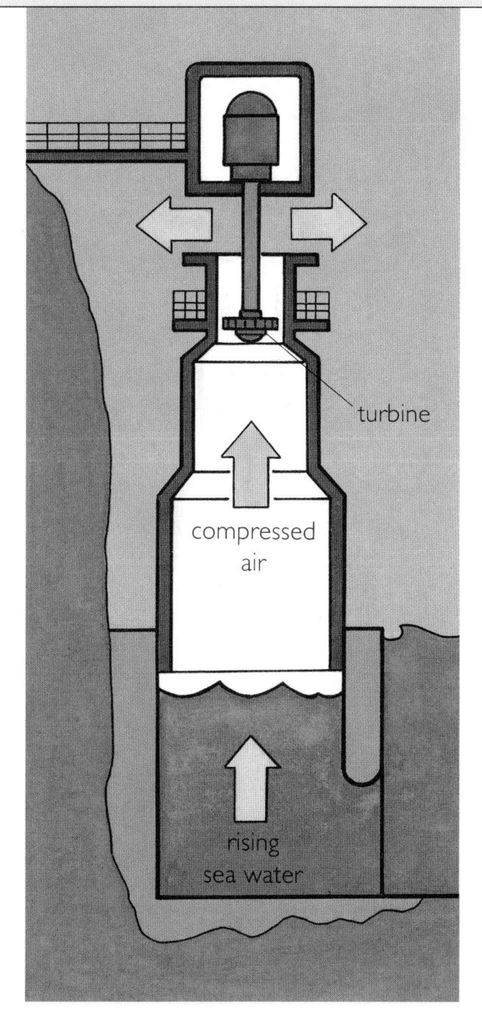

Wave power generators consist of cliff-face towers (above) *or 'bobbing-duck' devices out at sea* (below).

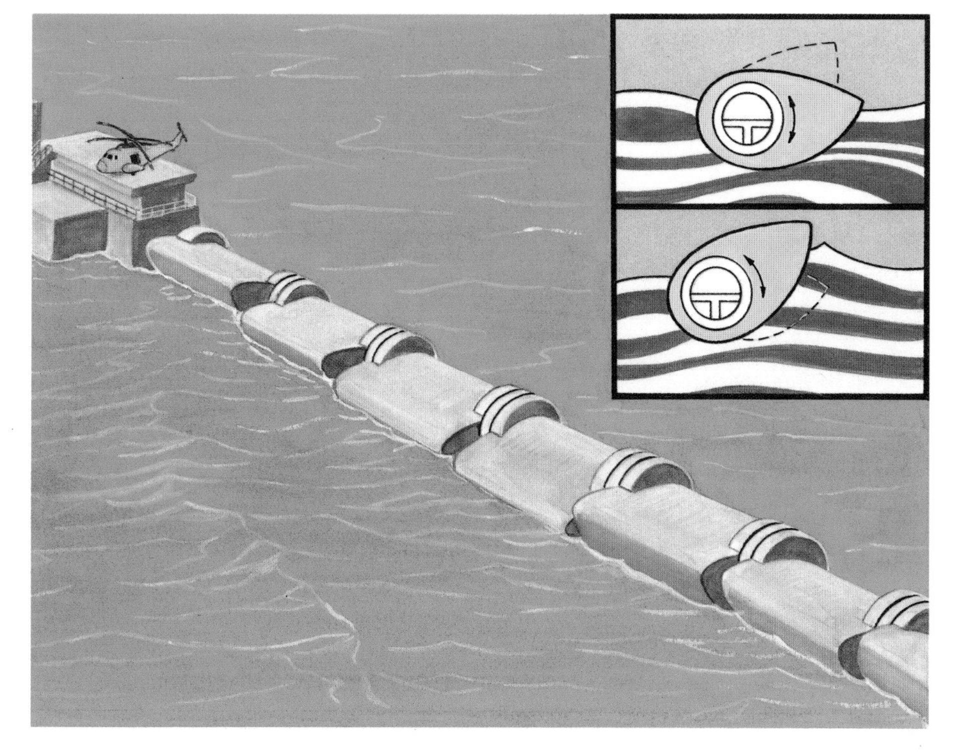

> ACID RAIN
>
> Some gases produced by power stations, such as sulphur dioxide and nitrogen oxide, mix with water in the atmosphere to produce acids which then fall as rain. In some parts of Europe and North America, the rain is as acid as lemon juice. It damages trees, destroying their leaves and eventually killing them and it kills fish and plants in lakes and ponds.

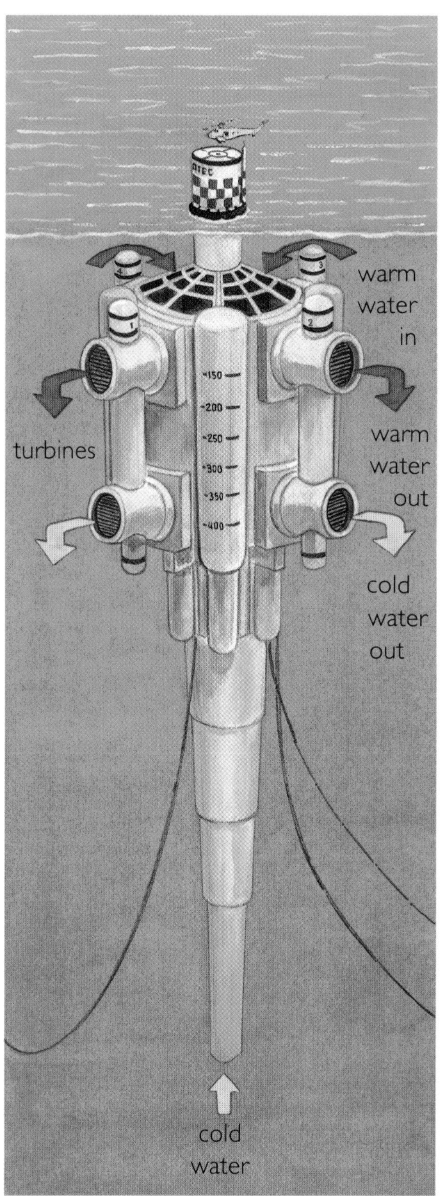

Above: *Diagram of an Ocean Thermal Energy Converter, or OTEC. It uses warm surface water to evaporate liquid ammonia and the vapour drives a turbine.*

Wind and Bio Power

The wind has long been a source of power. Windmills to grind corn were built in Iran as early as the seventh century BC.

Nature provides other sources of energy. Trees give firewood, and dried animal dung is burned as fuel in many countries. Power from living things is called 'bio power'.

Wind generators

Modern, large wind generators exist in several different types. Some look like bigger versions of a normal windmill. The sails, or blades, face into the wind. Often, there are only two giant blades, shaped like the propellers of an aeroplane. Another design consists of two flexible metal strips connected to an upright pole at the top and bottom, which catch the air currents whatever the direction of the wind. A third type has upright blades at the ends of arms attached to the top of a pole. If the wind becomes too strong, the blades fold outwards, which reduces the rotation to a safe speed.

In the Mojave Desert in California, USA, one electricity company is already using wind power commercially. The company has built a 'wind farm' which consists of hundreds of modern windmills, in neat rows across the desert, connected to an electricity generator. It produces electricity for the nearby city of Los Angeles.

Wind farms (below) *comprise many generators each with a rotor blade unit that can usually turn to catch the wind* (right).

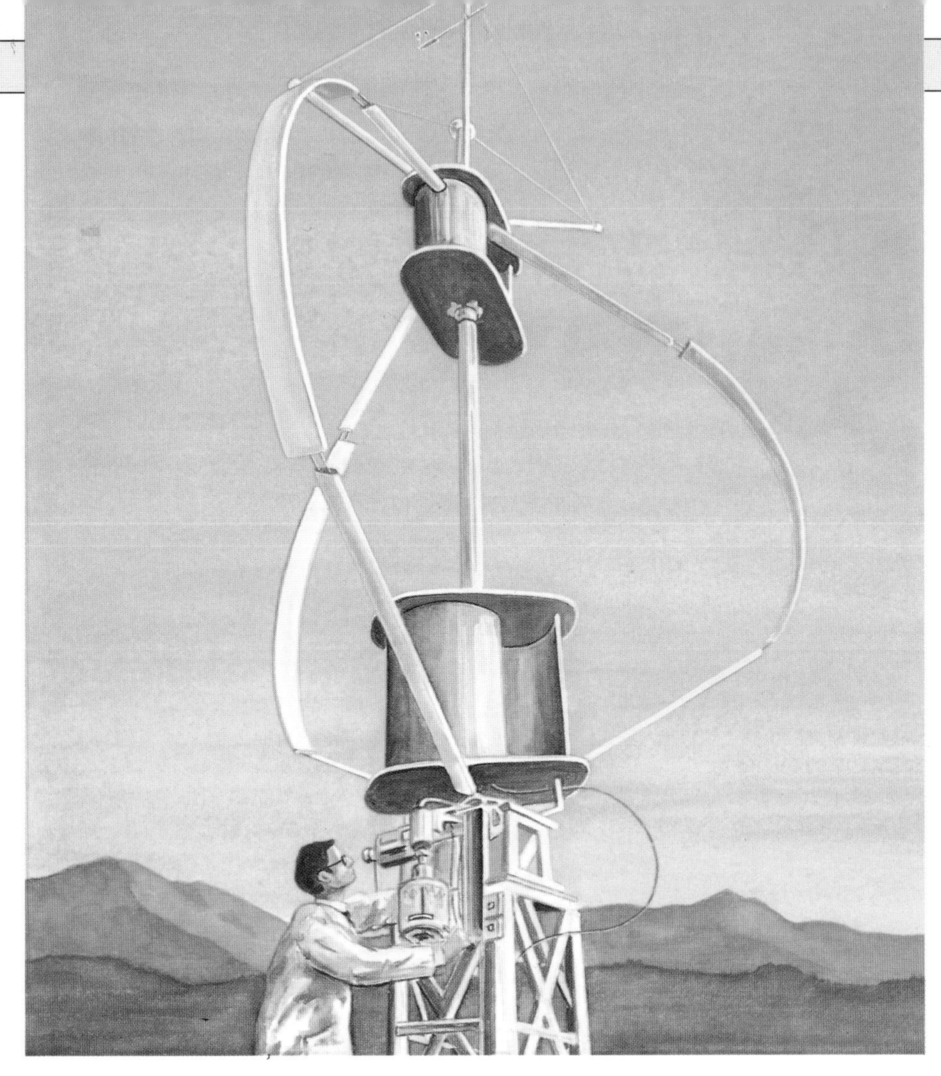

Power from rubbish

An energy-packed gas, called biogas, comes from natural sources such as rotting vegetable, animal and farm waste. It is produced in rubbish tips and swamps, for example.

Biogas consists mainly of methane mixed with some carbon dioxide. Because methane gas burns easily, biogas can be used as fuel. In some countries where other fuels are scarce or too expensive to use, biogas could be used as the main source of fuel. Unfortunately, it also contains small amounts of acids which would soon ruin an ordinary engine. However, special engines have been built that stop the acid gases from reaching delicate engine parts.

Above left: *A wind generator with vertical blades. This rotor unit spins in the horizontal plane so is ideal for places where the wind direction changes frequently.*
Below: *Domestic waste being taken from storage units to a refuse-burning incinerator to create heating for houses and offices.*

Plant power

Most of the world's people live in developing countries and rely on plants as their energy source, burning wood for cooking and heating.

In Brazil, liquid fuel is produced from sugar cane. The fuel is a form of alcohol, called alcool, and it can be obtained from cassava (a tropical plant from which we get tapioca), from grains such as wheat, and from seaweed and other plants. The plants are fermented in the same way that grape juice is fermented to make wine. The alcohol, which is boiled off from the resulting liquid, contains about half the energy of petrol and when mixed with petrol can be used in motor vehicles.

References

Acid rain Rain which is polluted by man-made waste gases forming a weak acid.

Alternating current (AC) An electric current that flows first in one direction, then in the opposite direction; normal household supply in Britain is AC.

Alternator *see* **Generator**.

Battery A source of electrical power which produces electricity from chemicals, usually containing many electrical cells linked together.

Biogas Gas, mainly methane, given off by rotting vegetation or decaying dung, which can be burned as fuel.

Bio power Energy from living sources, such as animal dung or rotting plants.

Cell In biology, the smallest piece of a living plant or animal. In physics, a cell is a device that produces, or stores, electricity from chemical changes.

Circuit-breaker A sensitive switch used in electrical circuits which switches off the electricity if the current grows too large.

Commutator A split ring used in a direct-current (DC) electric motor to keep the coil turning in one direction.

Diesel engine An internal combustion engine using diesel oil as fuel, in which the fuel is ignited by hot compressed air.

Direct current (DC) An electric current that flows in one direction only.

Dry cell A small electrical cell or battery, as used in a flashlight.

Dynamo *see* **Generator**.

Electrode A metal piece into and out of which an electric current passes, such as the terminals of a battery.

Electrolyte A liquid that conducts electricity, such as the liquid in an electrical cell or battery.

Energy The ability to do work. Energy takes many forms, such as heat, light or electrical energy.

Faraday, Michael (1791–1867) English scientist who studied the connection between electricity and magnetism and invented the transformer, the dynamo and the electric motor.

Force Something which makes an object move or change shape or direction. Examples are gravity and magnetism.

Fuel cell A type of cell that produces electricity from a continuous supply of fuel, such as hydrogen and oxygen, fed into the cell.

Fuse A thin wire which heats up and melts if a large electric current passes through it.

Generator A machine that converts movement into electrical energy. A dynamo produces direct current (DC) electricity. An alternator produces alternating current (AC) electricity.

Geothermal energy Energy that comes from the heat deep inside the Earth.

Greenhouse effect The way in which the Earth's atmosphere warms up, like a greenhouse, in sunlight. Sunlight passes through the atmosphere (or the glass of a greenhouse) and is converted into heat which cannot escape.

Grid system The system of linked cables and pylons that carries electricity from power stations to buildings and places all over the country.

Internal combustion engine A petrol or diesel fuel-burning engine, as used in most motor vehicles.

Jet engine A type of gas-turbine engine used in most large aircraft. Hot gases expelled from the rear drive the aircraft forward.

Methane A gas with no smell or colour, sometimes called marsh gas, which is produced naturally by rotting vegetation.

Newton, Isaac (1642–1727) English scientist who made many important discoveries, especially the laws of gravity and motion.

Pollution The harmful effects of waste materials that are released into the air, rivers, seas or ground. Pollution can be caused by chemical wastes from factories, nuclear waste from power stations, pesticides from farms, fumes from motor vehicles, oil spilled from tankers, etc.

Relativity The concept developed by Albert Einstein in his famous 'Theory of Relativity' that describes how objects behave when moving at very high speeds – near the speed of light.

Renewable energy Energy that can be used over and over again, such as wind power or solar energy.

Rotor The coil of wire that rotates in an electrical generator or motor.

Solar cell A device, usually made from materials called semi-conductors, that can convert light and heat from the Sun into electrical energy.

Stator The coil of wire or magnet in a generator or motor that does not move when the device is working.

Transformer A device for changing the voltage of an alternating electric current.

Transmission line A cable or thick wire that carries high-voltage electricity over long distances.

Turbine An engine in which a shaft is turned by a flow of water or gas directed through the blades of a kind of fan attached to the shaft.

Volt A unit used to measure the electrical pressure in a circuit, named after Alessandro Volta.

Volta, Alessandro (1745–1827) Italian scientist who made the first electric battery. The volt is named after him.

Watt A unit that measures electrical power, named after James Watt.

Watt, James (1736–1819) Scottish engineer and inventor who made important improvements to the steam engine. The watt is named after him.

Work The amount of energy used when a force moves an object.

Engineering and Construction

Building Materials

Until the Industrial Revolution began in Europe (about 200 years ago), stone, timber and brick were the main building materials. Iron became important by about 1800, but was soon replaced by steel. The past 50 years have seen increasing use of reinforced concrete, plastics and carbon fibre.

Architects and engineers choose their building materials on the basis of availability, strength, weight, ease of working, weather-resistance and insulation. Timber and bricks, for example, are good for houses but not for skyscrapers, for which steel and reinforced concrete are needed.

Bricks, stones and mortar

Most bricks are made by shaping wet clay into rectangular blocks which are left to dry then heated in a kiln to harden. Roof tiles are made in a similar fashion. Bricks were first made from mud, and in some places they still are. Mud bricks are quickly destroyed by damp, so they are only used in hot, dry countries.

Stone is more hard-wearing and weatherproof than clay or mud bricks and therefore more long-lasting. When cut and shaped into regular blocks and used like bricks it is known as ashlar. The other main type of building stone is rubble, which consists of rough lumps of rock laid in layers or piled on top of each other.

For strength, bricks or stones are usually bonded together with mortar, which is a mixture of sand, water and cement. Portland cement, the most common type of cement, is produced by burning together a mixture of lime or chalk, and clay, in a kiln, then grinding the product into a fine powder.

Concrete

Concrete is a mixture of cement, solid matter (such as sand and/or gravel), and water. It sets very hard and its strength increases with time. It can be cast into any shape, provides good insulation, and is fire- and weather-resistant. It cannot be easily crushed or compressed, but it breaks when under great tension. If you press hard in the middle of a 50mm (2in) concrete beam, it will snap in two. So, concrete is often reinforced by embedding in it steel rods.

Production and properties of reinforced concrete.

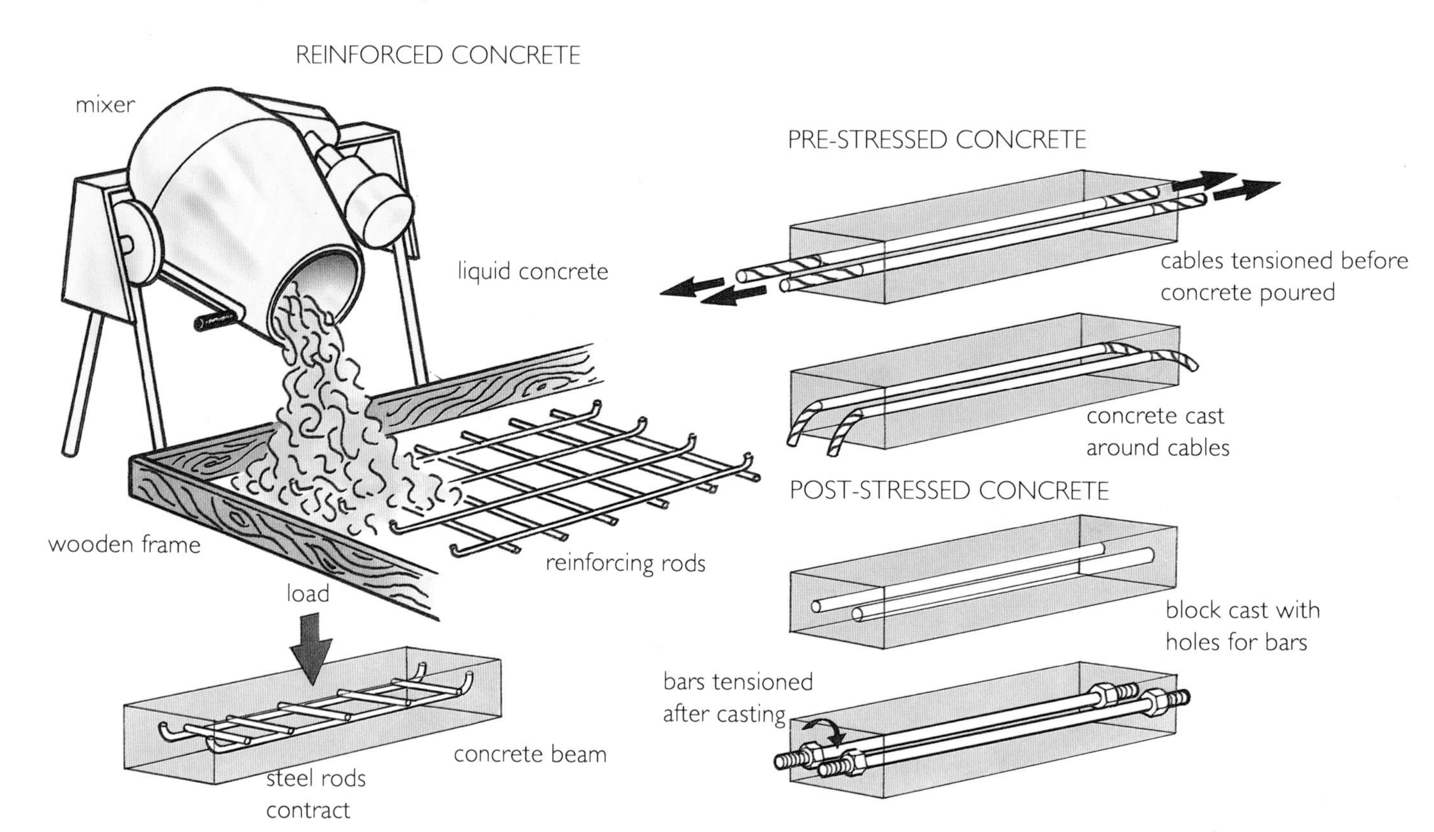

Timber

Wood is light yet strong, easy to cut, provides good insulation and is generally cheap and readily available.

Hardwoods, such as oak or mahogany, are tough and long-lasting. They are used mainly for the outer parts of buildings, such as window and door frames. Softwoods, like pine and spruce, are used for floorboards, wall panels and roof beams.

Steel

Steel is very strong. It can be cut and shaped into bars, rods and sheets, and it is very long-lasting. It is widely used in the construction of skyscrapers, bridges and tunnels, either on its own as a framework or girders bolted together, or in reinforced concrete.

WATTLE AND DAUB

Wattle is made by weaving twigs, thin branches or straw around upright wooden poles set in the ground. Mud, turf or farm-animal dung is then pressed into or smeared (daubed) on to this wooden framework. This form of building was common in ancient times and was still used in Europe in the Middle Ages. It is still used in parts of Africa and south-east Asia where timber and stone are scarce and bricks and cement too expensive.

BUILDING WITH PLASTICS

Plastics are generally strong, lightweight and resistant to rain or snow. They can be made in any colour, thickness or shape. They provide good insulation and are flexible. In buildings they are used to form outer cladding, insulation and roofing panels, and for gutters and pipes. They are also the basis of many adhesives and weatherproof sealants.

Recently, plastic domes have been made for sports arenas. The weight of a plastic dome – which may be up to 60m (200ft) across – is about 1/30th of a steel roof. It is, therefore, simpler to erect and support. However, its lifespan is shorter, maybe only 40 to 50 years, while steel should last more than four times as long.

Theatre building in India, constructed using concrete foundations, walls and supports, and a steel-panel roof.

Building Methods

Whatever the building, the stages of construction are much the same. First to be made is an underground base that can support the structure and spread its weight over a large area. Second, a solid outer framework is constructed. Third, the inner walls, floors and roof are built on this framework. Fourth, the windows, plumbing and electric wiring are installed. Finally, walls and ceilings are covered with plaster.

Foundations and floor
Houses are generally built on concrete foundations. Tall buildings are built on either a massive 'raft' of reinforced concrete or on huge posts set deep into the ground. The ground-level floor is made either of concrete slabs or wooden boards laid across timber beams, called joists.

Walls and ceilings
Brick walls are made by hand. The bricks are set in mortar and overlapped so that no joints are in line, which would weaken the wall. To reduce heat loss double walls are built, with an air space or insulation material between them. Inner walls, which will be invisible when the building is finished, are often made of cheaper material.

A timber-framed building consists of a strong wooden framework covered with timber or lightweight cement panels, or with brick, stone or tiles, and lined with timber sheeting or plasterboards. Wooden beams supporting each floor of the building – the ceiling joists – are fitted from wall to wall. Plasterboards are nailed underneath (ceilings) and floorboards nailed across the top (floors).

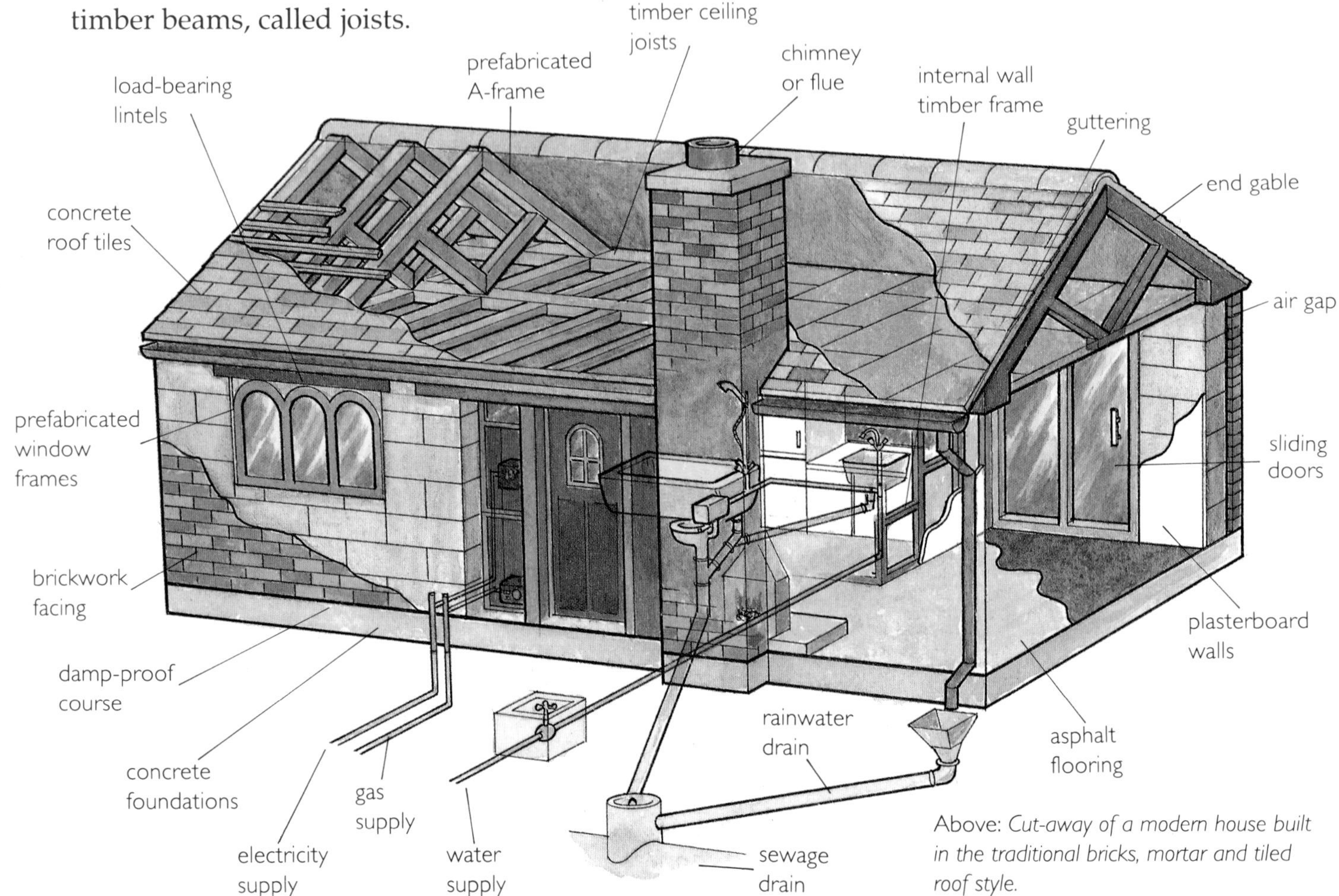

Above: *Cut-away of a modern house built in the traditional bricks, mortar and tiled roof style.*

INSIDE A HOUSE

A typical brick house has thick outer walls and thin inner walls. Water pipes and electricity cables are concealed in the walls and under the floorboards. The main water tanks are placed in the roof space to give the best possible water pressure in kitchen and bathroom taps.

To prevent damp from the ground soaking the bricks of the outer walls, a waterproof layer of slate or plastic, the damp course, is set in the walls slightly above ground level.

Adding the roof

Most small buildings have a pitched or sloping roof because it is easy to build and allows rain and snow to run off quickly. The timber frame of the roof rests on the load-bearing walls of the building. Horizontal wooden strips are nailed between the sloping beams, or rafters, of the frame, and the tiles are fixed to them. In large buildings such as warehouses, reinforced concrete beams or steel girders are often used instead of a timber frame. Where the roof-space is used as a living area, insulation boards and felt are fitted underneath the tiles.

PREFABRICATED BUILDINGS

In constructions such as office blocks, walls and ceilings – and most other components – are assembled from units built in the factory. These 'prefabricated' units are transported to the building site by lorry, lifted by crane into position, then bolted or bonded together. Nowadays, many timber-framed buildings, including houses, are constructed by this 'system' method.

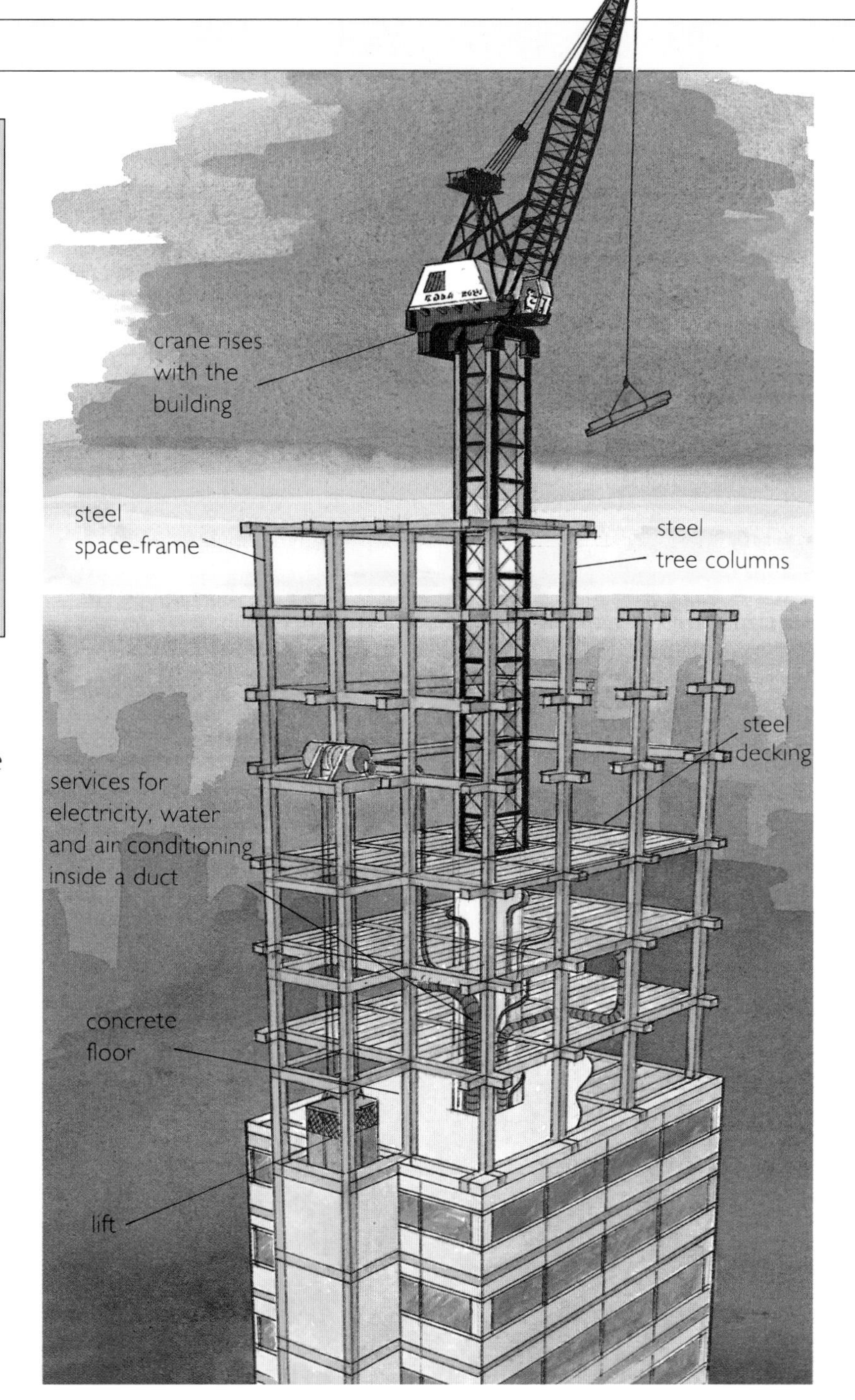

Above: *The basic construction elements and machinery of a modern skyscraper.*

Skyscrapers

Skyscrapers have a frame of steel girders, usually I-shaped or H-shaped in cross-section. This steel 'skeleton' supports the 'skin' and the internal walls and floors. Tower cranes, which 'grow' along with the building, place the sections of the framework one on top of the other.

Service and supply systems (water, gas, electricity, etc.) are concentrated together in tunnels and ducts running through the building. This makes them easy to install and repair. The main tunnel runs down the centre of the building, occupying the space once filled by the tower crane. At each floor service ducts run off this to all the rooms. Surrounding the main tunnel is an emergency staircase.

Roads and Bridges

Before work begins on a new road or bridge, surveyors and engineers study the geology of the land and the effect the construction will have upon the local community and the landscape. Several different plans are drawn up and the advantages and disadvantages of each assessed.

Preparing the site

Once the route or crossing point has been chosen the site is cleared and levelled. Explosives may be used to make cuttings through hillsides and to destroy buildings in the way. Huge bulldozers, earth scrapers and dumper trucks are used to remove thousands of tonnes of soil and rubble.

The next stage is the laying of pipes and channels in the ground to drain water away from the pavement or road surface to be built above. Soil is laid on top and made firm by heavy rollers.

In bridge-building, reinforced concrete bases are made for the towers or pillars that will support the horizontal parts of the structure.

Roadways

Road pavements consist of layers of gravel and crushed stone, topped with concrete, tarmac or asphalt. Tarmac is a mixture of stones and tar (extracted from coal) and asphalt is a mixture of stones and bitumen (made from oil).

As each layer is laid it is compacted and rolled flat. Motorways are finished in tarmac or in concrete reinforced with steel mesh. Joints between the sections are filled with a bitumen compound which allows them to expand and contract slightly. Ordinary roads are coated with hot tarmac or asphalt. Stone chippings are added to help prevent skidding, and the whole surface is rolled flat and allowed to cool and set hard.

Where little traffic is expected, roads are built in a similar method to that of the Romans, the first great road builders. A foundation of heavy stones is laid on top of compacted and rolled soil. A layer of smaller stones is then added, topped by gravel.

> ROADS AND MOTORWAYS
>
> The M6 motorway and main road interchange at Gravelly Hill, near Birmingham, England, has 18 routes on six different levels. This system is nicknamed 'Spaghetti Junction'.
>
> The USA has the world's largest road system, with a total of over six million kilometres (over three million miles).

An elevated section of concrete roadway leading across a wide valley. Inset: Layers in an ordinary road.

Bridges

Bridges used to be built from wood, stone or brick. These days, most modern bridges are built from steel and concrete. The choice of bridge design depends on many factors: the length of the span, the load to be carried, how far the beams must be above the surface, the possible sites for the supporting towers, and (not the least important), how much money can be spent.

Once the towers are in place and firmly anchored, the horizontal section is constructed. This is usually done in stages, working inwards from either side. The prefabricated concrete beams or steel sections are placed in position by giant cranes or hydraulic jacks.

To allow for expansion in hot weather, sections are joined by flexible compounds or movable plates like those linking lengths of railway track. On suspension bridges, each cable is made of many wires bound together. This is stronger than a solid rod.

Bridge types

There are five main types of bridge. In a beam bridge, a horizontal beam is supported at each end by pillars, or piers, or by the ground. In an arch bridge, the load is carried outwards along a curve to supports on either side. In a suspension bridge, the span is hung (or suspended) from cables attached to two much larger cables which are anchored in the ground and pass over the tops of the two supporting towers. In a cantilever bridge, two giant brackets are constructed on either side of the gap, and the main beam rests on these cantilever 'arms'. In a cable-stayed bridge the deck is suspended from cables or rods fixed to the top of a series of towers.

LONGEST BRIDGE

The world's longest bridge span is the main span of the road bridge between Honshu and Shikoku, Japan, with a length of 1,990m (6,527ft). Second longest is the centre span of the Humber Estuary Bridge, England, at 1,410m (4,625ft). The two main cables of the Humber Bridge each contain 14,948 wires.

The main types of bridge.

cantilever

beam

arch

Tunnels and Pipelines

Tunnels are built mainly to carry roads or railways underneath rivers or seas or through mountains. The longest road tunnel in the world is the St Gottard Tunnel through the Swiss Alps which is 16.3km (10 miles) long. Tunnels are also constructed in mines and beneath cities, for underground railways and sewers, etc. Pipelines may carry water from reservoirs to towns, or oil from the wells to the refineries.

Tunnelling through hard rock
The traditional way of tunnelling is by drilling holes in the rock face for an explosive charge. Each blast advances the tunnel a metre or two. After each blast, the roof of the tunnel is supported by steel or reinforced-concrete arches, or by a layer of quick-drying concrete, sprayed on at high pressure.

An alternative method is to cut the tunnel with a huge machine known as a mole. Recently, robot cutting machines have been invented. They are controlled from above ground via closed-circuit television, computer links and a laser guidance system fitted to the cutting head.

Tunnelling in soft ground
The most common method of tunnelling through softer material is with a machine called a 'roadheader' which has a large drill at the front and a conveyor belt behind to carry away the debris. It is also fitted with a unit that fixes steel arches and reinforced-concrete segments against the tunnel walls and roof as the roadheader advances.

Where a tunnel is being constructed below water, as in the case of the Channel Tunnel, the roadheader is supplied with compressed air. This prevents the tunnel from caving in before the supports are in place and keeps water out.

A tunnel boring machine used to drill the Channel Tunnel which runs beneath the English Channel.

THE CHANNEL TUNNEL

The rail tunnel between Folkestone, England, and Calais, France, is the longest undersea tunnel in the world at 50km (31 miles). The tunnel has three parallel tubes – two main tunnels each 7.6m (25ft) in diameter and a 4.8m (16ft) service tunnel between them. Cross-passages link the main tunnels to the central service tunnel every 375m (1,230ft).

The tunnel-boring machines used each weigh over 500 tonnes (492 tons). They are fitted with tungsten-carbide 'jaws' which crunch through rock at a speed of 5m (16ft) an hour. They are computer and laser guided to an accuracy of a millimetre or two.

Trains will run in the main tunnels at speeds of up to 160kph (100mph). Maintenance and emergency vehicles will drive along a roadway in the service tunnel.

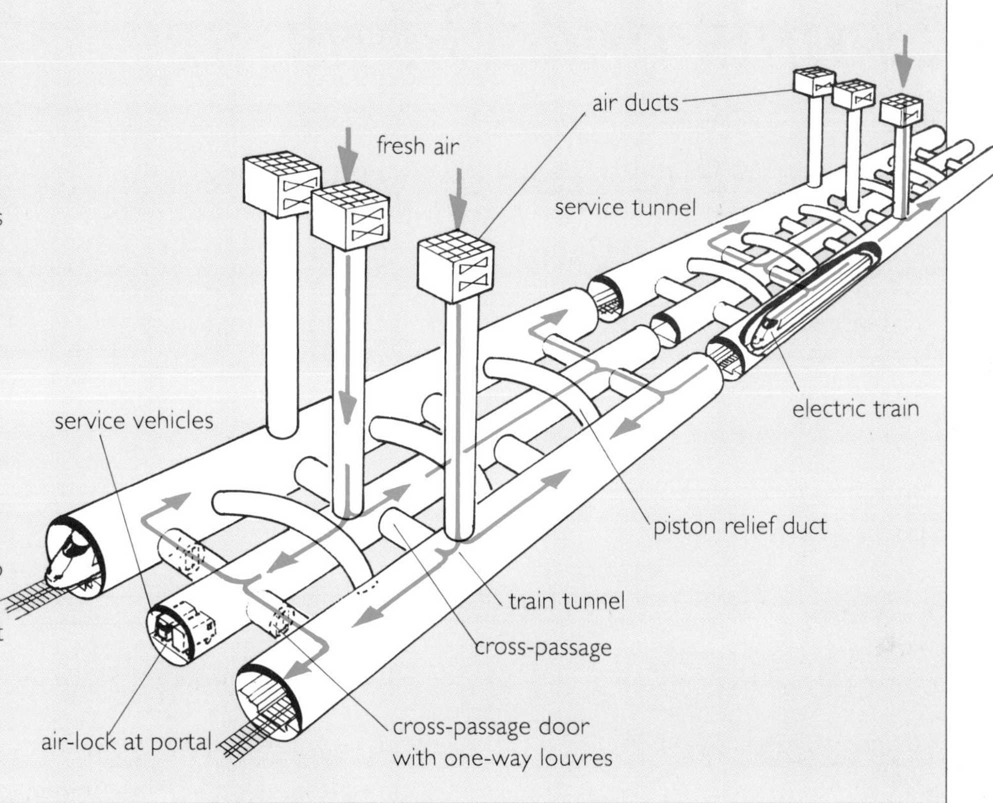

Another method of tunnel construction under water is to link together giant pre-fabricated sections of steel tubing. The sections are towed out to sea then lowered into a trench dredged out of the seabed. When all the sections are in place, the joints are sealed and the tunnel is pumped dry and covered with sand or gravel. The Hong Kong Cross-Harbour Tunnel, completed in 1972, was built by this method.

Building pipelines

Oil and gas pipelines are laid underwater in a similar manner. The special pipelaying vessels can transport the pipe sections, dredge the trench, lower the sections into place and seal and cover the pipeline all in one operation. The longest underwater pipeline in the world takes natural gas from an offshore drilling rig to Rayong in Thailand. It is 425km (264 miles) long.

On land, pipelines are usually laid in shallow trenches. Where the ground is too hard to dig a trench, as in the frozen ground of Alaska and Siberia, the pipeline is constructed above the surface on steel or concrete supports.

Below: *Pipeline laid above ground in Siberia.*

Straight and narrow

Nowadays, sewer pipes and oil pipelines are laid accurately by means of a laser beam, which is a very thin and almost perfectly straight line of light. It can be used like a ruler over distances of several kilometres, both to show a trench-digging machine where to dig, and to check that a pipeline laid in the trench is properly aligned.

Canals and Dams

Canals are artificial waterways usually built for drainage, irrigation or navigation. Before the railways were built, canals and waterways carried most of the inland freight in Great Britain and other countries.

Dams are constructed to hold back water flowing along rivers or out of lakes. They provide water for irrigation and hydroelectric power, and by storing water in reservoirs may prevent flooding.

Left: *A canal with lock, alongside a river and dam.*

Digging the trench

Canals are dug by a variety of earth-moving vehicles including excavators, power shovels, bulldozers, scraper and dumper trucks. These have caterpillar tracks or thick-tread tyres which allow them to move over the roughest and soggiest of surfaces, and usually a hydraulically operated bucket, shovel or tipper.

The largest of these machines is a bucket-wheel excavator. This consists of a wheel up to 10m (33ft) in diameter with 20 or more large buckets, fitted to the boom of a crane-like vehicle. The boom may be up to 100m (328ft) in length. As the excavator is driven forward the wheel rotates and the buckets scoop up great quantities of earth. The earth is carried away to dumper trucks by a conveyor on the boom. The bottom and sides of the trench are then lined with pre-formed sections of concrete to prevent erosion and the loss of water.

HOW BOATS CLIMB HILLS

Unless the ground is level, canals have to go up and down hills by means of steps called locks. A lock is simply a chamber in the canal with a gate at either end. A boat going up enters the lock, the gate behind it is closed and water let in through an opening in the other gate. When the level inside the lock has risen to the level above the gate, the gate is opened and the boat continues on its way.

upper gate closed
lower gate open
upper level
lower level
BARGE ENTERS LOCK
upper sluice open
upper gate closed
lower gate closed
boat rises
LOCK GATES CLOSED
lower gate closed
upper gate open
BARGE LEAVES LOCK

DIFFERENT KINDS OF DAM

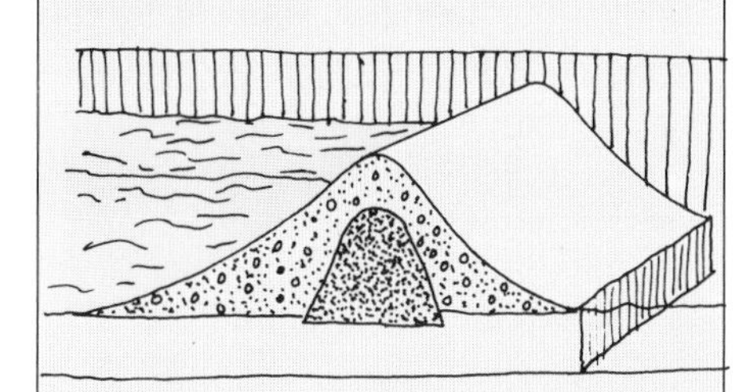

Earth fill: soil is built up into a gigantic mound, with a clay or concrete centre to prevent water seeping through.

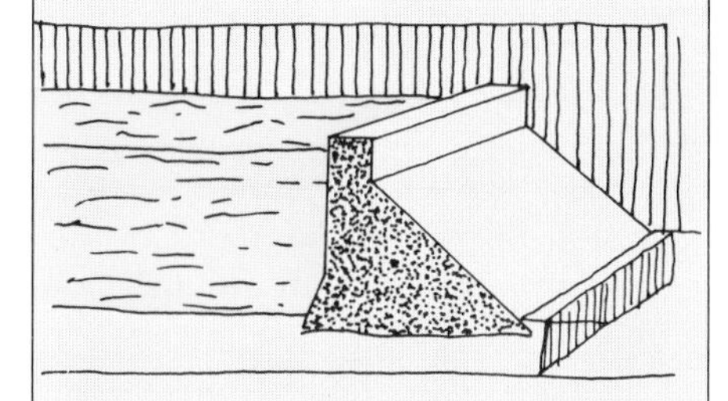

Gravity dam: a giant concrete structure, triangular in cross-section, which resists water pressure by its weight, transmitting it to the foundations.

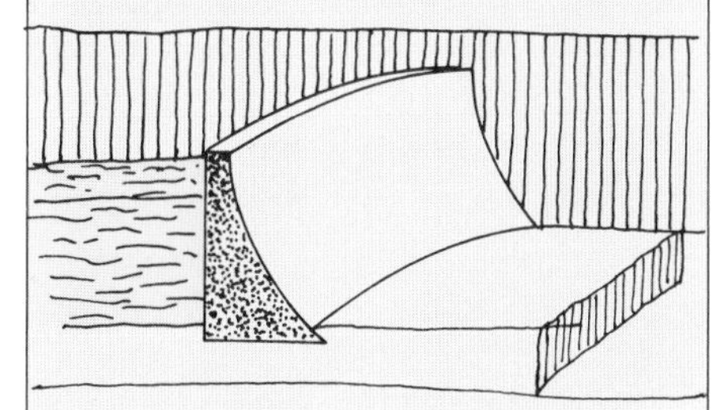

Arch-gravity dam: the curved form transmits some of the pressure to the sides, as well as to the foundations.

Buttress: the reinforced concrete wall is supported by triangular buttresses.

Dams

A dam is simply a very large, strong wall, thicker at the bottom, which is built across a waterway (usually a river) to check the flow and build-up of water in a reservoir. Dams can be as small as the mud-and-sticks barriers made by beavers or they can be gigantic concrete structures up to 300m (1,000ft) high. Water is allowed to flow through slipways or holes in the dam, and the flow can be controlled by changing the size of the holes. Water may also be channelled through turbines to generate hydroelectric power.

Dams are built of masonry (nowadays usually concrete) or of earth and broken rock. Dams can be of many types, depending on their purpose and the place where they are built. A low dam is called a barrage. One example is the Thames Barrier which crosses the River Thames, London. It has tilting gates that can be lowered to prevent water flowing up-river at high tide.

Dams are built with the aid of caissons, large reinforced-concrete cylinders which are sunk into the river to form foundations. Earth is excavated from a chamber, which is pressurized to keep water out, at the bottom of the caisson, and raised to the top to be carried away. Eventually the caissons are filled with concrete and form supports for the dam wall.

Below: *An arch-gravity dam.*

References

Adobe Bricks of clay which are dried in the sun rather than in a kiln.

Aqueduct Bridge carrying a canal or channel of water across a valley.

Bogardus, James (1800–74) US engineer. He invented the technique of using a metal framework to support the weight of buildings, now used for skyscrapers.

Brunel, Isambard Kingdom (1806–59) English engineer. He built the first London to Bristol railway, including its bridges, tunnels and stations. He also built steamships.

Canal A man-made waterway used for transport of goods by barges and ships.

Cladding The external covering or 'skin' applied to the outside of a building for protective purposes or for decoration. Most modern skyscrapers consist of a steel framework and cladding for outer walls.

Concrete Cement mixed with aggregate (pebbles, brick, crushed stone), sand and water. On drying, it forms a very hard, weather resistant building material.

Course A single line of bricks, stone or other material running along a wall or building.

Dam Structure built across a river to stop the flow of water, usually to aid irrigation, produce hydro-electricity or store water for household use.

Deck The horizontal surface of a bridge.

Eiffel, Alexandre-Gustave (1832–1923) French engineer. In 1889 he designed the iron-girder Eiffel Tower in Paris which is 320m (1,050ft) high. He also designed the iron framework of the Statue of Liberty in New York harbour and many iron bridges.

Flashing A strip of metal, usually lead, which prevents a roof leaking at joints and around chimney stacks.

Foundations The solid base on which a building rests. Most foundations are made below ground level and consist of thick rafts of concrete or reinforced concrete pillars.

Girder Iron or steel beam; large ones are used in building bridges.

Hydraulic jack A machine for raising heavy loads which uses the power of resistance created when liquid is forced through a small hole.

Insulation Material that reduces the transmission of heat, electricity or sound.

Jib The long arm of a crane; also known as a boom.

Keystone A wedge-shaped brick or stone at the centre of an arch.

Lesseps, Ferdinand de (1805–94) French engineer who planned the construction of the Suez Canal in Egypt, linking the Mediterranean and the Red Sea.

Maillart, Robert (1872–1940) Swiss engineer. He pioneered the use of steel reinforcement to construct large, strong, but inexpensive bridges.

McAdam, John Loudon (1756–1836) Scottish surveyor. He invented the macadamized road surface still used today.

Plasterboard A thin board of plaster with fibrous surfaces pressed on to it, used as a basis for plaster on ceilings and walls.

Plumbline A weight on a string used to check that a wall is vertical.

Prefabricated Ready-made building materials such as steel girders, roof trusses and skyscraper cladding units are factory-built then transported to the construction site for quick and easy assembly.

Pre-stressed concrete Concrete formed around steel rods held under tension, or stretched. When the concrete sets the tension is released, compressing the concrete.

Reinforced concrete Concrete in which steel rods are inserted before it hardens to give additional strength. *see* **Pre-stressed concrete.**

Skyscraper Any tall building, but usually refers to very high office buildings built on a steel framework and cladding design.

Spirit level A wooden or metal bar, holding one or more tubes of liquid in each of which an air bubble is trapped. When the bar is put against a structure the bubble should be in the centre of the tube. If not, the structure is not level.

Steel A mixture of metals – an alloy consisting mainly of iron and carbon, but with other elements such as silicon, chromium and nickel. Steels with a high content of chromium produce stainless steels.

Swing bridge A bridge in which a section of the deck swings sideways or upward to allow boats to pass by.

Telford, Thomas (1757–1834) Scottish engineer. He built roads, bridges and canals including the Menai Suspension Bridge, Wales, and the Caledonian Canal, Scotland.

Ties Lengths of wire or metal rods which hold the inner and outer walls of a building together, making the structure stronger and preventing it from bulging under pressure.

Trésaguet, Pierre-Marie Jerome (1716–96) French engineer. In the 1770s he developed the basis for modern road construction. McAdam's methods were a development of his work.

Tungsten-carbide An extremely hard substance from which cutters and rock drills are made.

Viaduct A long series of arches carrying a roadway or railway track.

Wattle and daub Primitive building material comprising twigs, branches or straw woven around upright wooden poles and covered with mud, turf or animal dung.

Transport on Land

Motor Cars

Since the invention of the internal combustion engine, motor vehicles have become the chief form of land transport in industrialized countries. There are now about 400 million cars in use in the world, and every day 100,000 new ones roll out of factories in Japan, Europe and the USA.

Almost all cars today are made from steel and powered by an internal combustion engine using petrol as its fuel. But future cars will be different.

Plastic cars

Already, some cars are made partly from plastic or fibreglass. These materials have several advantages over steel. They are lighter, yet they can be just as strong and are more resistant to damage from minor knocks. They don't rust as steel does. But so far, manufacturers have been slow to introduce plastic and fibreglass because parts made from them can be more expensive to produce.

New fuels

Petrol is extracted from oil, which is a fossil fuel. At some time in the future, oil reserves will begin to run dry and vehicles will have to use a different fuel. Car manufacturers have experimented with several new fuels, including hydrogen, which has some advantages over petrol. As one of the constituents of water, hydrogen is in plentiful supply in the oceans. When hydrogen is burned in air, it combines with oxygen to make water again, which is harmless compared with the toxic gases that result from burning petrol. Existing car engines can be modified to run on hydrogen, but while relatively cheap petrol is still available, the hydrogen-powered car remains a dream of the future.

Electronics

Electronic and computerized systems are making cars more efficient and safer to drive. An engine-management system can monitor an engine and control many of its functions, including its temperature regulation and lubrication, to achieve the best engine performance.

Mechanics of a modern car with rear-wheel drive and manual gearbox.

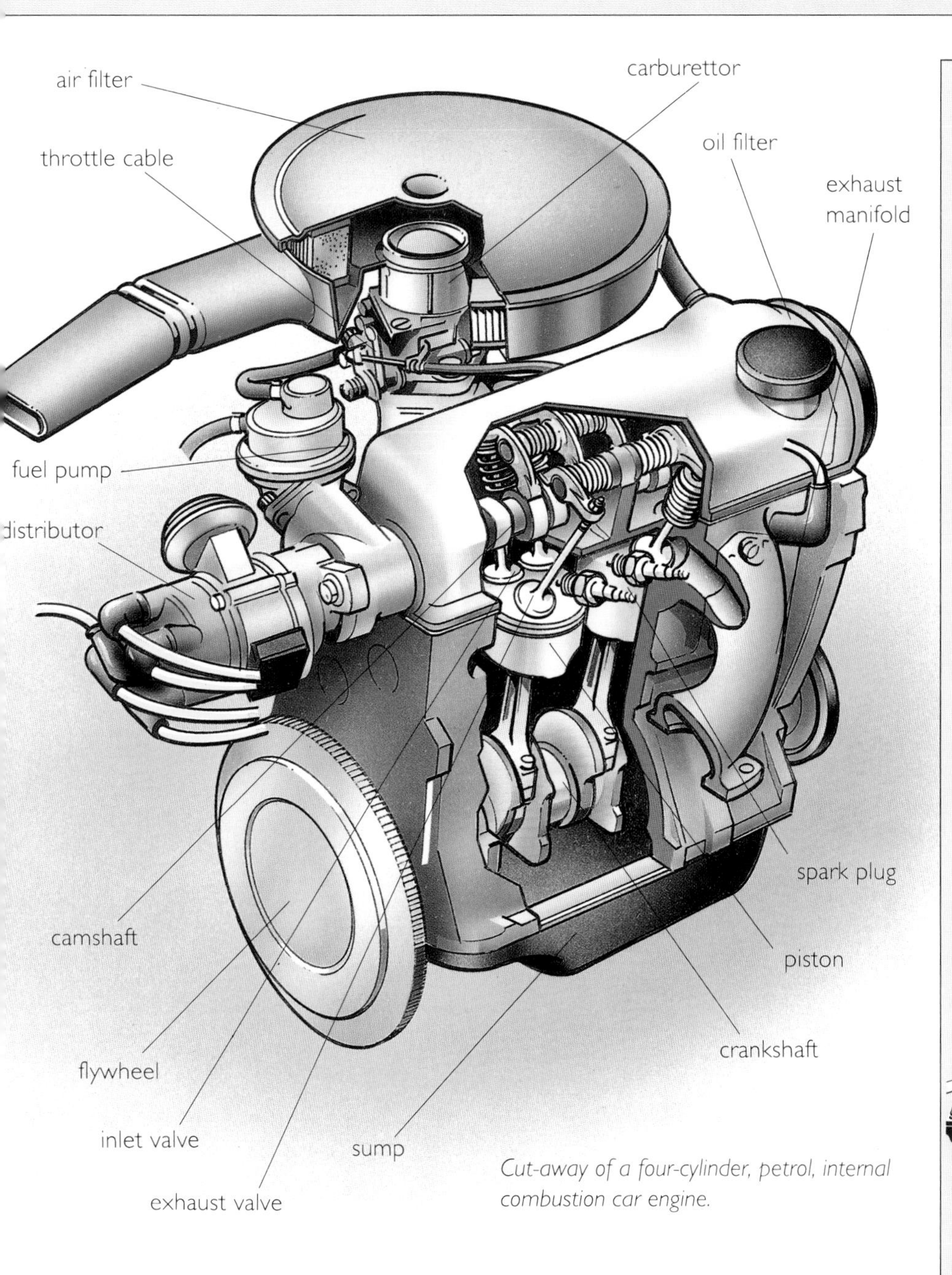

Cut-away of a four-cylinder, petrol, internal combustion car engine.

The simplest engine-management system replaces the ordinary engine's distributor and carburettor, the mechanical parts which control spark timing and fuel supply. The most advanced systems can receive and analyze signals from sensors all over a car up to 400 times a second.

Navigation systems can help the car reach its destination safely by the best route. Transmitters beside the road, or buried under it, send information to a receiver inside the car, and the car's position can be shown on a screen or 'spoken' to the driver by a computer-generated voice. If the system is also programmed with the destination, it can advise the driver which route to follow. Advanced systems can modify the route they recommend to the driver if they receive news of a road blockage ahead.

AERODYNAMICS

The shape of a car affects its fuel consumption, safety, stability and the noise level inside. If it resists the air flowing over it instead of allowing the air to slip easily around it, the engine has to work harder and uses more fuel. By shaping the body carefully, a car can be 'streamlined' to reduce air resistance.

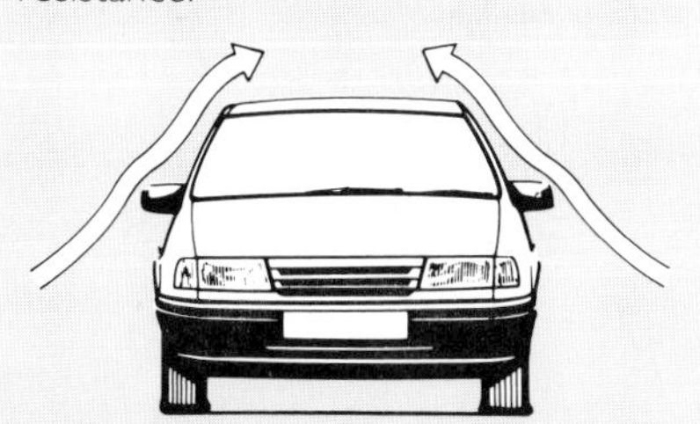

Small projections from the car, such as aerials, rain gutters and door handles, break up the smooth air-flow, creating turbulence that results in noise inside the car. If they are smoothed out, the noise can be minimized. A car can also be shaped so that the downward force pushing it towards the ground increases as it travels faster, improving its road-holding.

A few cars have moving 'spoilers', flaps or strips on the bodywork, to adjust the car's aerodynamic characteristics automatically to match its speed. A car's aerodynamic efficiency is given by a number called its drag coefficient. The more streamlined the car is, the lower its drag coefficient.

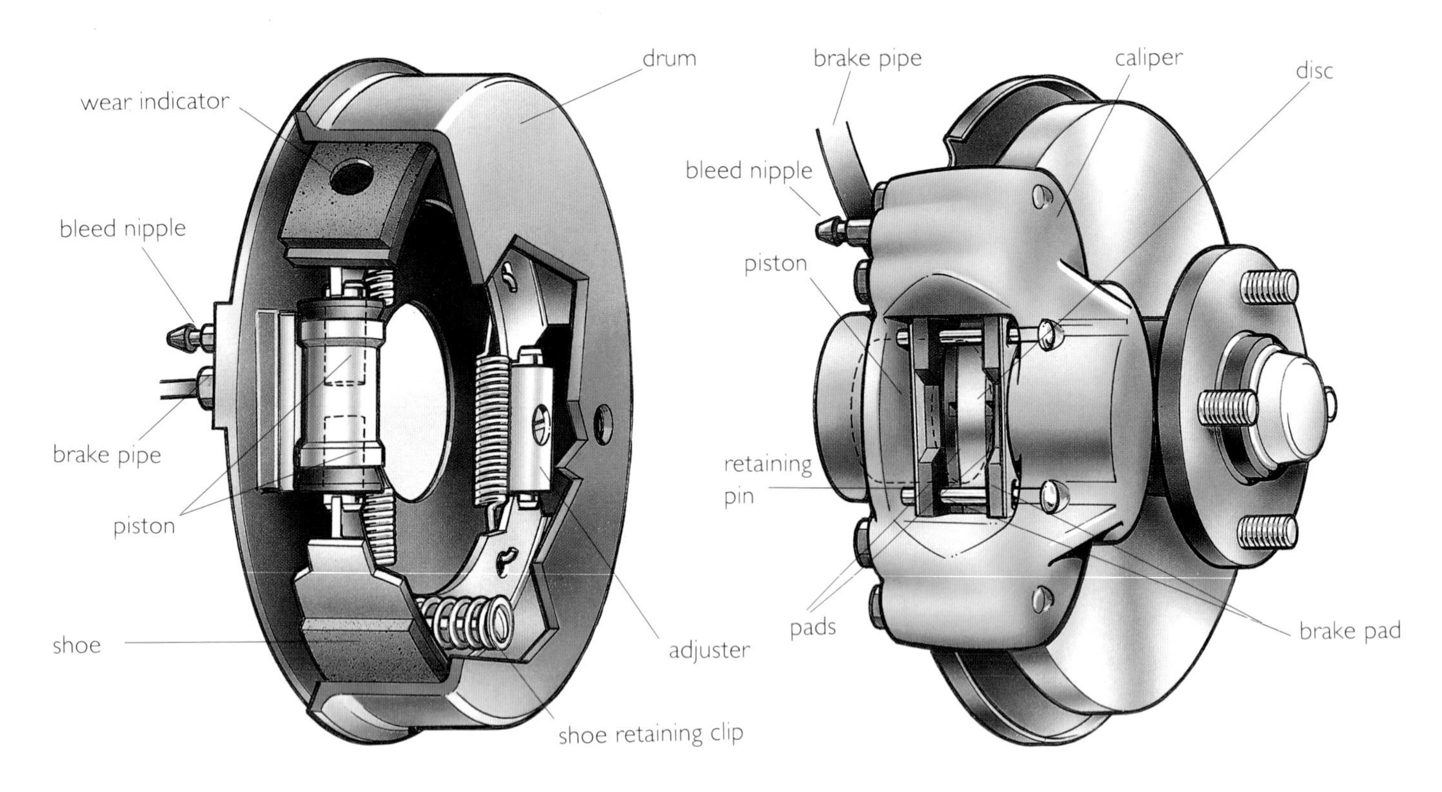

Above: *Comparison of a drum brake* (left) *and a disc brake* (right).

Brakes

To be safe, cars must have good brakes. Drum brakes have shoes which press against a drum fixed to the rotating wheel. Disc brakes have pads which press against a disc with a clamp-like action.

Electric cars

Electric cars are quieter and cleaner than petrol- or diesel-powered cars. They need less maintenance because they have fewer moving parts; they have no pumps and filters, no cooling system and no ignition system. They are much simpler vehicles.

However, electric vehicles have disadvantages. They must carry very large, heavy batteries which have to be recharged often. Unless a much smaller, more powerful battery is invented, electric batteries are unlikely to replace internal combustion engines in the future.

CONCEPT CARS

Car manufacturers often build strange, futuristic-looking cars to demonstrate how future technology might affect car design. Most of these 'concept cars' never go into mass production, but they enable manufacturers to make experiments and to spot potential problems caused by the new designs.

One recent example, the Volkswagen Futura, has a large area of glass, giving better visibility. A new kind of glass is used, which is just as transparent as normal glass but cuts out 60 per cent of the heat – otherwise the car would get as hot as a greenhouse.

A highly aerodynamic concept sports car incorporating carbon fibre, toughened glass, ceramic and plastic components.

A solar powered vehicle which, because it does not burn fuel, does not produce exhaust fumes that pollute the air.

Solar power

Some experimental electric vehicles use solar energy to produce electric power. 'Solar cells' fixed to the car convert sunlight directly into electricity. A road vehicle cannot be powered by solar energy alone because it will only work when the Sun shines, but solar cells can be used to generate extra power in a battery-powered vehicle.

ACTIVE SUSPENSION

The suspension system links the car's body to its wheels through a series of springs and oil-filled pistons called dampers or shock absorbers. They allow the car to remain relatively steady while the wheels bounce up and down over bumps in the road surface. The same flexibility also allows a car to 'roll' towards the outside of a curve as the car drives around it. But this can be uncomfortable for the car's occupants.

One solution to this is an active suspension system. Sensors monitor the height of the car above the road surface. If one side begins to dip as the car rolls in a corner, the sensors alert the system's computer. Within a fraction of a second, the computer stiffens the suspension on that side of the car by pumping extra oil into the pistons on that side, and the car remains level.

Cornering in a car without active suspension (left) *and with active suspension* (below). *Active suspension gives a more comfortable ride.*

Cycles and Motorbikes

The bicycle has been a popular form of transport since it appeared in the early nineteenth century. It evolved from the earlier 'hobby-horse' which consisted of two wheels linked by a wooden beam on which the rider sat. The hobby-horse was pushed along by the rider's feet on the ground. The present-day shape and construction of the bicycle (a diamond-shaped frame with wheels driven round by pedals) has remained almost unchanged since 1900.

The motorcycle is almost as old as the push-bike. Gottlieb Daimler built the first internal combustion motorcycle in 1886. Like the push-bike, the motorcycle's basic structure has changed little since the beginning of the century.

Modern machines

During the 1980s new materials and studies of how air flowed around a bicycle changed the shape and appearance of bicycles, especially competition cycles. Solid wheels made from carbon fibre slip through the air more easily than spoked wheels and a frame made from oval tubing is much more aerodynamic than a circular-tube frame. Bicycle frames are now being built from lighter materials such as titanium or magnesium.

Motorbikes have also benefitted from new technology. Today designers are making use of computer-aided design, new lightweight materials and new devices developed for the car industry to transform the traditional motorcycle. Many of the improvements in road motorcycles are the result of developments tested first for racing bikes. These bikes can

Modern lightweight racing bicycles.

LESS WORK, MORE SPEED

Most machines, whether they are electrical, mechanical or muscle-powered, work best within a small range of speeds. The output speed, such as the speed of a bicycle's wheel, can be increased or decreased while the machine itself still operates at its normal rate by using gears.

A bicycle is moved along by pedals connected to the centre of a gearwheel (1). A chain links this to a second gearwheel fixed to the hub of the bicycle's rear wheel (2). If the two gearwheels are the same size, one turn of the pedals makes the rear wheel turn round once. But if the rear gearwheel is smaller than the pedal gearwheel, it turns round more than once; the bicycle travels further for the same pedal movement.

In practice, the rear wheel is fitted with a series of gearwheels of different diameters (3). When the rider operates a gear lever, the chain slips from one rear gearwheel and on to the next. The number of gears can be doubled by replacing the single gearwheel connected to the pedals with two gearwheels of slightly different size. The most popular system of this type is the Derailleur system, introduced in France as long ago as 1909. An alternative system houses all the gearwheels inside the rear-wheel hub.

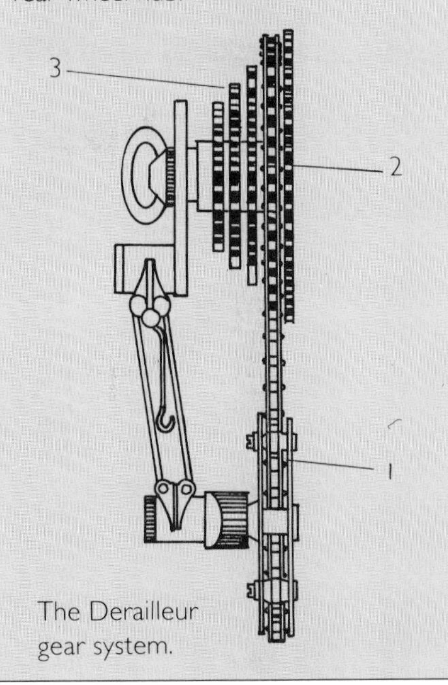

The Derailleur gear system.

now reach speeds of up to 250kph (155mph). Their designers are trying to reduce weight, improve engine performance and shape the bike more aerodynamically.

Motorbikes and safety
In general, motorbikes are more dangerous to drive than cars, partly because, having only two wheels, they are less stable. As the rider is also unprotected by a car body, skids are a special danger. The type of skid in which one or both wheels 'lock', which means they stop turning although the bike continues to go forwards, can be prevented by an anti-lock braking system (also available on some cars).

A small computer monitors the wheels and controls the brakes. When the wheels are in danger of locking, the computer reduces the brake pressure momentarily, but increases it again as soon as the wheels begin to turn again. The computer repeatedly 'pumps' the brakes in this way several times every second which brings the bike to a controlled stop without skidding.

BMX and mountain bikes
BMX is short for Bicycle Motor Cross. These tough, light bicycles were designed for children too young to cycle safely on roads. They became popular in the 1980s and special 'dirt tracks' were made for them in cities. They are designed to do tricks such as leaping into the air, turning and stopping quickly.

Mountain, or 'all-terrain' bikes have become equally popular for adults. These chunky, wide-wheeled bikes with solid frames and flat handlebars were designed for rough country, but they have proved useful on city streets. They usually have a wide range of gears, and plenty of space below the frame to clear obstacles or ride through mud.

The Pan-European ST 1100 touring motorbike – a heavy machine with a large engine (shown in cut-away), designed for comfortable long-distance cruising.

Trucks and Buses

The transport of raw materials, products and people is vital to our society. Some of the goods are carried by railways, but most of them travel from port to factory, and from factory to shop, by road, in lorries or trucks.

Trucks

Trucks come in all shapes and sizes, from small electrically powered vehicles, such as milk floats, up to the giant 'road-trains' used to transport goods across continents. The biggest transporters in the world are two crawler transporters used to move the US Space Shuttle from its assembly building to the launch pad. Each weighs over 2,722 tonnes (2,678 tons) and can carry over 6,500 tonnes (6,300 tons).

Such vehicles would not be allowed on ordinary roads! Strict rules limit the size and weight of commercial vehicles and control their loading, equipment and maintenance. A special driving licence is required for heavy vehicles, and the maximum number of hours for which a driver may work is checked by a special instrument called a tachograph in the cab.

Trucks travel slowly compared with racing cars and aircraft, but aerodynamic design can reduce fuel consumption. A test comparing a normal box-shaped freight truck and the same truck fitted with an aerodynamic body shell resulted in fuel savings of up to 26 per cent.

KEEPING TRACK OF TRUCKS

There are several reasons why a transport company likes to keep in touch with its drivers on the road: breakdowns can be reported, or a driver with an empty lorry can be diverted to pick up a load. Sometimes the only contact is by telephone, but better systems are now in use.

One type of truck-tracking system has sensors on the truck's wheels and an electronic compass to monitor the truck's position, which is sent back to base via a small radio transmitter. A second type uses a network of radio transmitter beacons located all over the country. A computer in the truck receives signals from the beacons to calculate its position, which is then transmitted to base.

Left: *A dumper lorry with a rear section that can tip up using hydraulic pistons.*

Above: *A double-decker coach used for long-distance motorway travel.*

Computer systems also help to improve a truck's safety and performance. Sensors monitor brakes, suspension, engine temperature, oil and fuel levels, speed, etc., and the driver is alerted if anything goes wrong.

Buses

Although more people own cars now than ever before, many millions of people rely on buses for transport. There are good reasons for encouraging car owners to use buses more often. They reduce traffic and cause less pollution, and one 'double-decker' bus can carry as many people as 22 cars.

In some cities, 'park and ride' bus services have been introduced. Cars are driven to a large car park on the outskirts, where the occupants board buses to take them into the city.

Different types of buses are preferred in different places. Double-deckers are rare outside Britain. Long-distance buses have comfortable seats, toilets and refreshments on board. Small buses, seating 20 people or less, run on special routes and in towns where they can be 'hailed' like a taxi.

Below: *A single-decker articulated bus for city passenger transport.*

Railways

The first railways were built in coal mines as early as the sixteenth century. The rails were wooden, and the carts were drawn by horses. Early in the nineteenth century, one or two public lines, with iron rails but horse-drawn carriages still, were opened.

The Red Devil – a steam locomotive from South Africa.

The age of steam
In 1809 Richard Trevithick exhibited a steam engine on wheels towing a passenger carriage in London – on the site of today's Euston Station. Twenty years later, George Stephenson's famous *Rocket* was built to carry passengers on a railway between Liverpool and Manchester, the first public railway which was run with steam-driven locomotives. The *Rocket* could travel at 46kph (36mph), faster than a horse, and some people feared the passengers would be suffocated whilst travelling at such a high speed!

During the next 50 years or so, railways were built at astonishing speed all over the world. By 1866 a railroad linked the east and west coasts of the United States. Railways became the chief means of land transport, for passengers and goods. Steam continued to provide the power for about 100 years, and in some countries, such as India, steam engines are still at work today.

In the more advanced industrialized countries, they were replaced after about 1950 with internal combustion engines, burning diesel as fuel, or by electric engines.

Electricity

Electricity was especially suitable for short distances and was almost a necessity for underground railways in cities (although smoky steam engines worked on the first underground lines). More recently, many long-distance railway lines have been electrified. Electric locomotives have good acceleration and hill-climbing power, and they are cheaper to run than diesel trains, but the cost of installing special tracks or overhead power lines to carry electricity makes them expensive. The sharp rise in oil prices (and therefore in diesel fuel) in the 1970s made electric trains a more attractive investment.

Trams

Trams are vehicles like buses except that they run on rails in the streets and draw power from overhead electric cables. They were an important form of city transport from the late nineteenth to the mid-twentieth centuries, but the increase in motor traffic and the competition from buses made many cities scrap them after World War II. Today, however, trams, or something very like them, seem to be returning, in the form of light electric railways, sometimes automatic, running without a driver. These tram-like vehicles are often the best way of providing quick passenger transport in large urban areas.

TRACK LAYING

Apart from normal wear and tear, the old railway tracks, some laid as long ago as the last century, have to be replaced because they are not suitable for modern trains. The fastest trains of today cannot cope with sharp bends or steep changes in level. Modern tracks must also be very stable, so they do not move too much under the weight of the passing train. The 'sleepers', the cross-pieces on which the tracks rest, which were formerly made of wood, are now concrete, while the rails themselves are high-grade steel.

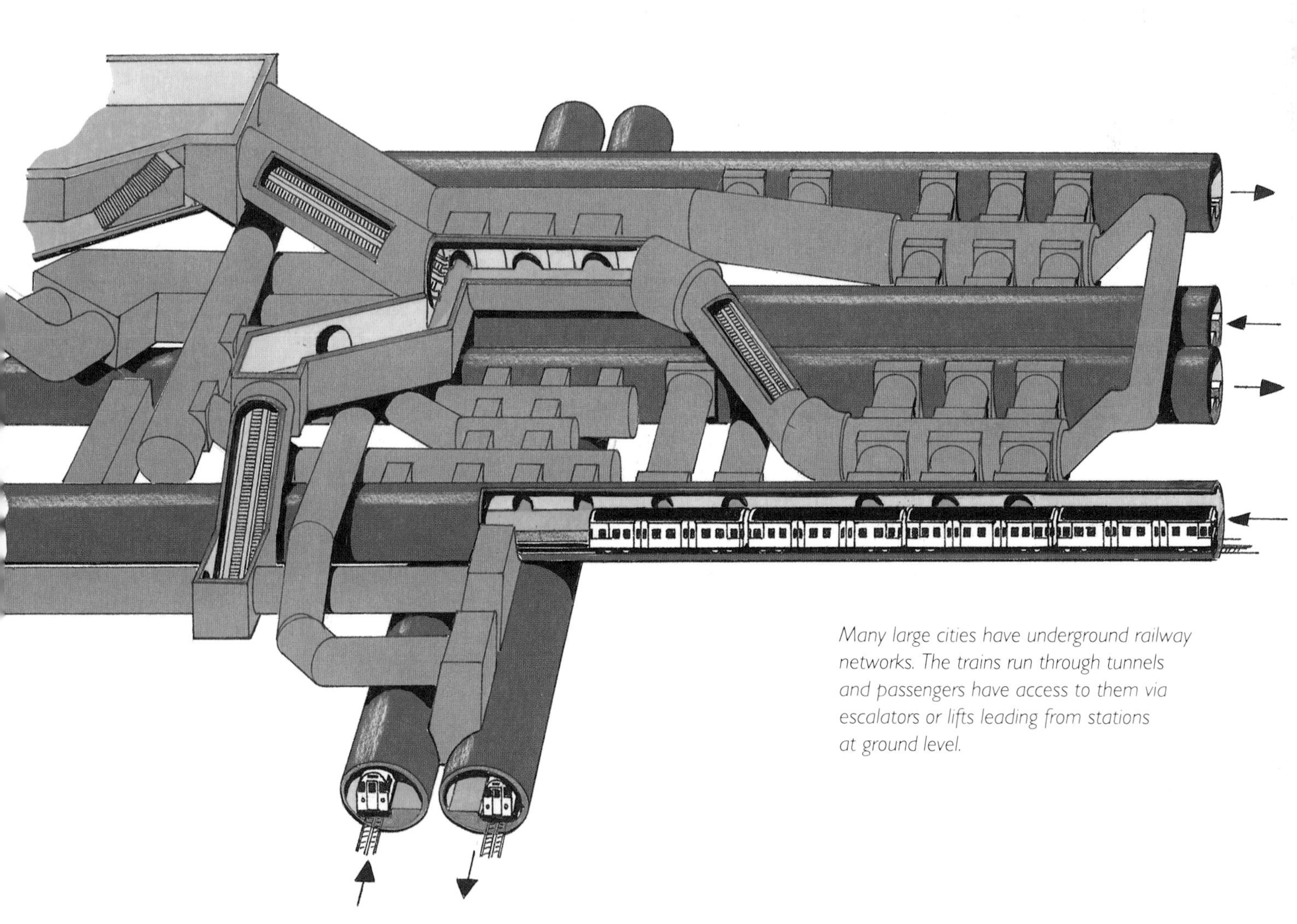

Many large cities have underground railway networks. The trains run through tunnels and passengers have access to them via escalators or lifts leading from stations at ground level.

FUNICULAR RAILWAYS

A special type of railway carries people up or down very steep hills. Normally, two carriages run on parallel tracks, connected by a cable running from one carriage to the top of the hill, through winding gear, and down to the second carriage. When one carriage is at the top and the other at the bottom they balance each other's weight. The winding gear then draws the lower carriage up the hill, while the second carriage moves down. The word 'funicular' comes from the Latin *funiculus*, a thin rope.

Intercity express

Today's express trains between distant cities travel at speeds of up to about 270kph (165mph). The French TGV (*Train Grand Vitesse*, 'great speed'), the German ICE (Intercity Express) and the Australian VFT (Very Fast Train) can run at speeds up to about 400kph (250mph). Japan and Germany are developing trains for the next century which will run at 500kph (310mph), which is close to the speed of some aircraft.

Floating trains

These trains run in the old way, with wheels on tracks, but at very high speeds this causes problems. Wheels and track both wear out in time, of course, but more important, the track can never be perfectly straight and level, and the faster the speed, the greater the noise and vibration transmitted by the wheels.

The answer may be Maglev, short for 'magnetic levitation'. This system makes use of a magnetic field, on which the train floats. The magnetized track and train repel each other

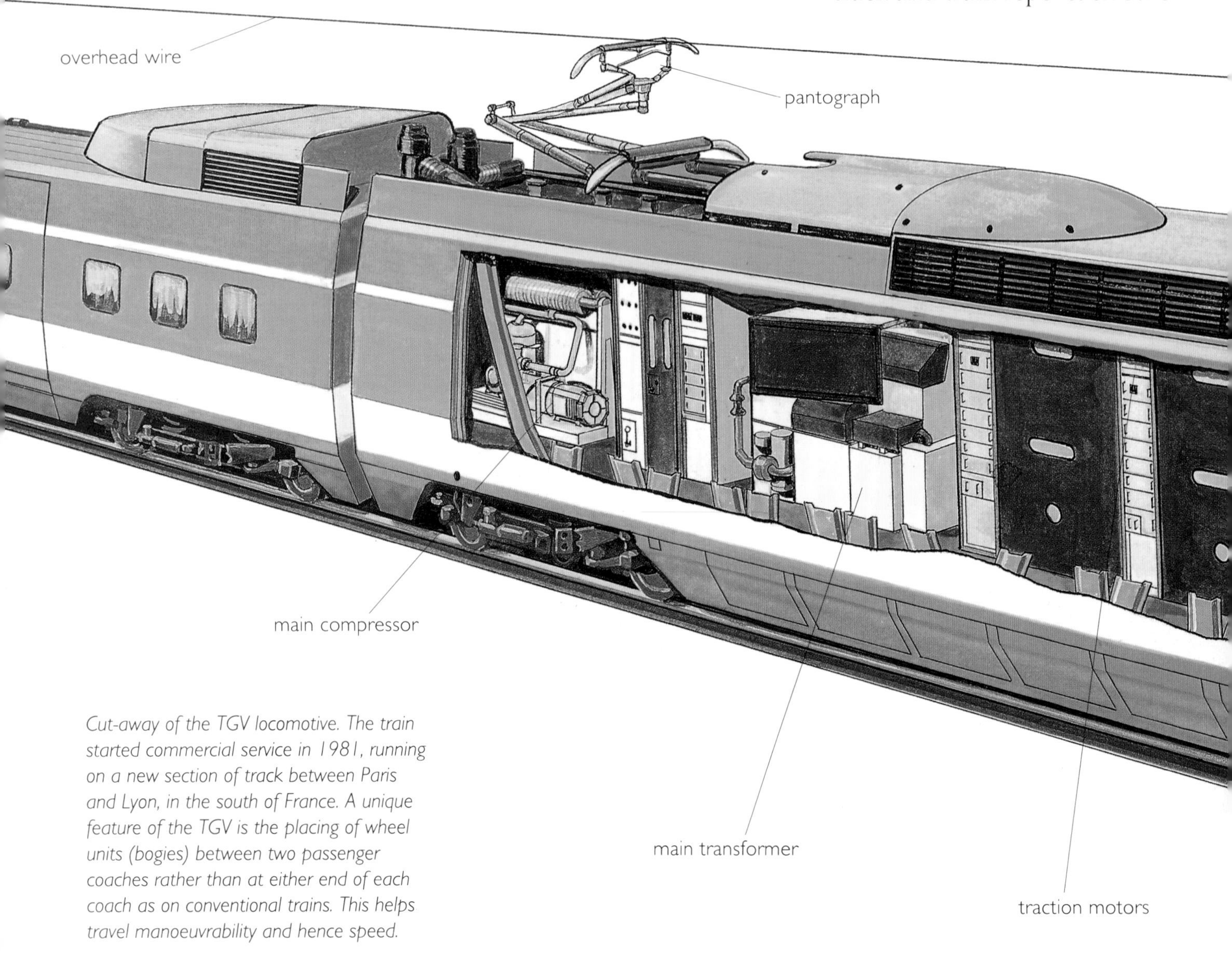

Cut-away of the TGV locomotive. The train started commercial service in 1981, running on a new section of track between Paris and Lyon, in the south of France. A unique feature of the TGV is the placing of wheel units (bogies) between two passenger coaches rather than at either end of each coach as on conventional trains. This helps travel manoeuvrability and hence speed.

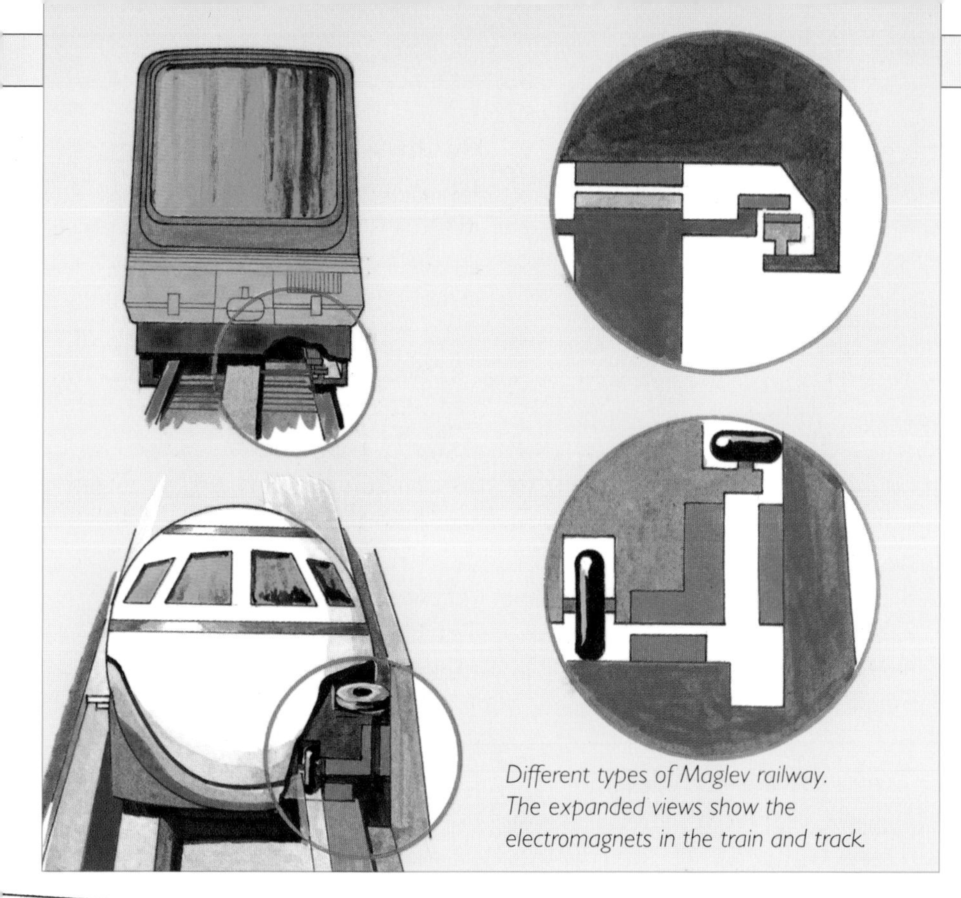
Different types of Maglev railway. The expanded views show the electromagnets in the train and track.

in the same way as the north poles of two bar magnets. As the track cannot move away, the train moves up. Japan's experimental Maglev vehicles rise about 100mm (4in) above the track.

The force to move the train forward is also provided by magnetism. This time, the principle that opposite magnetic poles attract is used: magnets in the track ahead are switched to the opposite polarity of the train's magnets. High walls on each side of the track are also fitted with magnets to keep the train on course.

Because the train cannot carry large power generators, superconducting magnets are used. A superconductor loses its electrical resistance when it is cooled to a low temperature. Once its resistance disappears, the magnetic coil can be disconnected from its power source and the electric current will continue to flow.

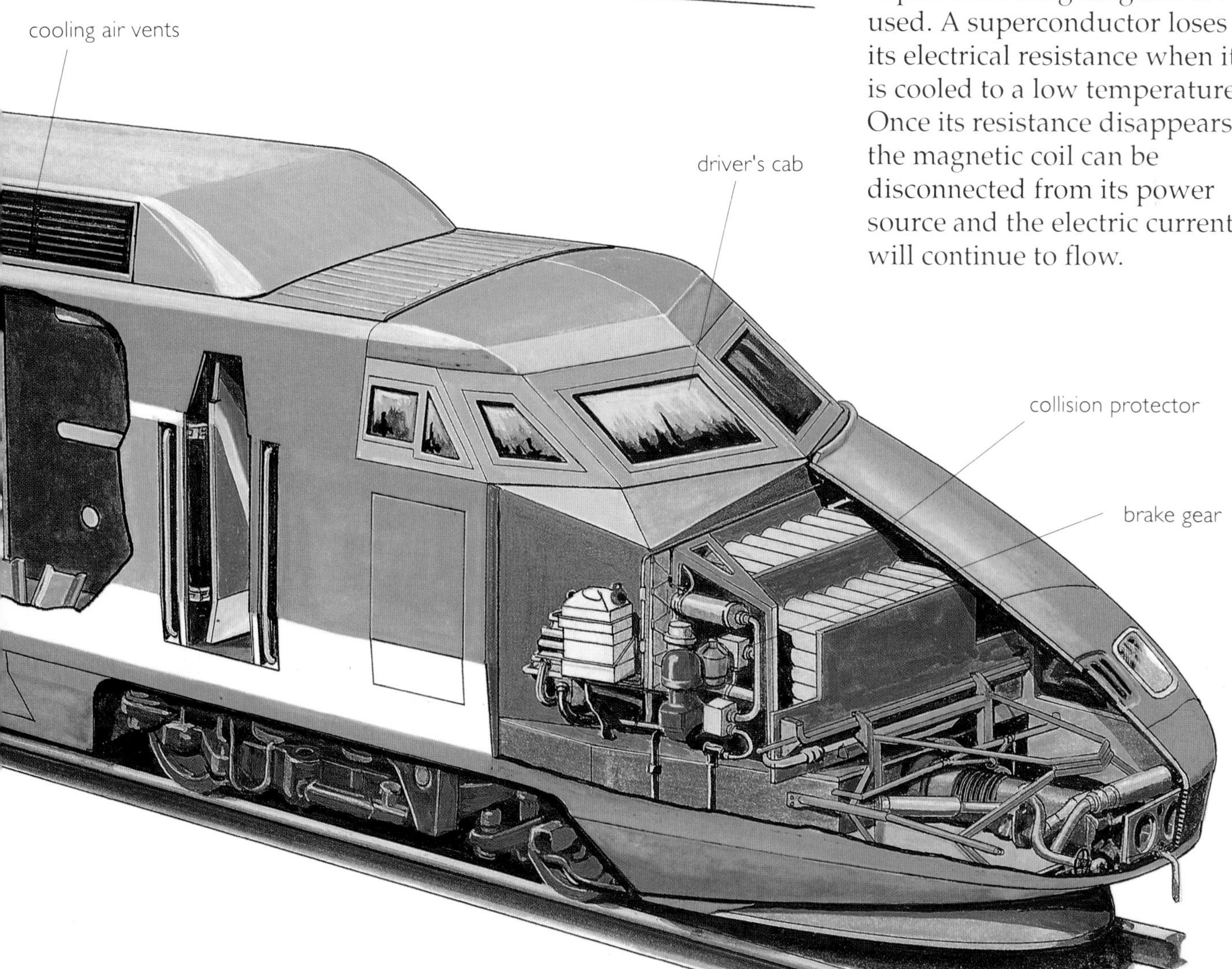

Tanks

A tank is an armoured vehicle with a powerful gun, which can move easily across country on its 'caterpillar' tracks. The first tanks were used in World War I, although the tank is really just a modern, mechanical version of the war chariots of ancient times. The earliest British tank, built in 1916, had a crew of eight, four of whom were needed to drive it. Today's tanks are a lot easier to control – some only require a crew of two – and they are also a lot more powerful!

The battle tank
When one tank meets another, the first one that fires an accurate shell survives. So modern tanks have computer-assisted firing systems. The range, speed and direction of the target are automatically measured by a laser range-finder, while wind direction is measured by sensors outside the tank. The tank's computer uses this information to aim the gun. The sights and the gun are held rock-steady by gyroscopes, so that the gun remains 'locked' on the target whatever movements the tank is making.

Tanks are carried along by tracks driven by toothed wheels connected to the diesel engine. The tracks are as wide as possible so that the tank can travel over any type of surface. Tanks can even cross rivers. If the river is too deep to ford, light tanks, which are air-tight, 'swim' across using their tracks for power, while heavier tanks submerge and cross underwater, using a snorkel to draw air into the crew compartment.

The armoured car is a lighter vehicle than the tank. It usually has wheels rather than caterpillar tracks and is faster but less powerful.

Armour
Tanks are armoured with nickel-chrome steel, up to 120mm (4.7in) thick. A more recent development is Chobham armour, made up of layers of titanium, nylon and granular material.

Cut-away of a modern tank, showing gun and drive controls.

ARMOUR-PIERCING SHELLS

Special armour-piercing shells are designed to destroy tanks. Some shells have a high explosive head that does not actually penetrate the armour but creates a great shock as it hits the target. Splinters of metal are detached from the inside of the armour, doing great damage. Another type of armour-piercing shell has a narrow, explosive dart in its centre. In flight, the outer parts of the shell fall away, leaving the narrow dart, which penetrates the armour of the target.

Anti-tank weapons

The main defence against tanks is the guided missile. It is launched from a light, shoulder-held tube. The operator tracks the target through a telescope while the missile is in flight, and information about the target's position is fed to the missile through a wire trailing behind it. The missile changes direction if the target moves.

Another anti-tank weapon is the mine. Simple mines are large charges of explosives buried beneath the ground, which explode when a tank passes over them. More complex mines have sensitive microphones to listen for an approaching tank. When the tank is within range they fire an armour-piercing warhead.

An armoured car, a small tank with road wheels instead of caterpillar tracks.

An anti-tank weapon with two types of armour-piercing shell.

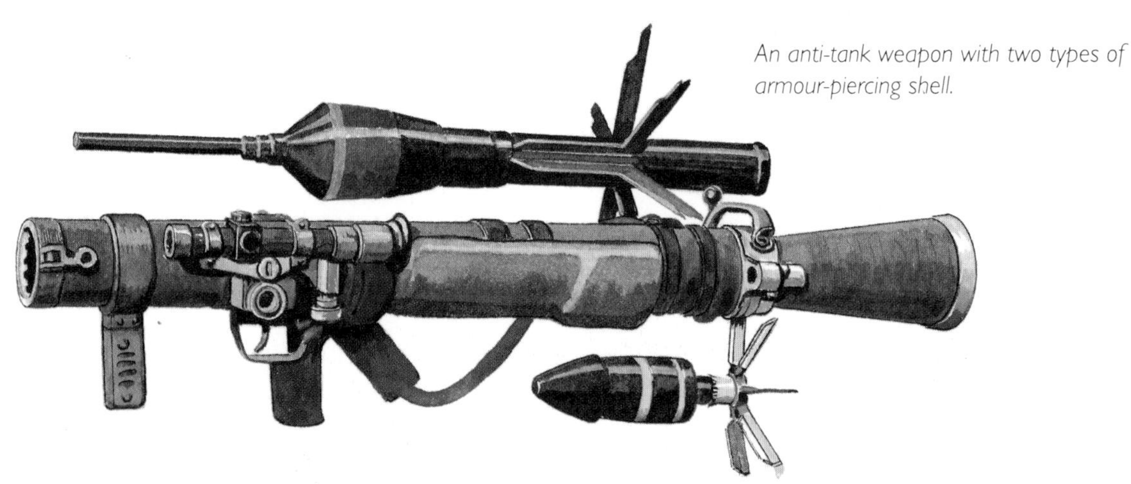

References

Articulated lorry A large lorry in which the tractor (or cab) can be detached from the trailer, to which it is linked by a pivot joint.

Benz, Karl (1844–1929) German engineer who built what was probably the first petrol-driven car in 1885.

Carburettor In an internal combustion engine, the part that controls the petrol/air mixture supplied to the cylinder.

Catalytic converter A canister containing a metal honeycomb which, when fitted to a car's exhaust pipe, extracts some of the harmful, waste gases in the car's exhaust.

Centre of gravity The point in a body, or object, where all the parts exactly balance each other.

Clutch In a motor vehicle, the part that transmits the engine power to the wheels. The power can be disconnected from the wheels by pressing the clutch pedal inside a car or squeezing a lever on a motorcycle.

Cugnot, Nicolas (1725–1804) French engineer who built the first mechanically powered passenger vehicle, a steam-driven carriage which went at 4kph (2.5mph), in about 1769.

Cylinder A motor vehicle's combustion chamber where the fuel/air mixture is compressed by a piston and ignited by an electrical spark to generate power. Most cars have four to eight cylinders.

Daimler, Gottlieb (1834–1900) German engineer who built one of the earliest cars and probably the first internal combustion motorcycle (1886).

Diesel, Rudolf (1858–1913) German engineer who invented the diesel engine in 1892.

Dunlop, John Boyd (1840–1921) Scottish veterinary surgeon and inventor who developed the world's first pneumatic (air-filled) tyre in 1888.

Ford, Henry (1863–1947) US car manufacturer who pioneered mass production. His Model T car was first built in 1908, and 15 million were produced in the next 20 years.

Fuel injection A system for forcing fuel under pressure into an engine's cylinders. This system is an improvement on the carburettor.

Gearbox The part of a motor vehicle that transforms the speed of the engine into the slower speed of the wheels via a series of interlocking, toothed gear-wheels. The right gear for a car's road speed is selected by a gear lever, operated by hand, or in some cars automatically.

Hydraulics Any system that transmits a force by using a fluid, usually oil, under pressure. For example, hydraulic brakes transmit the force of the driver's foot, as it presses the brake pedal, to the brakes through a pipe full of compressed oil.

Lean-burn engine A type of engine that uses less petrol and thus emits less toxic gases.

Locomotion No.1 The first locomotive to pull the world's first regular steam train service, between Stockton and Darlington, England, in 1825. It was built by George Stephenson and his son, Robert.

MacMillan, Kirkpatrick (d.1878) Scottish blacksmith who was the inventor of a pedal-powered bicycle (perhaps the first) in 1839. He won a race against a coach and horses in 1842.

Maglev 'Magnetic levitation', an experimental system for high-speed trains. Electromagnets in the base of the train and in the single rail lift the train clear of the track.

Newcomen, Thomas (1663–1729) English inventor of an early type of steam engine which was chiefly used for pumping water out of mines.

Pantechnicon A large lorry, especially the type used for transporting furniture.

Pantograph A spring-loaded frame on top of an electric train or tram that presses against overhead cables to pick up electric power.

Rocket The locomotive built by George and Robert Stephenson that won time trials near Liverpool in 1829 and established the steam train as a superior form of transport to the horse.

Shinkansen Japan's high-speed train service which began in 1964. It is often better known as the 'bullet train'.

Shock absorber A device used to soften the action of a car's springs; it prevents the springs recoiling violently after they are compressed when the car hits a bump.

Sleeper One of the blocks that help to support a railway track.

Spark plug A component screwed into the top of each cylinder in a petrol engine to provide an electrical spark, which ignites the fuel in the cylinder.

Throttle A motor vehicle's fuel control in the form of a valve, operated by pressing the accelerator pedal of a car or twisting the hand-grip of a motorbike, to increase fuel supply to the engine.

Trevithick, Richard (1771–1833) British engineer who developed one of the first steam locomotives about 1800.

Turbocharger A turbine used to increase the pressure inside an internal combustion engine in order to develop more power.

Viaduct A bridge supported by a series of arches built to carry a road or railway track across a valley.

Watt, James (1736–1819) Scottish engineer who developed and improved Newcomen's steam engine, by using a separate condenser. The watt, a unit of power, is named after him.

Transport by Sea and Air

Ships

The first boat was probably a log, propelled by a man sitting astride it and paddling with a branch. Soon, someone must have discovered that the 'boat' was more stable if several logs were joined together, making the first raft. Hollow tree trunks, or dug-out canoes, were another early invention. The Ancient Egyptians were the first people to use a sail, and the first to build ships from wooden planks. For thousands of years, all ships were built of wood and driven by sails or oars (sometimes both).

Methods of shipbuilding and navigation improved steadily, but not until the 19th century did wooden sailing ships begin to give way to ships which were made of iron and steel and driven by coal-burning steam engines. There are plenty of sailing boats today, but they are kept for sport and recreation. Warships, passenger ships and cargo ships are driven by engines, although no longer by steam engines.

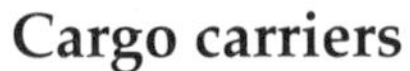

Cargo carriers

Most of the world's trade, especially large and heavy products, still travels by sea. The largest type of ship afloat is the oil tanker or VLCC (Very Large Crude Carrier). They may be over 350m (1,120ft) long and weigh up to 500,000 tonnes (490,000 tons).

The oil tanker is an example of a ship designed to do one special job. Another is the gas carrier, which transports liquified gas in high-pressure tanks at very low temperatures.

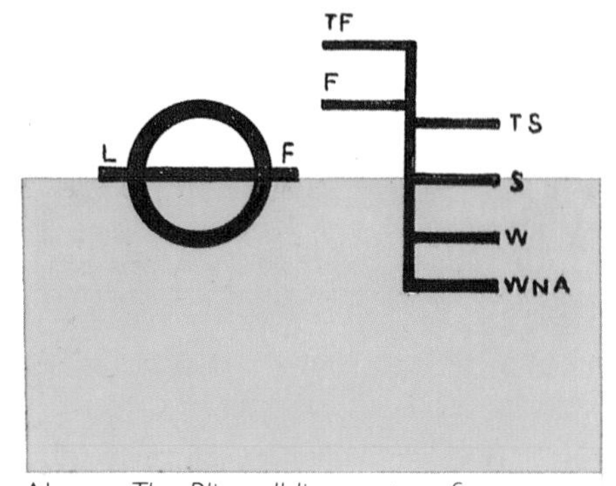

Above: *The Plimsoll line system for measuring a ship's load and loading capacity.*

A third type, widely used today, is the container ship. It can carry any kind of cargo providing it fits into standard-sized containers. The containers travel to or from the port by road or rail, and can be loaded directly on to (or off) the container ship by crane.

Passenger ships

Since air travel became popular, most of the great passenger liners which crossed the oceans regularly before World War II have disappeared, but similar ships take holiday-makers on luxury

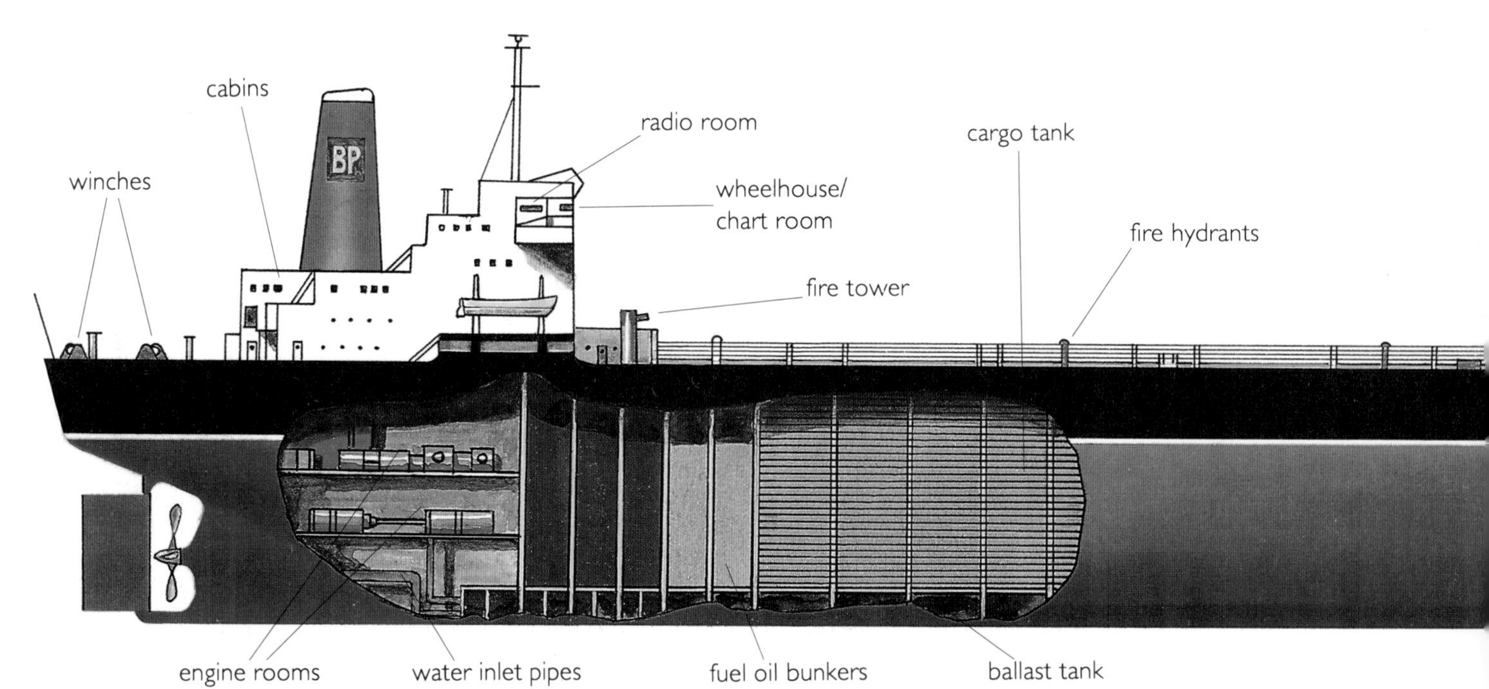

Below: *Cut-away view of a giant ocean-going oil tanker.*

cruises. A much greater number of people travel for short distances on various kinds of ferry, like those that cross the English Channel between Britain and the continental mainland. Roll-on roll-off ('ro-ro') ferries have large doors at bow and stern so that vehicles can be driven straight from the quayside on to the ship.

In harbour

Large passenger or cargo ships are too big and clumsy to navigate in the confined space of a harbour. They are moved by small, powerful boats called tugs. In the larger ports, the movements of all ships are monitored on radar screens, and the port traffic controllers can communicate with the ships' captains by radio.

Power at sea

Although there are still coal-burning steamers working in some parts of the world, most modern commercial vessels are driven by diesel engines. For greater speed, but with larger fuel consumption, they may have gas turbines, which work like the engines of jet aircraft. The jet thrust turns a turbine which is connected to the ship's propeller. A few ships, especially warships, are nuclear-powered.

Ship designers have experimented with other ways, cheaper or more efficient, of propelling ships. One example is the wing-sail, which looks like an aircraft wing standing on end. The wing-sail rotates in or out of the wind to control the amount of force it produces, and 'pulls' a ship through the water just as an aircraft wing 'lifts' an aircraft.

Multi-hulls

A ship with more than one hull, or body, is more stable, which makes it suitable for carrying passengers. Catamarans (two hulls) and trimarans (three hulls) travel easily through the water, and such designs are used for very fast sailing craft.

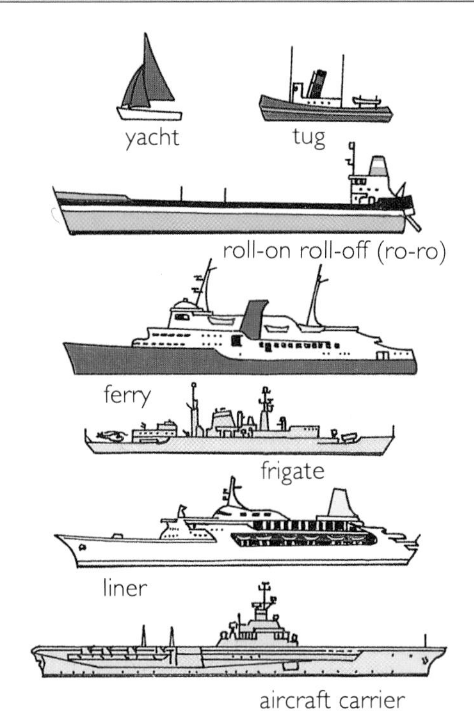

Above: *Profiles of the main types of boat and ship.*

Below: *Nautical terms for various on-board locations and vessel measurements.*

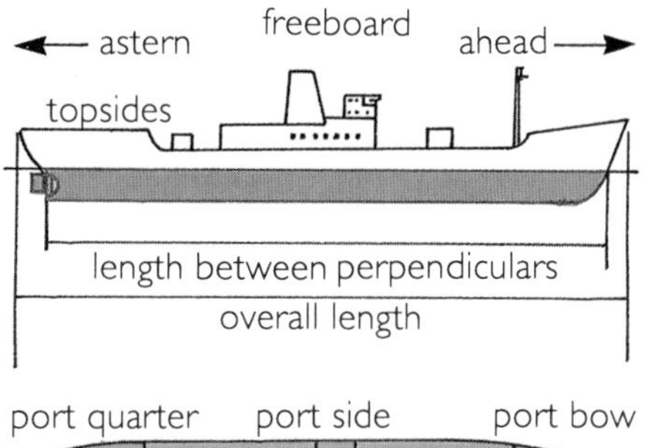

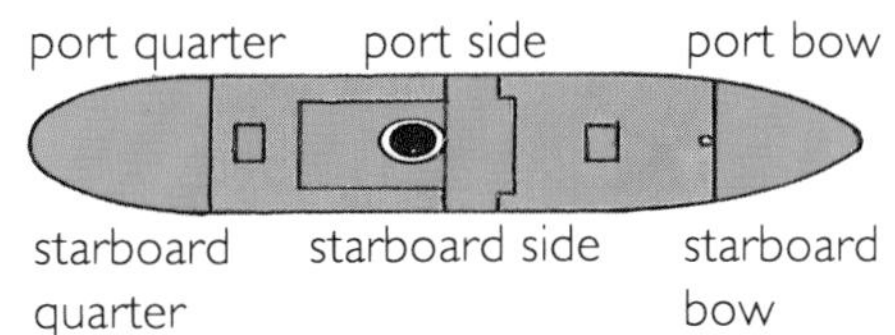

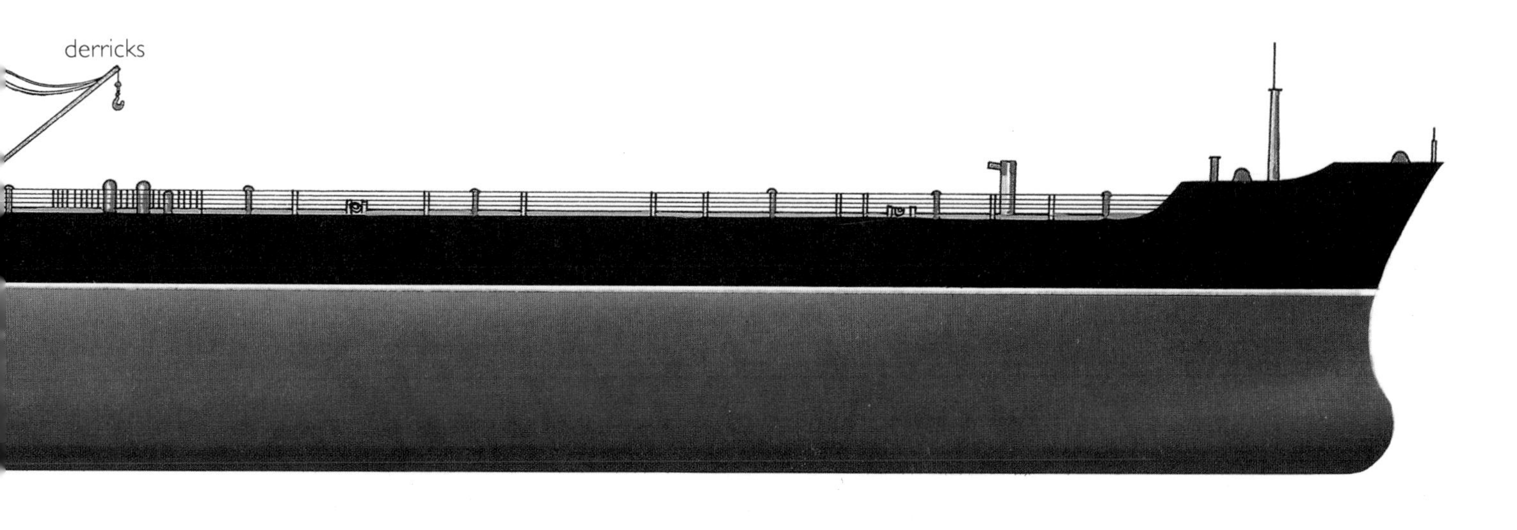

Submarines and Submersibles

Most vessels float on the sea's surface, but submarines are designed to travel underwater as well, and submersibles to descend to great depths.

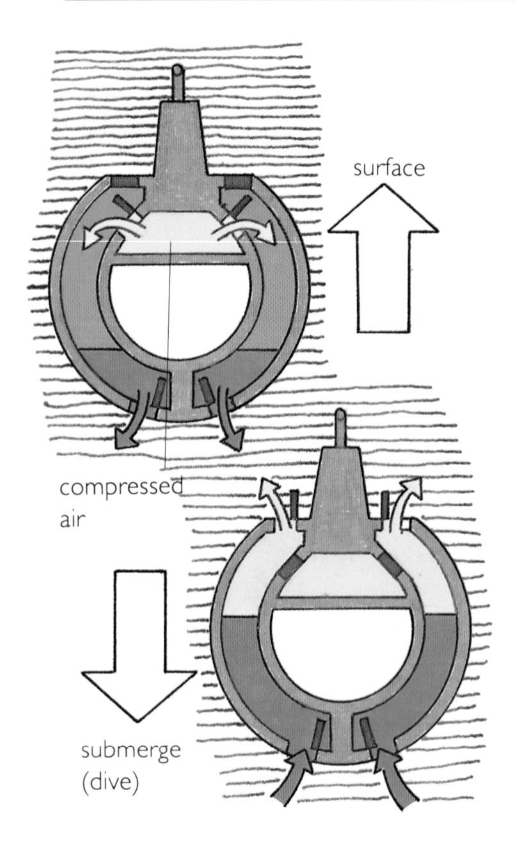

Above: *Submarines fill and empty their ballast tanks of water to dive and surface.*

Submarines

Submarines dive underwater by becoming heavier than the water around them, which is done by flooding the ballast tanks, which contain air when the subs are on the surface. To come to the surface again, the water in the ballast tanks is replaced by air from high-pressure air tanks.

Most submarines are warships, armed with missiles and torpedoes. The smallest are short-range vessels powered by diesel/electric engines. Diesel engines need air and produce poisonous fumes so they cannot be used underwater. When a submarine dives it switches from diesel to an electric motor, powered by batteries. The submarine must return to the surface every few hours or days to recharge its batteries.

Nuclear power

The largest and most powerful naval submarines are nuclear-powered, and use uranium for fuel. A nuclear submarine can remain submerged for several months. Its job is to remain concealed, and its ability to surface and attack from anywhere at any time is intended to prevent any hostile country making an attack. The fastest nuclear submarines are thought to be the Soviet Union's Alfa class submarines, which travel at over 45 knots (83kph/51mph).

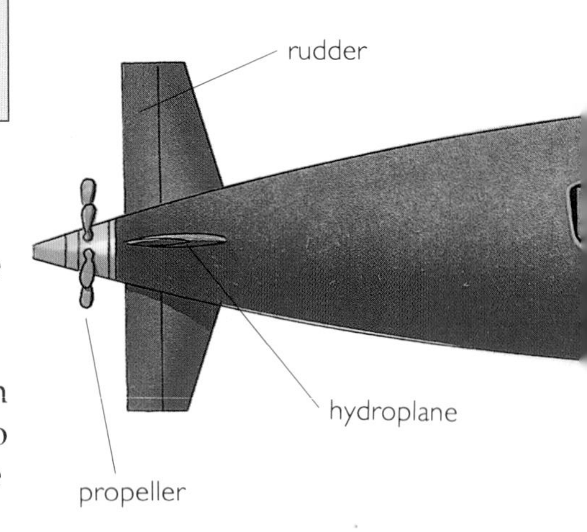

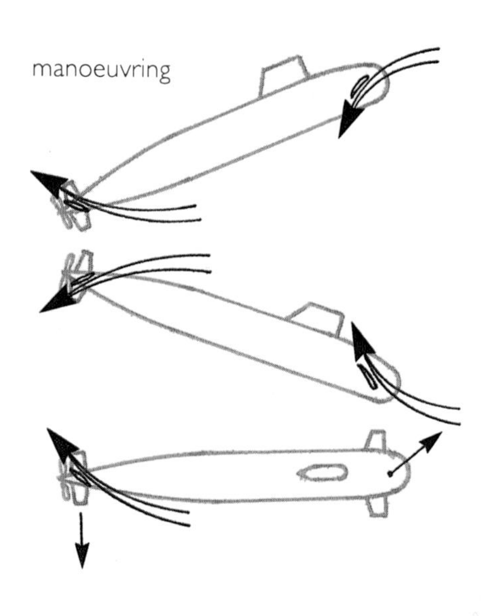

Left: *To manoeuvre underwater, submarines adjust the position of their hydrofoils front and back.*

SUBMARINE DEVELOPMENT

The earliest record of a submarine is a craft driven by oars in about 1620. It was built by a Dutchman, Cornelius van Drebel. The first naval submarine was a wooden, egg-shaped craft built in the USA by David Bushnell in the 18th century. It was unsuccessful in its mission to fix explosives to British ships during the American War of Independence.

Submarines were used in large numbers during World War I to attack enemy shipping. Since then, the world's major naval powers have competed with each other to build faster, quieter and more powerful submarines.

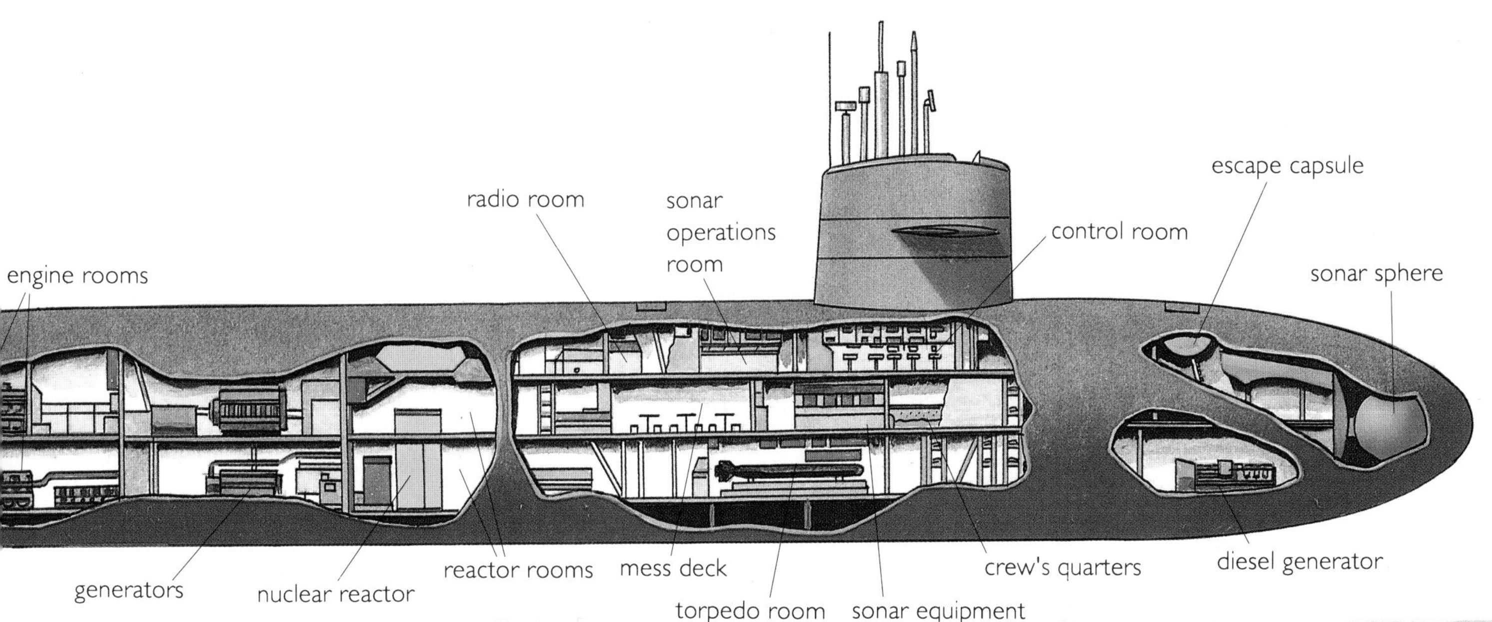

Above: *Cut-away of a nuclear-powered submarine, showing nuclear reactor, engine rooms and crew's quarters.*

Submersibles

Different types of underwater vessels are built to explore the ocean depths. They are small and very strong – to withstand the enormous pressure of the water. The bathyscaphe or 'deep boat' designed by the French inventor Auguste Piccard after 1945 could descend to 3,000m (nearly 10,000ft). More recently, even greater depths have been reached by manned submersibles, as well as by unmanned robot vessels controlled from the surface. The liner *Titanic*, which sank to the bottom of the Atlantic on its maiden voyage in 1912, was photographed on the sea-bed by a US submersible, the *Alvin*, in 1988.

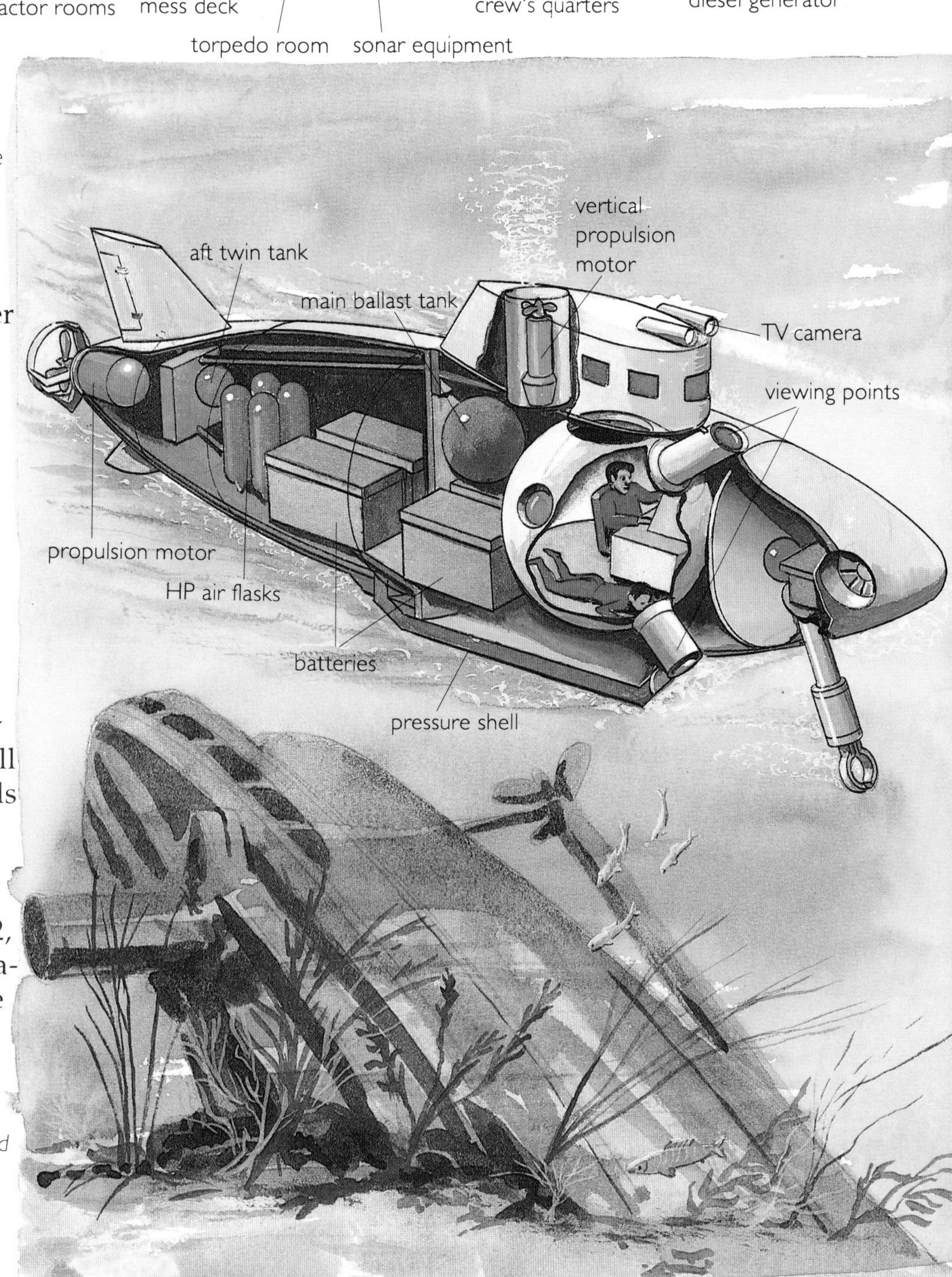

Right: *A two-person submersible being used to inspect a sunken wreck.*

Hydrofoils and Hovercraft

As a boat travels through water the friction of the water on its hull produces a force called drag that resists the boat's movement. Drag limits a boat's speed to about 35 knots (64kph/40mph). Speedboats travel much faster than this because their hulls are shaped to rise out of the water at speed. When the hull is raised, drag disappears and speed increases.

Air-cushion vehicles

About 1953, the British inventor Christopher Cockerell developed a new type of vehicle that became known as a hovercraft or Air-Cushion Vehicle (ACV). The first practical hovercraft, the SRN-1, made the first crossing of the English Channel in 1959.

Hovercraft ride on a cushion of high-pressure air, which is trapped beneath the vehicle by a flexible 'skirt'. Hovercraft are thus amphibious: they can travel over water or land. Large ones are used extensively as passenger ferries, others as military craft.

Below: *A cross-Channel car and passenger hovercraft ferry. Inset shows details of the air-cushion system.*

Hydrofoils

These vessels also travel with their hull out of the water. The hull itself stands on legs attached to underwater 'wings' (hydrofoils). At rest and at low speeds, a hydrofoil boat floats on the surface like an ordinary boat. As its speed increases the underwater wings produce an upward force called lift, in the same way as an aircraft wing. The whole vessel rises until the hull is clear of the water.

Most hydrofoil boats use surface-piercing hydrofoils, which are shaped like a letter V underneath the boat, extending out to each side of the hull. As the boat's speed increases, it rises, until the

Above: *A hydrofoil with its underwater wings in the surface-piercing configuration for high-speed cruising.*

HYDROFOIL LIMITATIONS

The hydrofoil solves the problem of hull drag, but it has some limitations. Hydrofoils can suffer from a problem called cavitation. If the water flowing over the foil is turbulent, tiny bubble-like 'cavities' of very low pressure continually form and collapse. If there are enough of them they reduce the amount of lift produced by the hydrofoil, and in time the constant collapse of cavities against the hydrofoil can damage it.

The foil's shape creates a lifting force by reducing water pressure above and increasing it below the foil. At high speed, especially if the boat is riding very high in the water, the pressure over the hydrofoil can be so low (less than atmospheric pressure) that it sucks air down through the water surface on to the hydrofoil. 'Ventilation', as this is called, also reduces lift.

angled hydrofoils themselves begin to rise out of the water. This reduces lift, and the boat then sinks a little again, so that the height of the boat is automatically regulated.

A second type of hydrofoil boat uses totally submerged, horizontal hydrofoils mounted on the end of vertical struts. The amount of lift they produce is controlled by a computer, receiving a signal from a height sensor in the bow, which alters the angle of the hydrofoils. The Boeing Jetfoil has this system. It is called a jetfoil because of its propulsion system. Water is sucked in through an intake in the rear hydrofoil, accelerated by a turbine and ejected at the back of the boat as a high-speed jet of water, providing thrust. The Boeing Jetfoil can carry up to 250 passengers or 25 tonnes (24 tons) of cargo at 43 knots (80kph/50mph).

Below: *Front views of jetfoils with hydrofoils angled and straight. These vessels can ride waves 3.5m (10ft) high.*

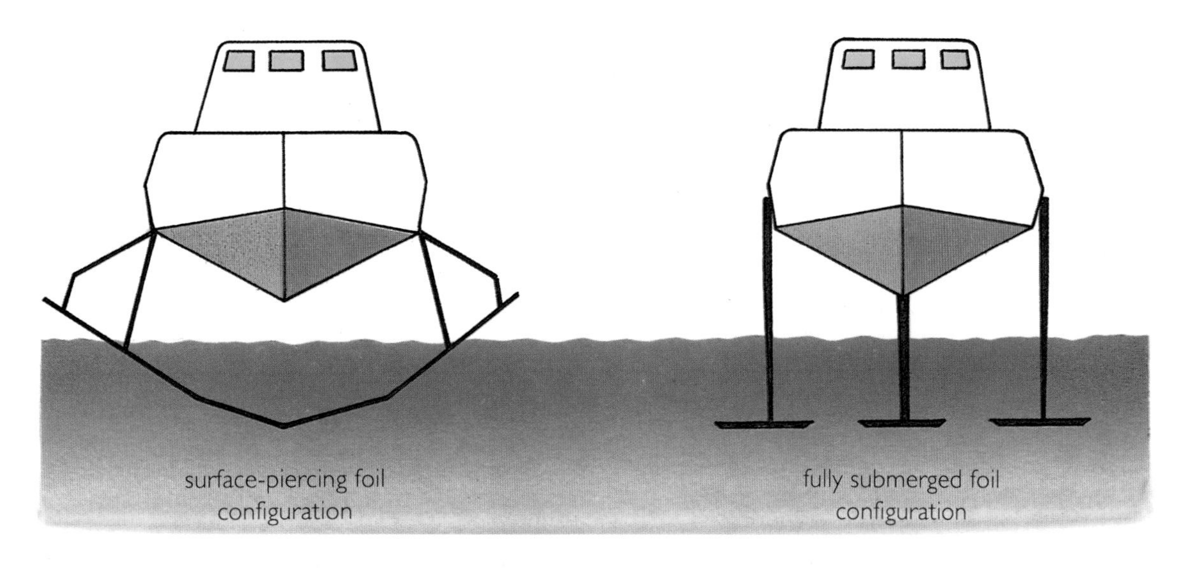

Aeroplanes

Before the modern jet airliner was developed, it took days or weeks to reach distant countries. Now it is possible to fly anywhere in the world within a day.

The Boeing 747 'Jumbo Jet' is one of the most successful airliners. The largest version can carry over 500 passengers. With a full load it weighs up to 350 tonnes (345 tons), and its four engines produce 100 tonnes (98 tons) of thrust to push it through the air at up to 980kph (608mph).

How aeroplanes fly
Despite the Jumbo Jet's great size, power and complexity, it flies according to the same principles as the world's first successful aeroplane – the Wright brothers' 'Flyer'. Orville Wright made the first successful flight in a powered, heavier-than-air aircraft in 1903 at Kitty Hawk in North Carolina, USA.

Aeroplanes are able to fly because their wings generate an upward force called lift. As the aircraft travels forwards, air flows faster over the curved top surface of the wings than the flatter lower surface. This causes a difference in air pressure. The pressure is lower above the wings and greater below them, forcing the wings upwards.

An aircraft's wings are shaped to suit the speed at which the aircraft will fly. The smallest and slowest aeroplanes that fly at speeds of around 300kph (180mph) have wings at right angles to the plane's fuselage (body). A jet airliner which can fly at up to about 1,000kph (620mph), has swept-back wings. Supersonic aircraft such as Concorde, which can fly at over 2,300kph (1,400mph), have wings swept back so far that they form a triangular shape, or delta. Some military aircraft that have to fly efficiently at both low and high speeds have hinged wings that can swing forwards for low flying speeds and backwards into a delta shape for supersonic flight.

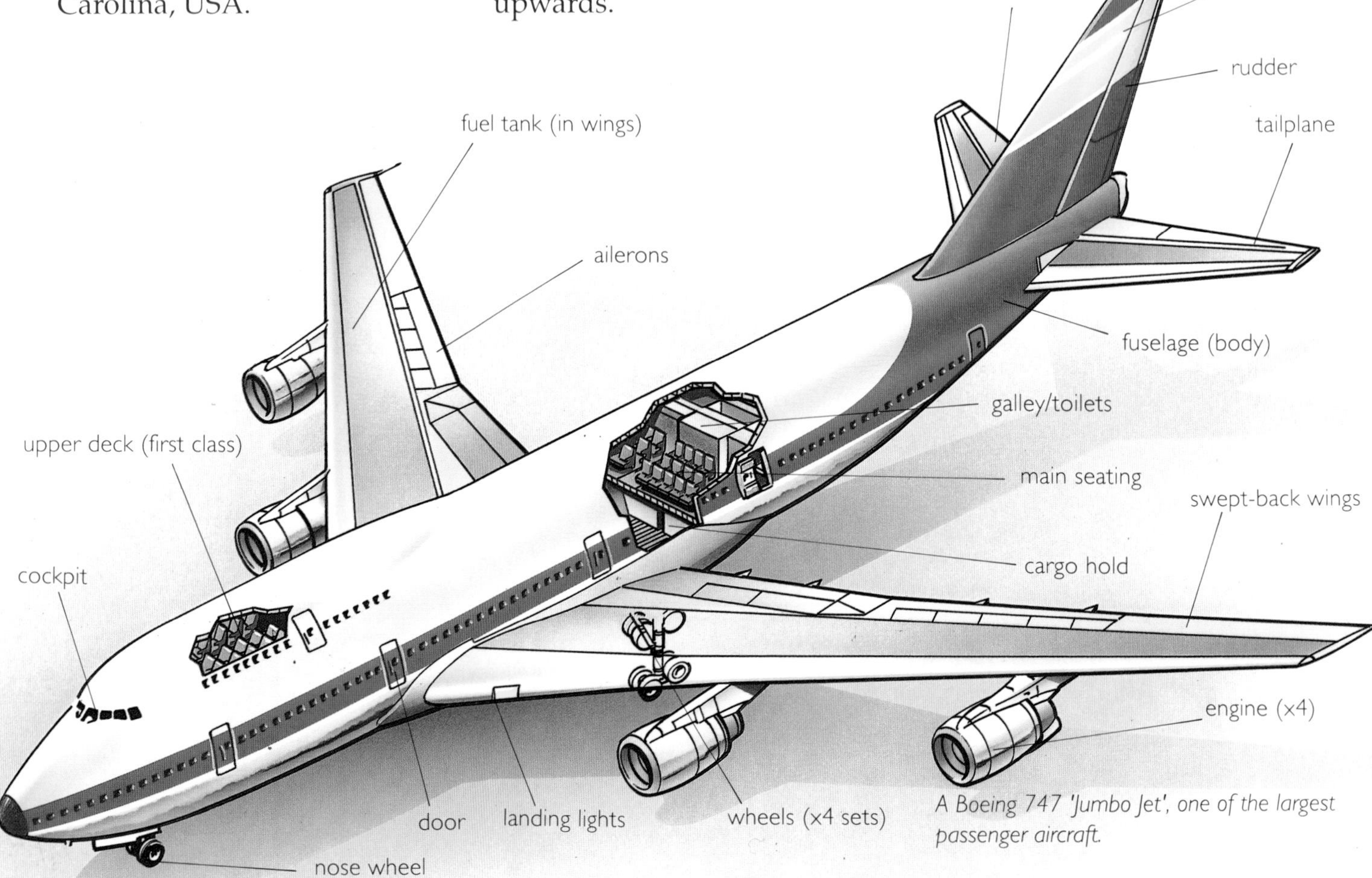

A Boeing 747 'Jumbo Jet', one of the largest passenger aircraft.

Roll, pitch and yaw

An aeroplane's 'attitude' – its position in the air – is controlled by a series of hinged 'control surfaces' – ailerons on the wings, elevators on the tail-plane and a rudder on the vertical tail-fin. If the aileron on one wing is raised and the other lowered, one wing rises and the other falls and the aircraft rolls to the left or right. Elevators control the aircraft's 'pitch': both elevators are raised or lowered together to make the aircraft's tail rise or fall. The rudder controls 'yaw': it pushes the aircraft's tail to one side or the other, making it turn, with help from the ailerons.

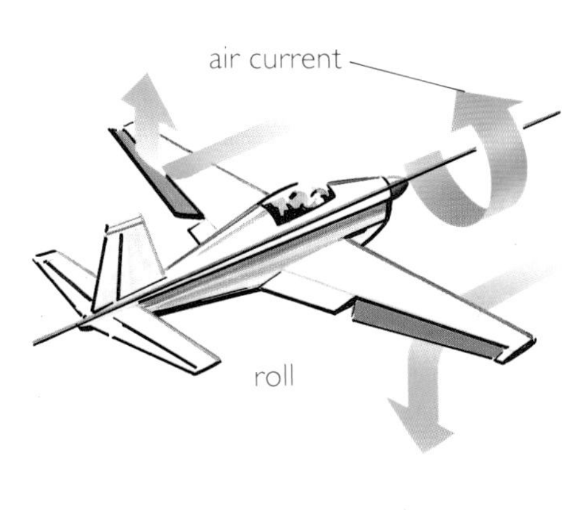

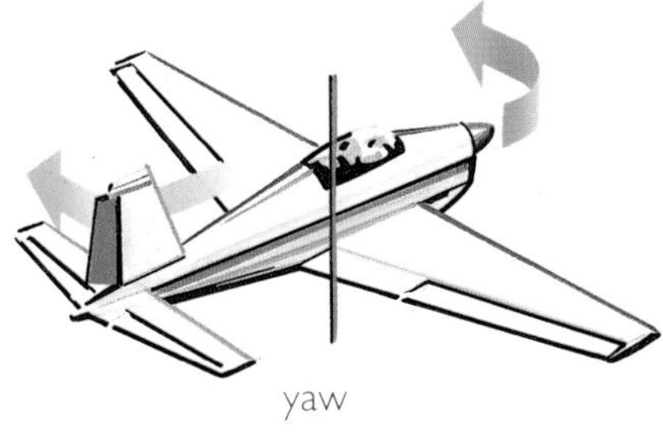

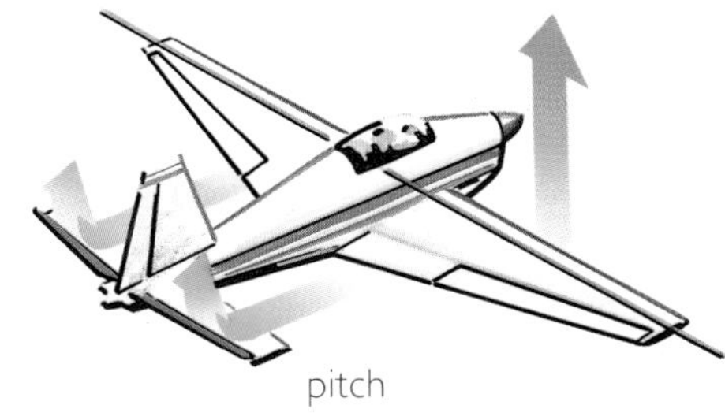

Engines

Most large modern aircraft are powered by jet engines. A fan at the front of each engine sucks air in. The air is compressed by another fan to increase the pressure inside the engine. Fuel is burned in the air to heat it and make it expand. The rapidly expanding hot gases rush out of the back of the engine, producing thrust to push the aircraft forward.

This, the commonest type of jet engine, is actually only one type of gas turbine engine. Power can be taken from a gas turbine in several ways. In a turbo-fan engine, the jet exhaust drives a large fan, which generates thrust. Another type of gas turbine called a turbo-prop, uses the burning fuel/air mixture to drive a fan connected through a gearbox to a propeller. Yet another type, the turbo-shaft, generates power via a shaft rotating at high speed to drive a helicopter's rotor blades around.

The prototypes of large passenger airliners fitted with a new type of propeller engine called a prop-fan will enter service during the 1990s. A prop-fan looks like a jet engine with two propellers at the back.

Left: *The manoeuvrability of an aircraft in flight.*

FLY-BY-WIRE

Military fighter aircraft are now very agile. They can twist and turn very quickly to escape enemy missiles. To make them so manoeuvrable, they are deliberately built to be unstable in the air – that is, they are constantly trying to tumble out of the sky. They can only be kept airborne by making frequent tiny corrections to their control surfaces. A human pilot cannot react quickly enough to control the aircraft, but a computer can. The computer senses the way in which the pilot is moving the controls and operates the control surfaces in the best way to make the plane do what the pilot wishes. The system is called fly-by-wire. Civil airliners such as the A320 Airbus are beginning to use fly-by-wire systems too.

WING DESIGN

Some experimental aircraft, such as the Grumman X-29, have forward-swept wings. They look as if fitted back to front, but this arrangement works well on agile fighter aircraft. The wings must be strong and yet thin, and only the development of new materials, based on plastics, glass fibre and carbon fibre, has made this type of aircraft possible.

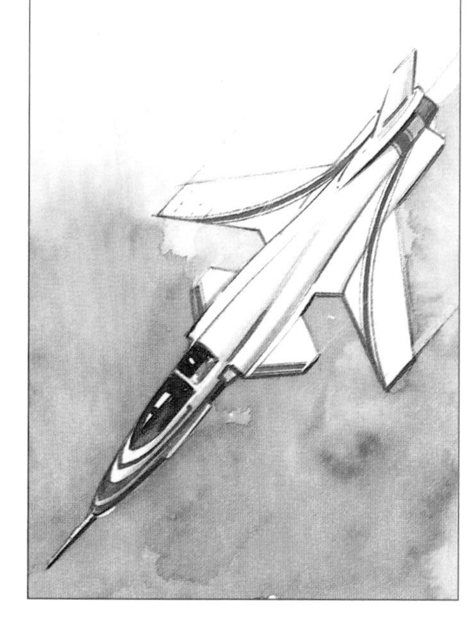

Helicopters and other Aircraft

An aeroplane wing can only produce lift when it is travelling forwards at speed. That is why an aeroplane must get up speed on the ground before it takes off. Certain aircraft *can* create lift when stationary, by means of rotating wings, or rotors.

Helicopters
The helicopter is the most common type of rotorcraft. Most helicopters have a single overhead rotor assembly (some large helicopters have more than one), and a smaller tail rotor. The overhead rotor blades provide lift. In the air, the helicopter itself would spin as the rotor blades turn; the tail rotor provides the force to prevent this.

A helicopter is flown by controlling the speed and angle of the overhead rotor blades with a pitch lever in the cockpit. Once the rotors are spinning fast enough, their leading edge is tilted up to produce more lift, and the helicopter rises vertically.

A second control, the cyclic control stick, controls direction. To fly forward, the pilot pushes the cyclic control stick forwards, which tilts the rotor blades up in the rear half of their circular path and down in the front half. This has the effect of angling the downdraught from the blades towards the rear, pulling the helicopter forward.

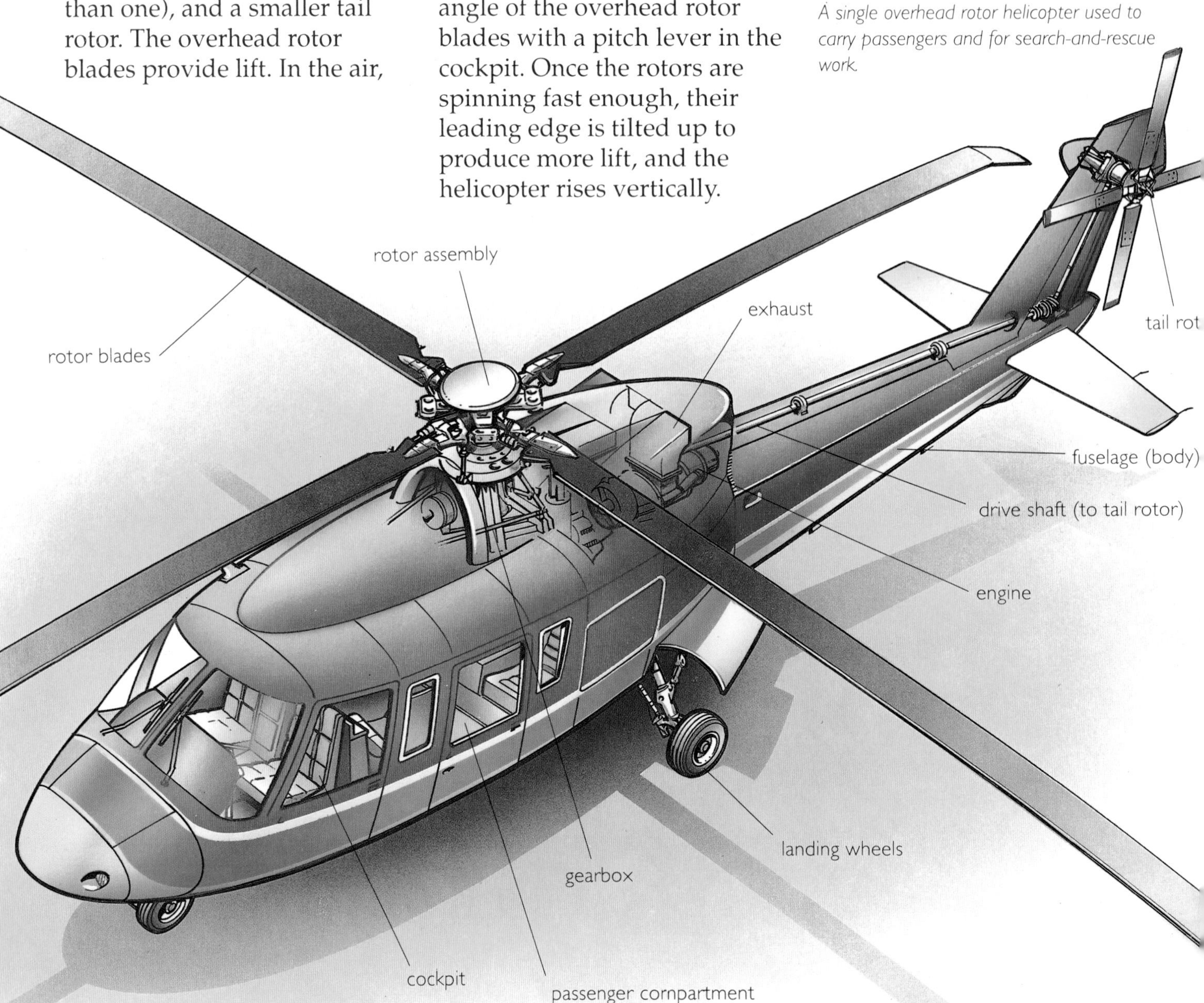

A single overhead rotor helicopter used to carry passengers and for search-and-rescue work.

Tiltrotor and X-Wing

New types of rotorcraft are being developed, such as the tiltrotor. This is an aircraft that combines the vertical take off and hovering ability of a helicopter with the forward flight of a fixed-wing aeroplane. A tiltrotor is faster than a comparable helicopter and can travel nearly twice as far.

Another new type of rotorcraft is the X-Wing, which has four broad overhead wings instead of long, thin rotor blades. The wings spin like rotors for vertical take off. Forward thrust is provided by propellers or a jet engine. When the X-Wing is flying forward fast enough, the overhead wings stop spinning and behave like fixed wings.

AIRSHIPS AND BALLOONS

Airships ceased to be built following a series of accidents in the 1930s, but recently they have become popular again. Nowadays they are filled with helium, which will not catch fire, instead of hydrogen which the old airships used. The gas they are filled with must be lighter than air to provide the necessary lift to overcome the weight of the airship's structure.

Modern airships are used as passenger transports, especially for sight-seeing, as flying advertisements, and as platforms for television cameras.

The Sentinel 5000, designed for the US Navy in the 1990s, will be the size of a 15-storey building, over 120m (394ft) long. It will carry a gondola similar to the fusilage of a Jumbo Jet.

Hot-air balloons, which, unlike airships, have no engine, have become very popular as sporting vehicles and tourist transports. Gas burners under the balloon's open canopy warm the air inside the canopy. As the air warms it becomes lighter than the surrounding air and the balloon floats upwards. In 1988, Richard Branson and Per Lindstrand crossed the Atlantic in the largest hot-air balloon ever made. They travelled a distance of 4,947km (3,074 miles) at speeds of up to 209kph (130mph) at a height of over 8km (5 miles).

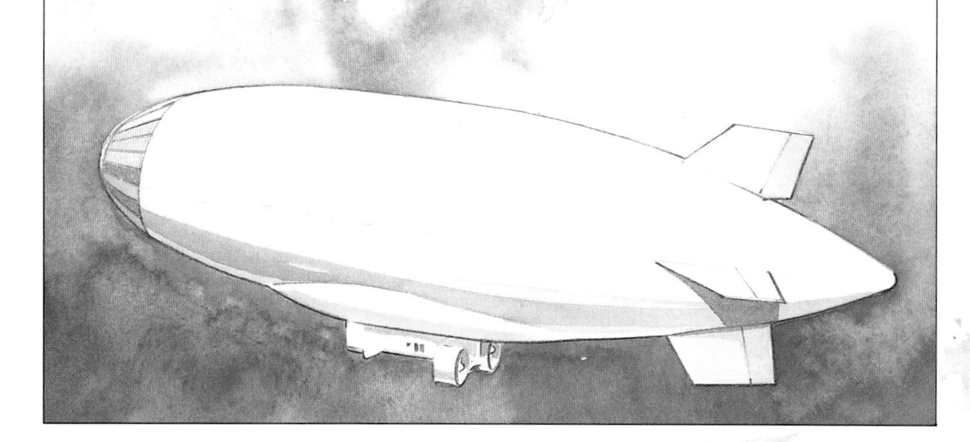

Various types of helicopter, glider and light aircraft.

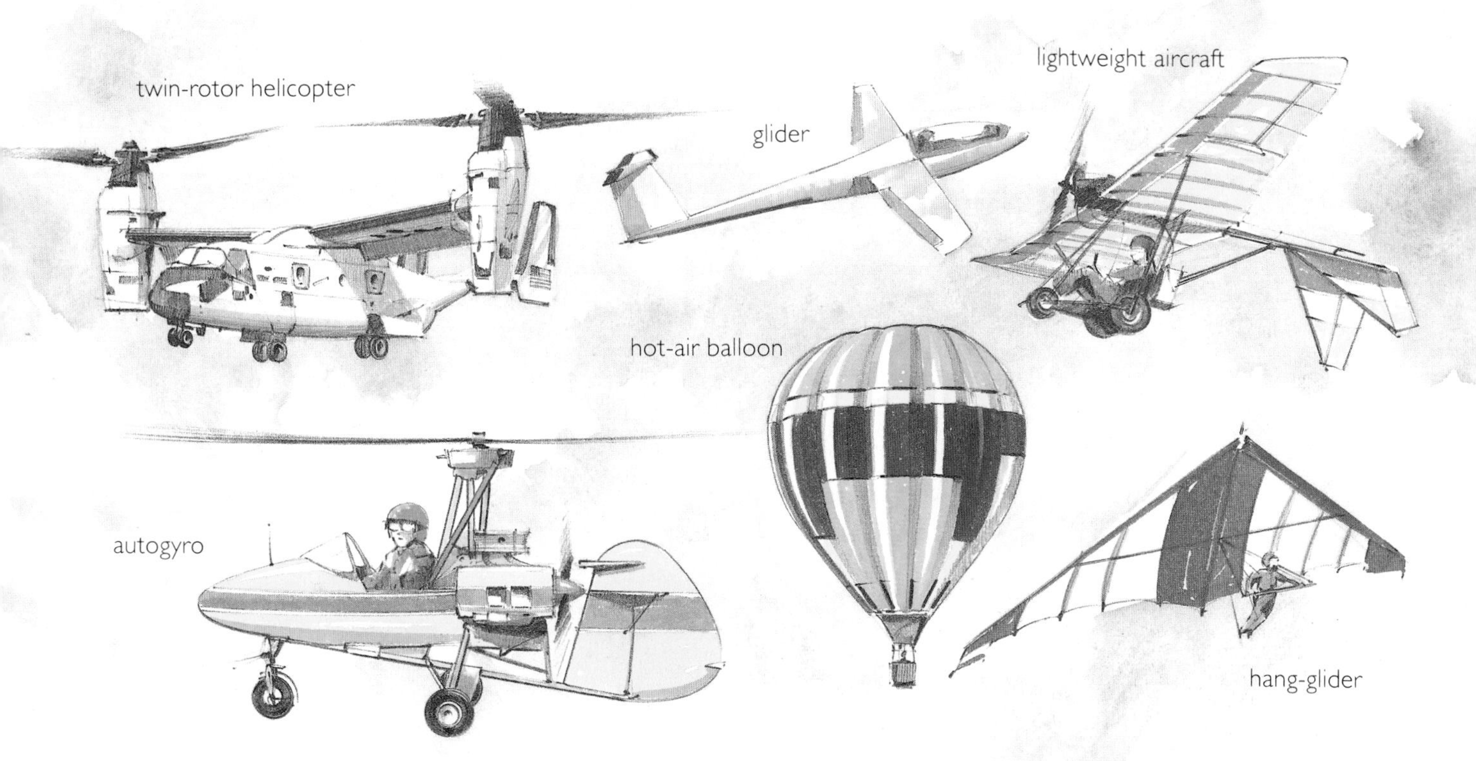

Space Transport

Since the first artificial satellite was launched in 1957, we have come to make use of space in many ways. Hundreds of satellites now orbit the Earth. Many of them are communications satellites that relay sounds and pictures around the world; others do different jobs, such as mapping the Earth, assisting ships to navigate, watching weather developments, etc.

All these satellites, and all other space vehicles, must be launched by rockets, because rockets are the only kind of engines that work in space. Until 1981 the rockets – and the spacecraft – could only be used once. This was wasteful and very expensive.

The Space Shuttle
US scientists at NASA set out to develop a spacecraft that could carry satellites, materials and people to a space station in orbit and back to Earth again.

The Space Transportation System (STS), better known as the Shuttle, has three parts: the spacecraft itself; an external fuel tank, which holds 2 million litres (435,000 gallons) of liquid hydrogen and oxygen; and a pair of booster rockets, which provide the extra power needed for launching. When they have used all their fuel, the boosters drop away, falling into the ocean, and are later collected by a ship. The fuel tank, when empty, also falls away, but it cannot be recovered because it is destroyed by the atmosphere as it falls. The spacecraft, or Orbiter, descends under its own power, landing like an aeroplane.

Five shuttles were built between 1981 and 1985, but one, *Challenger*, was destroyed in an explosion shortly after launching in 1986, killing its crew of seven.

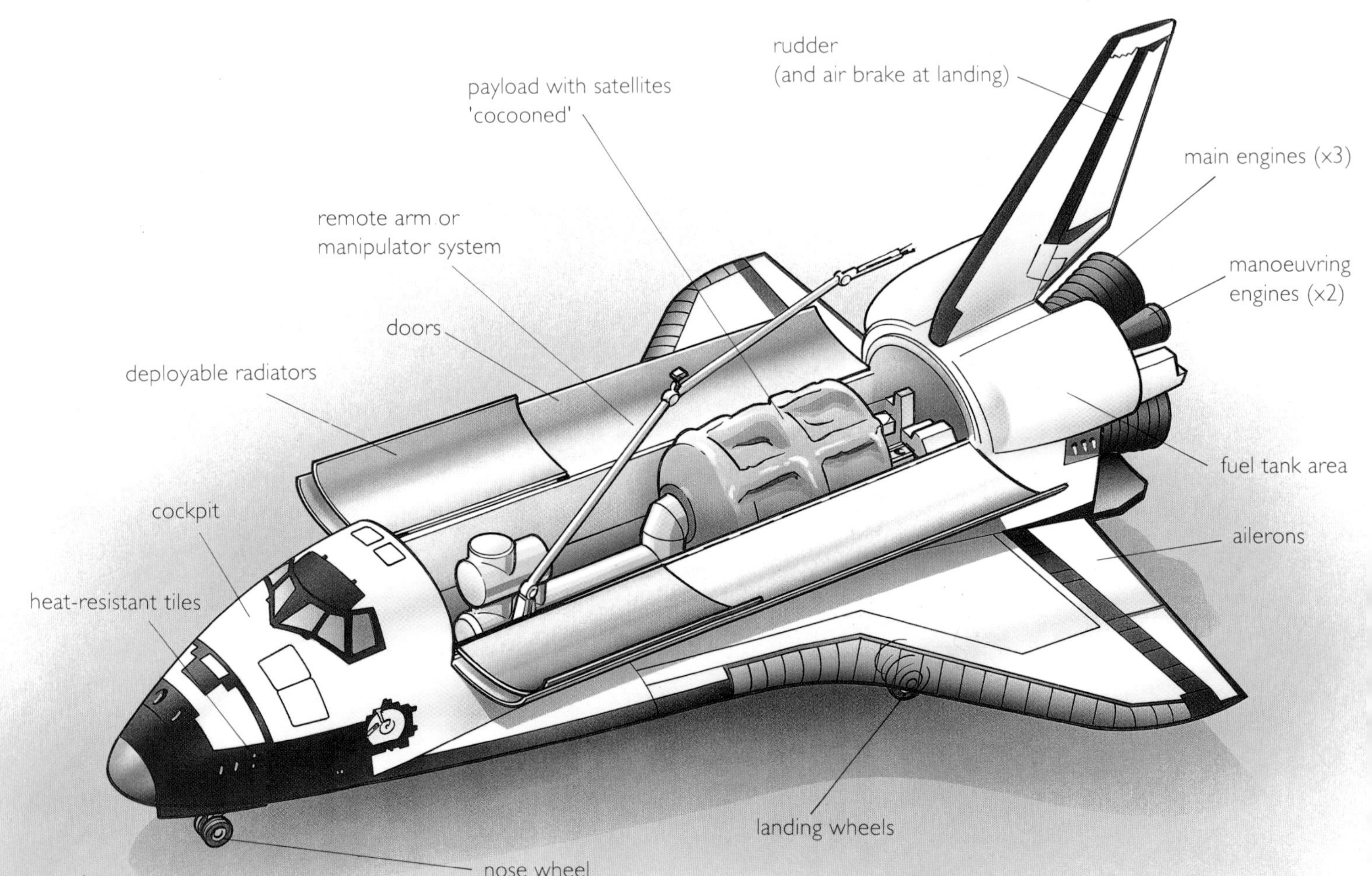

The US Space Shuttle Orbiter with payload bay doors open.

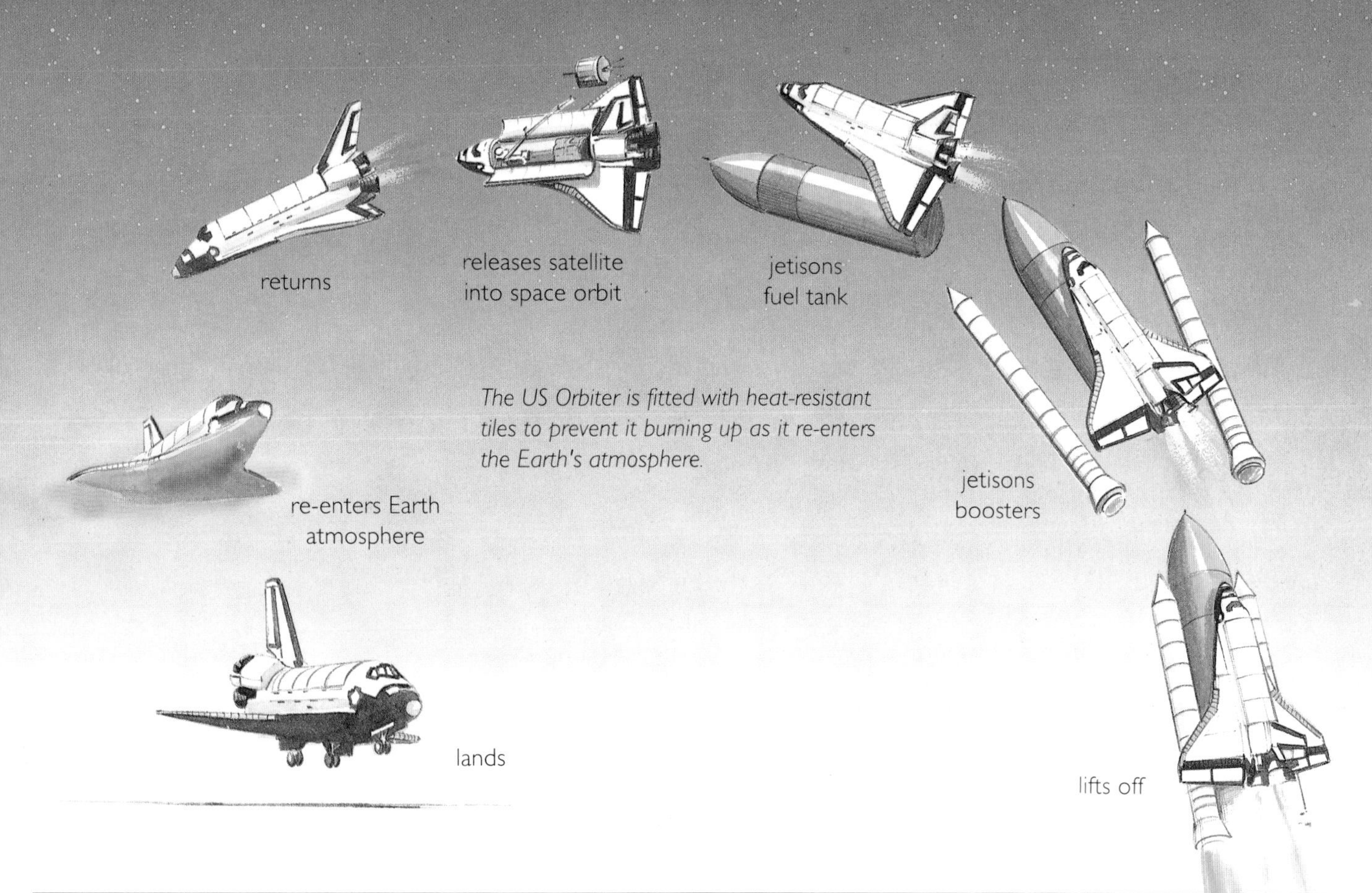

The US Orbiter is fitted with heat-resistant tiles to prevent it burning up as it re-enters the Earth's atmosphere.

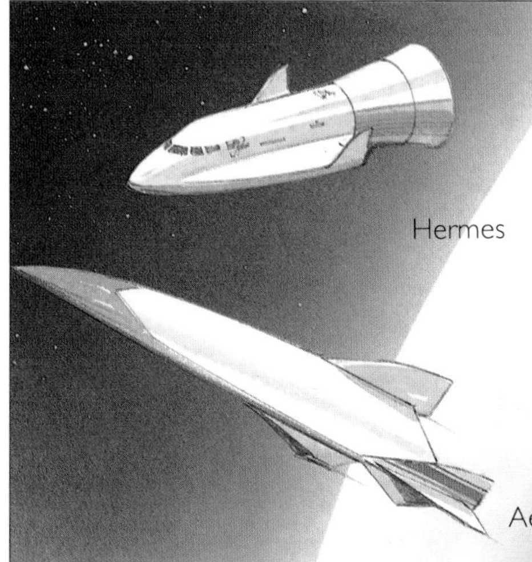

FUTURE SHUTTLES

Plans are underway in other countries to develop space shuttles. The European Space Agency is building the French-designed *Hermes*, which looks like a smaller version of the US shuttle and will be launched by the European Ariane rocket. A German company has plans for an orbiter which will fly 'piggy-back' on a booster craft.

The most ambitious project is the US National Aero-Space-Plane (NASP). It will need no booster craft, no additional fuel tank, and no booster rockets, climbing into space under its own power alone. There is also a British design for a one-stage-to-orbit spaceplane called HOTOL (Horizontal Take-Off and Landing).

The Soviet Union has concentrated on other types of space programme, especially its orbiting space laboratories where men and women can live for months at a time. But in 1988 a Soviet shuttle began tests; it was called *Buran*, or 'Snowstorm'.

Space shuttles, or ferries, are likely to become more numerous in future. At present, however, there are only enough to launch a small number of the satellites sent into space. Most satellites are still carried by expendable rockets, which can make only one flight.

The US Shuttle lifts off from its launch pad on its first flight.

References

Aileron A hinged flap on the rear edge of an aircraft wing, used to roll the aircraft to one side or the other.

Altimeter An instrument in an aircraft for measuring height above the ground.

Aqualung Breathing equipment carried by a diver, consisting of a tank full of compressed air (carried on the back), and a regulator to control the pressure of the air, which is delivered to the diver through a tube with a mouthpiece.

Autogyro An aircraft that looks like a cross between a helicopter and an aeroplane. It has rotor blades, not wings, which are turned by the pressure of the air as it flies. They provide only lift; an engine driving a propeller gives forward movement.

Autopilot Electronic system in an aircraft that keeps the aircraft flying automatically along a pre-set course.

Biplane An aeroplane with two sets of wings, one above the other.

Blériot, Louis (1872–1936) French airman who made the first flight across the English Channel in 1909. It was probably the first successful flight by a monoplane (having one pair of wings).

Charlotte Dundas One of the first reliable steamships, built for use on the River Clyde. She had a single paddle wheel near the stern.

Cockerell, Sir Christopher (b1910) British inventor of the first sea-going hovercraft, the SRN-1, in 1959.

Comet The world's first jet airliner, the de Havilland Comet entered service with the British Overseas Airways Corporation in 1952.

Concorde The first commercial supersonic airliner, built jointly by French and British companies, which entered service in 1976 and still flies from London and Paris.

Elevator A hinged flap on an aircraft's tailplane, used to make the aircraft dive or climb.

Fly-by-wire A system developed first for military aircraft that uses the rapid information processing power of computers to help fly the aircraft.

Friction The resistance to movement when two bodies rub against each other. Friction makes a ball stop rolling; friction also slows down a ball (or an aeroplane) travelling through the air.

Gagarin, Yuri (1934–68) Russian cosmonaut, the first man to travel in space and orbit the Earth, in 1961.

Gondola The passenger-carrying cabin slung underneath an airship, named after the type of boat seen on the canals of Venice.

Gyroscope An instrument used in navigation, consisting of a wheel spinning inside a frame in such a way that it can turn in all three dimensions; it therefore remains in the same position despite the movements of ship or aircraft.

Hydroplane A hinged flap on a submarine, similar to an aircraft's elevator, used to make the submarine rise or sink.

Knot A unit of speed used at sea, equivalent to one nautical mile per hour (1.853kph).

Lindbergh, Charles (1902–74) US airman who made the first solo flight across the Atlantic in 1927 in his own aeroplane, *The Spirit of St Louis*.

Montgolfier, Joseph (1740–1810) and **Etienne** French inventors who made the first hot-air balloon to carry passengers, in 1783.

Morse code A code composed of groups of short and long pulses (dots and dashes) invented by the American, Samuel Morse, for transmitting messages by electric telegraph, which was also invented by Morse.

NASA (National Aeronautics and Space Administration) The organization responsible for US space research and space flights.

Nautilus A US submarine which was the world's first nuclear-powered, sea-going vessel, launched in 1955. In 1958 she became the first vessel to reach the North Pole, sailing under the ice.

Radar (RAdio Detection And Ranging) An electronic device which locates an object by measuring the time taken by the 'echo' of a radio wave to return from it, and the direction from which it returns.

Rocket An engine like a jet engine which works in space because it carries its own oxygen.

Rudder A hinged flap on an aircraft's tailfin or a ship's stern or a submarine's tail used to steer the craft to the left or right.

Savannah The first steamship to cross the Atlantic Ocean in 1819; also the first nuclear-powered merchant ship (1962).

Sextant An instrument for navigation which measures the angle of the Sun or another star above the horizon, from which the ship's position can be calculated.

Sikorsky, Igor (1889–1972) Russian-born US engineer who built the first practical helicopter in 1940.

Sonar (SOund Navigation And Ranging) The sound equivalent of radar, a system for locating objects at sea by transmitting pulses of high-frequency sound waves and analyzing any 'echoes' or reflections that bounce back.

SOS The radio message transmitted in Morse code by ships in distress: three short bleeps (S), three long ones (O) and three short (S).

Submersible A small submarine, usually one designed for deep water, that needs a ship to transport it to and from the place where it will be used.

Wright, Wilbur (1867–1912) and **Orville** (1871–1948) US brothers who built the first heavier-than-air aeroplane to make a controlled flight, in 1903. Their aircraft was powered by a motorcycle

Manufacturing Industry

Iron and Steel

The most widely used metal in modern industry is steel, which is an alloy of iron and small amounts of carbon and other chemicals. The hardness and strength of steel, which is greater than iron, depends upon how much carbon it contains. Small amounts of other elements may be added to change the properties of steel in various ways, for example, to make it tougher, or easier to work, or more resistant to attack by chemicals ('stainless steel').

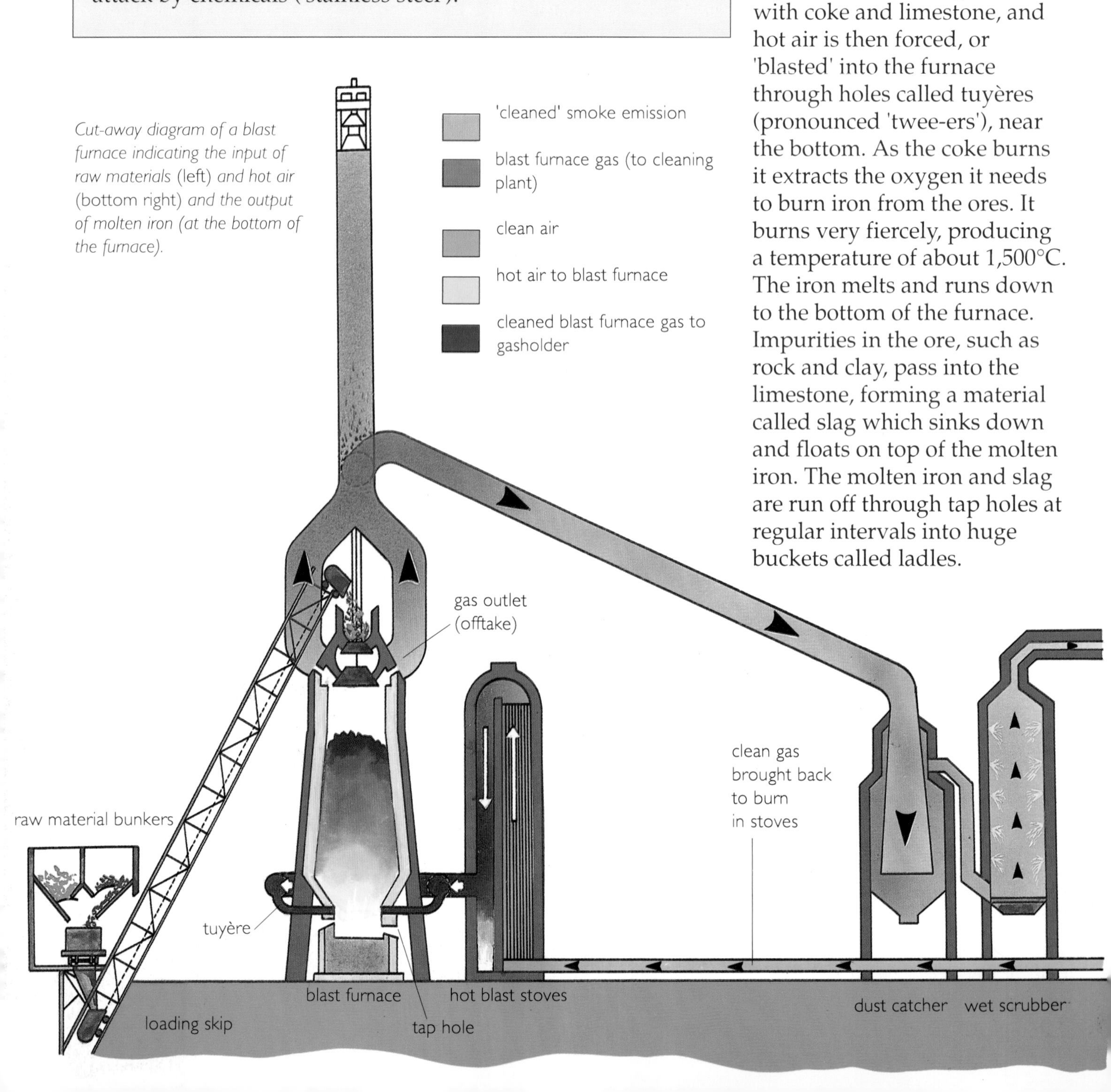

Cut-away diagram of a blast furnace indicating the input of raw materials (left) *and hot air* (bottom right) *and the output of molten iron (at the bottom of the furnace).*

The blast furnace

Most of the world's iron is produced from mined ores called haematite and magnetite. The iron has to be extracted from the ore in a blast furnace, which is a huge oven shaped like a tower, 30m (100ft) high and 9m (30ft) across, and lined with fire-proof bricks.

The iron ore is fed into the top of the furnace together with coke and limestone, and hot air is then forced, or 'blasted' into the furnace through holes called tuyères (pronounced 'twee-ers'), near the bottom. As the coke burns it extracts the oxygen it needs to burn iron from the ores. It burns very fiercely, producing a temperature of about 1,500°C. The iron melts and runs down to the bottom of the furnace. Impurities in the ore, such as rock and clay, pass into the limestone, forming a material called slag which sinks down and floats on top of the molten iron. The molten iron and slag are run off through tap holes at regular intervals into huge buckets called ladles.

Steelmaking

The molten iron produced by a blast furnace is called pig-iron and contains about five per cent carbon. Some pig-iron is melted and purified again to make cast iron, which is used for making items that can be cast in moulds, such as car engine blocks. But most pig-iron is turned into steel.

Most steel is made by the basic-oxygen process. Molten pig-iron is poured into a large converter lined with fire-proof bricks; some steel scrap may also be added. A water-cooled tube, called a lance, is lowered into the converter until its tip is just above the molten pig-iron. Then oxygen is blown through the lance at high pressure and the blast burns the impurities out of the molten metal, producing pure steel. The converter is then tipped on its side and the steel run off into a ladle.

The electric furnace

High-quality steel is usually produced in an electric furnace. Scrap steel is melted in the furnace by an electric arc, a large, continuous electric spark. Lime and iron ore are added to remove impurities from the molten steel.

> REFINING STEEL
>
> Some steels need to be refined further before they can be used. For example, trapped gases have to be removed from steels used in oil refineries. This can be done by melting the steel inside a special chamber. When air is removed from the chamber, the gases are released from the steel and can be pumped out.
>
> In one process called vacuum-arc remelting, an electric arc flows between a bar of the steel being refined and the bottom of a water-cooled mould. The end of the bar melts into droplets which fall into the mould, releasing the unwanted gases in the process. Another method is electroslag refining in which a special slag 'washes' the metal in a mould.

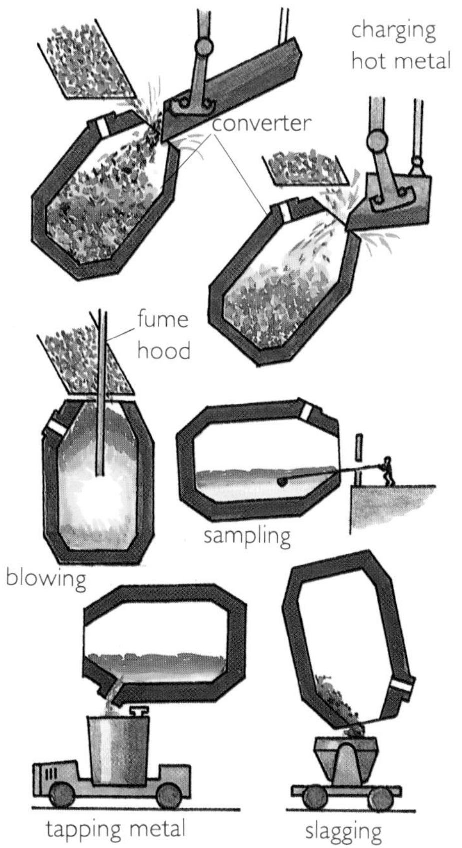

Stages in the basic-oxygen process. When ready, the pure steel is tapped – poured from the converter into containers.

Metal Working

Besides iron and steel, many other metals are used in industry, including aluminium, copper, nickel, tin and zinc. Metals are useful because, as well as being strong, they can be shaped in various ways. The most common methods are: casting molten metal in moulds; forging or hammering hot metal; rolling metal into sheets; and machining with tools which cut, drill or grind.

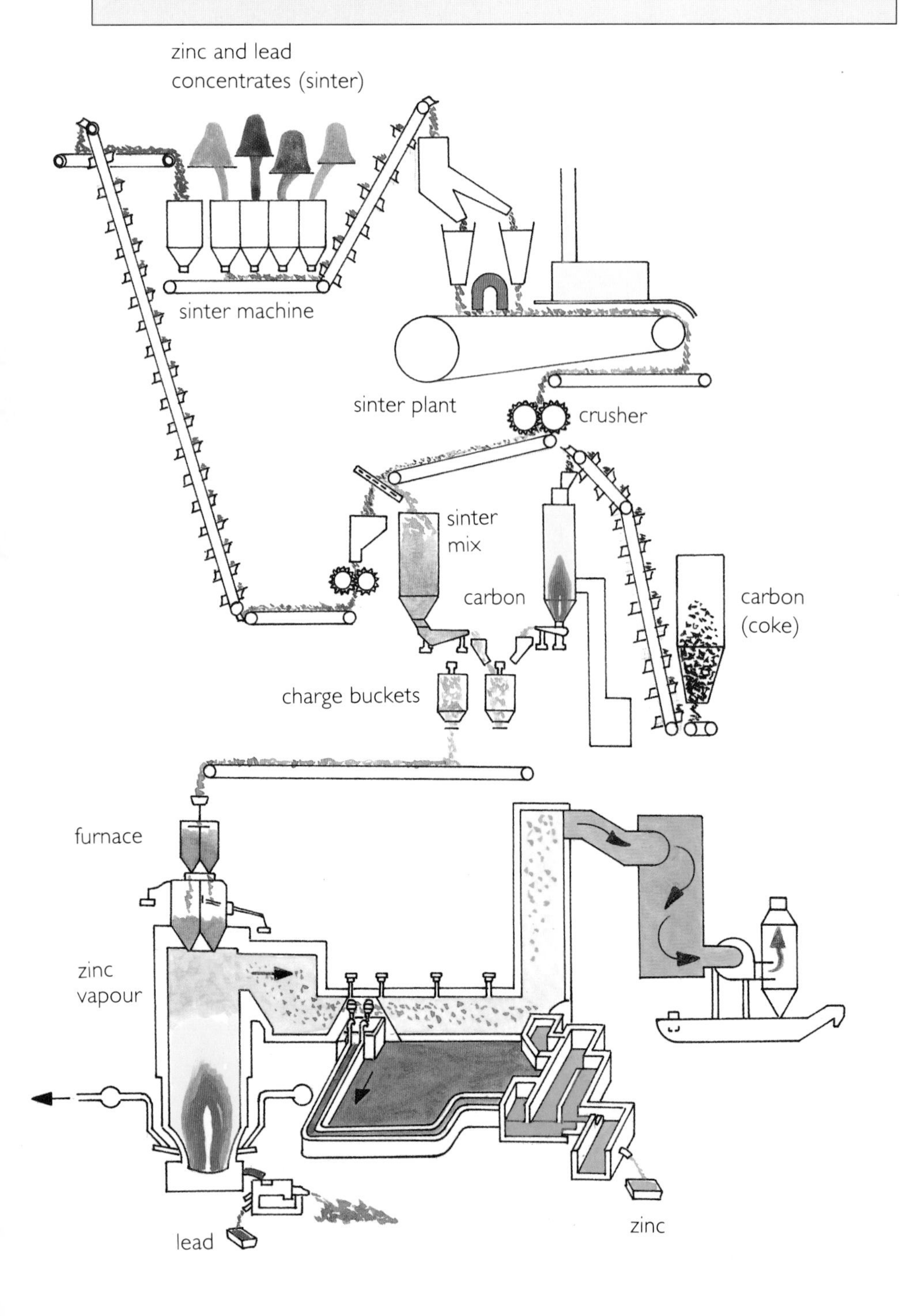

Stages in the production of zinc and lead. Sinter – lumps of the metal oxides – is mixed with carbon then heated in a blast furnace to separate the molten zinc and lead vapour.

Casting

In casting, liquid metal is allowed to solidify in a mould. Steel is sometimes cast into bars or ingots in this way, but a more modern process is continuous casting. The molten steel is poured into a water-cooled mould which has a slot in one side. The metal cools and emerges from the slot as a continuous slab.

More complicated castings are made with moulds of sand and clay. A model of the object to be cast is placed in a box and clay packed around it. When the clay has dried the model is removed leaving a cavity of the shape required. Molten metal is then poured into the cavity, after making holes in the casting box to allow the air inside to escape. When the metal has cooled the mould is broken and the casting removed.

Rolling

The slabs of steel made by continuous casting can be turned into thinner sheets by rolling. The slabs are first heated until red-hot and then passed between a series of heavy rollers. Each roller reduces the thickness of the slab by a certain amount until the desired thickness is reached.

Forging

Red-hot metals can be shaped by hammering, as a blacksmith does. This process is called forging. In industry today, the common method is called drop forging because a heavy, mechanical hammer is allowed to drop on to the heated metal.

In die forging the hot metal rests on a type of mould called a die. The metal is shaped by the die as it is struck by a hammer.

Press forging relies on pressure rather than sharp blows, and slowly 'squeezes' the hot metal into shape.

Above: *Flat sheets of steel for car bodies are cut and pressed into shape under great pressure.*

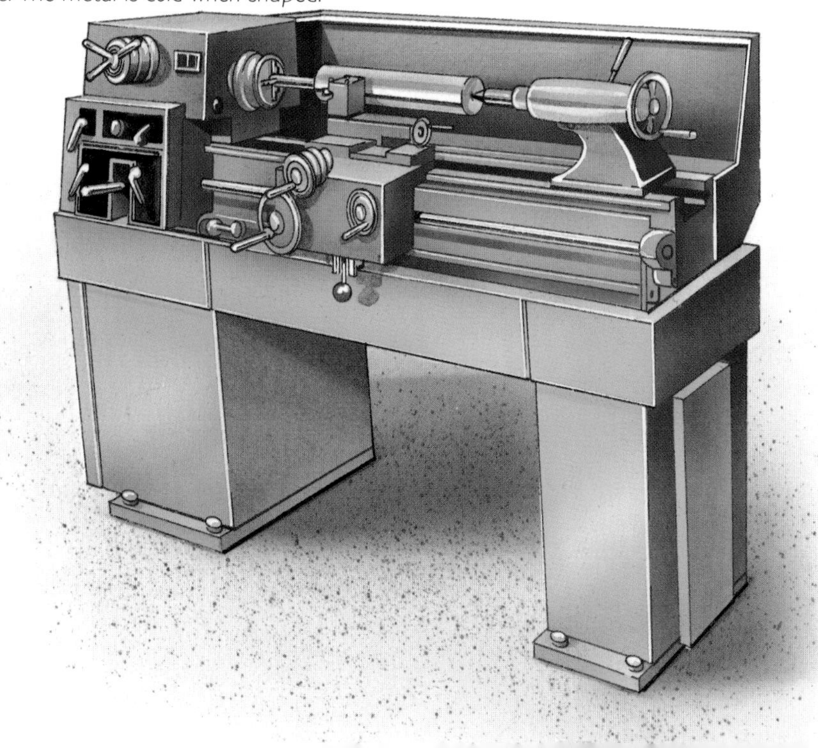

Below: *Machining a metal cylinder on a lathe. The metal is cold when shaped.*

Machine tools

Machine tools with powerful electric motors are able to cut, grind and drill metal parts very accurately. Often they are controlled by computers to ensure the greatest accuracy.

Among the most useful machine tools are the lathe, which shapes metal rods by turning them so that they rub against a sharp cutting tool, and the milling machine, which cuts grooves or slots with a toothed cutting wheel.

Mass Production and Robots

Factories must make goods – motor cars, television sets, lawn mowers and thousands of other articles – cheaply and in large numbers. This is called mass production. The secret of mass production is to break down the manufacturing process into small, simple steps. Each step is carried out by a machine and today the process is often controlled by computers.

Computerized machine tools
A machine tool such as a milling machine or a drill can be controlled by a computer. Once programmed with its instructions the computer works the tool unaided. Computer-controlled machine tools are called CNC (Computer Numerical Controlled) machines.

In modern car factories robots are used to weld together and paint body components.

Flexible systems

More complicated methods are used in some factories. The CNC machines are grouped together in FMS (Flexible Manufacturing System) cells.

In an FMS cell, the machine tools are supplied with rough metal parts called blanks. The blanks are carried to the cell by conveyor belts, or AGVs (Automatically Guided Vehicles). A computer-controlled robot arm passes the blank to the first machine tool. When this tool has done its work, the robot arm passes the blank to the next tool. After all the tools in the cell have done their individual jobs, the finished product is removed by conveyor belt or AGV. The factory floor can seem a ghostly place – hardly a human being in sight.

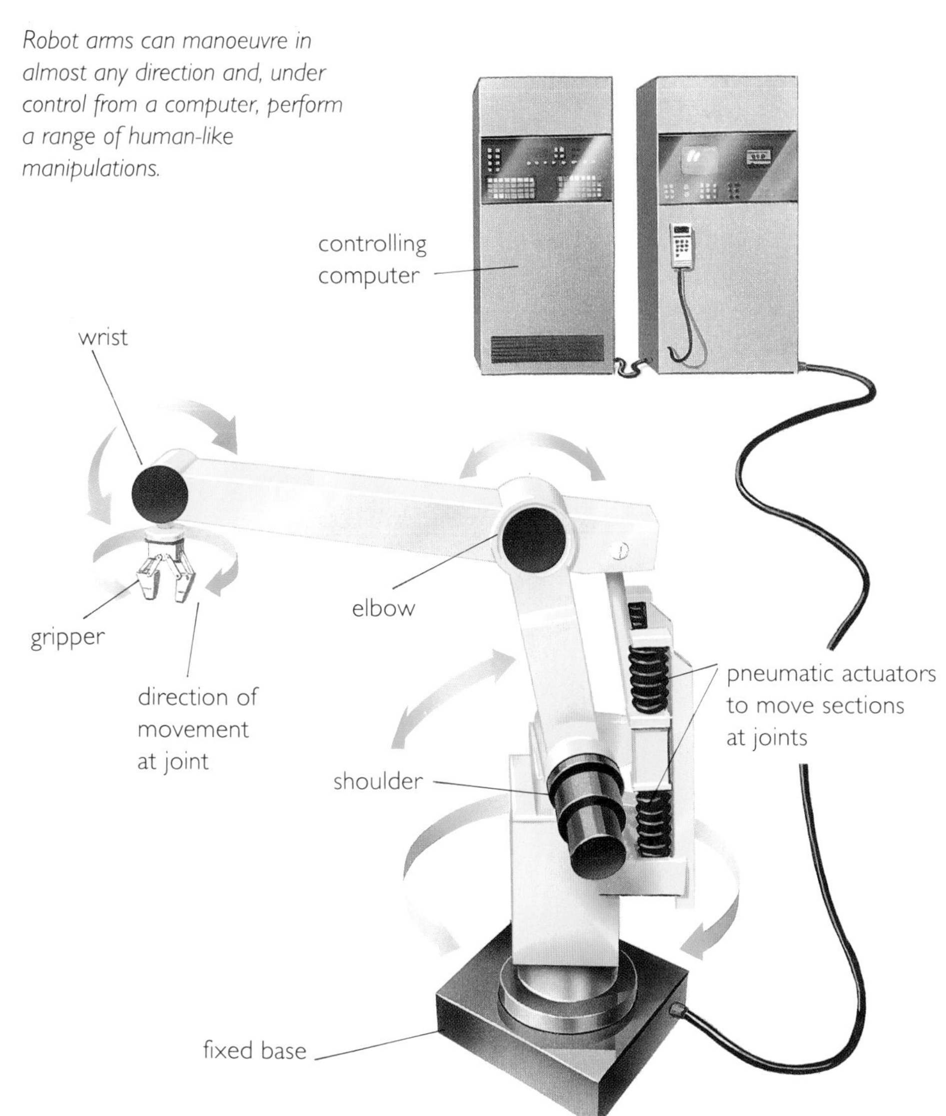

Robot arms can manoeuvre in almost any direction and, under control from a computer, perform a range of human-like manipulations.

The US Space Shuttle Orbiter has a mechanical arm for collecting satellites from orbit to repair.

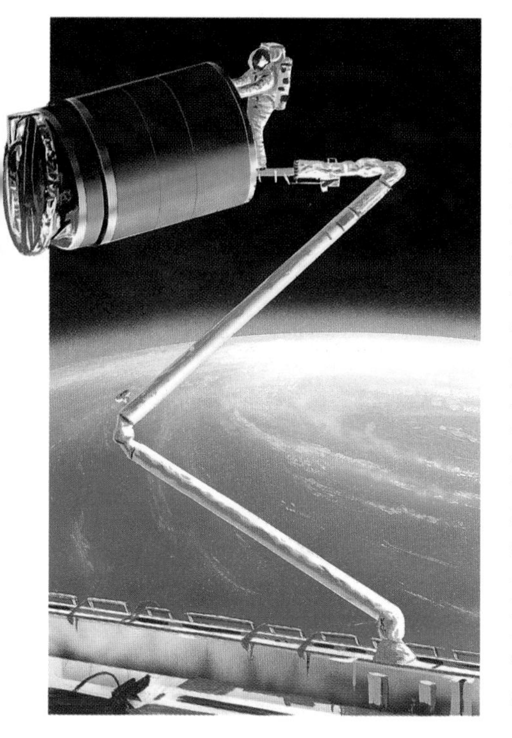

Robots

Robots in factories are nothing like those in science-fiction films. They are mostly mechanical arms which can move like a human arm. They have a joint in the middle, like an elbow, and a joint near the end, like a wrist. Instead of a hand they have a gripper which can pick up objects or hold tools. The arm and gripper are moved by small electric motors or by liquid pressure systems, called pneumatics, and they are controlled by a computer called the system supervisor.

A list of the exact movements that must be made is programmed into the computer. This may be done using an input keyboard, but some systems are 'taught' what to do by moving the arm through the sequence of moves it is to follow. The computer memorizes the moves.

The latest AI (Artificial Intelligence) robots have television cameras attached, so that they can recognize a part by sight. If they notice a small fault in a part, for example, they can decide whether to mend it or call for help.

Textiles

Clothmaking is one of the oldest crafts. People first learned how to spin fibre into threads and how to weave the threads into cloth on a loom about 10,000 years ago. Until mechanical looms, driven by water or steam power, were invented, most spinning and weaving, and the making of clothes, was done by ordinary people in their homes.

Natural fibres
Threads are made up of millions of tiny hair-like fibres. Until the 19th century these fibres came from natural sources: cotton fibre from the cotton plant; wool from sheep; linen from the crushed stalks of the flax plant; silk from silkworms.

Artificial fibres
Fibres such as rayon, Tricel, nylon, Terylene, Dacron, Acrilan and Dralon are not found in nature. Rayon is made from cellulose extracted from wood pulp and cotton waste. The liquid cellulose is squirted through fine holes in a device called a spinneret into a bath of weak acid, where it solidifies into threads. This process is called wet spinning. A similar process, called dry spinning, is used to make acetate fibres such as Tricel. Cellulose is dissolved in a liquid which evaporates as the filaments are spun in dry air.

Nylon and most other artificial fibres are made from plastics produced from crude oil. Nylon is made from a plastic called caprolactam, which is melted and forced through a spinneret into cold air. The filaments form as the plastic cools. This process is known as melt spinning.

Polyesters such as Terylene and Dacron are made by melt spinning a plastic called polyethylene terephthalate. Acrylics such as Acrilan and Dralon are made from a plastic called polyacrylonitrile, by wet spinning.

wood pulp and cotton waste – rayon

sheep – wool

cotton plant – cotton

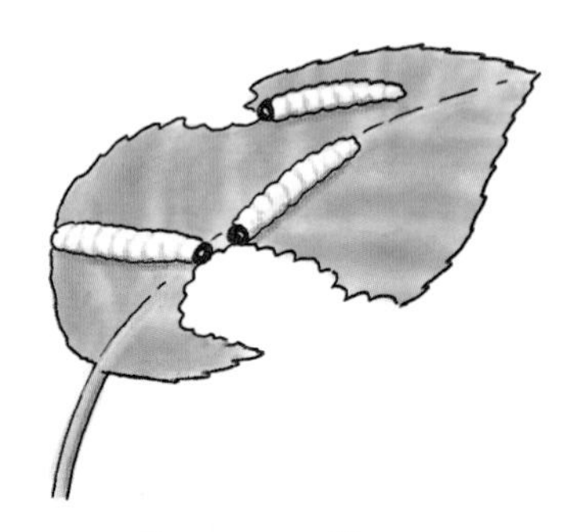

silkworm – silk

flax – linen

crude oil – nylon

Natural sources of threads and fibres used in cloth manufacture.

Spinning and weaving
A spinning machine turns short lengths of fibre into thread. The fibres are first drawn through rollers into a loose rope, or sliver. The sliver is then stretched and twisted until it becomes a strong, fine thread or yarn. Finally the thread is twisted again as it is wound on to a reel or bobbin.

Looms weave the threads together to make cloth. One set of threads, the warp, pass lengthwise, or up and down along the loom. Each thread goes through a hole in a wire frame, called a heddle. There are two heddles and they move up and down, separating the threads vertically as they move. A shuttle carries the other set of threads, the weft, to and fro across the warp threads as they move up and down. When the shuttle travels across the warp one way, it passes under the threads in one frame and over the threads in the other. On the way back, the frames have changed position, and so the shuttle passes under the threads it earlier moved over, and over the threads it had moved under.

Some modern machines use jets of air or water, or long thin wires called rapiers to pass the weft thread across the warp.

Different arrangements of warp and weft used in various materials.

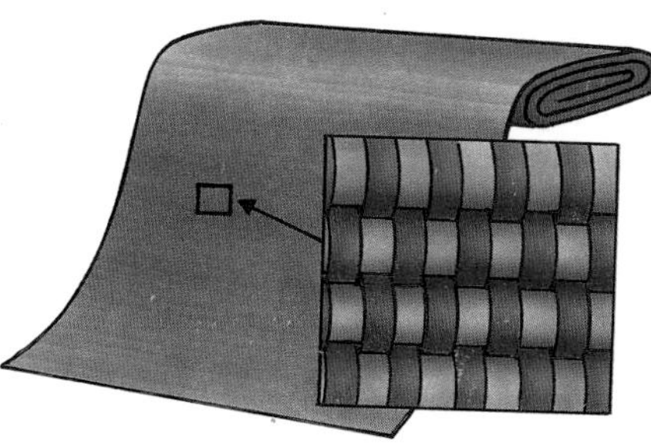

ribbed weave

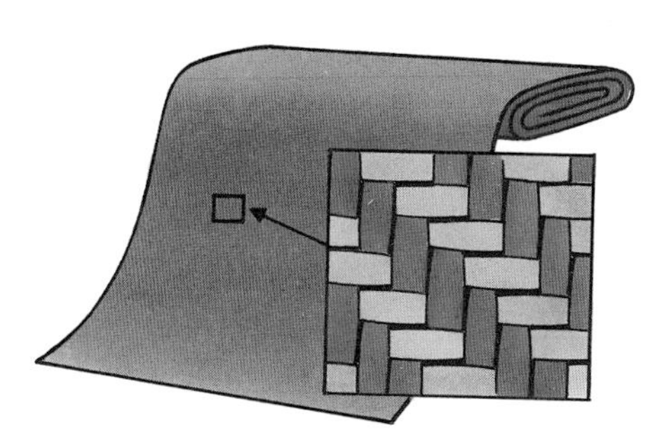

twill weave

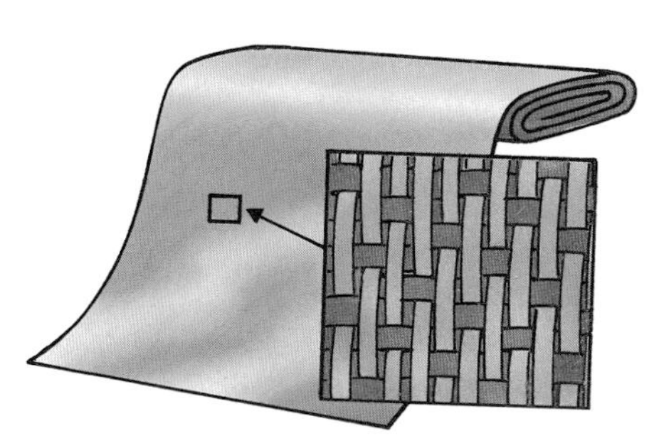

satin weave

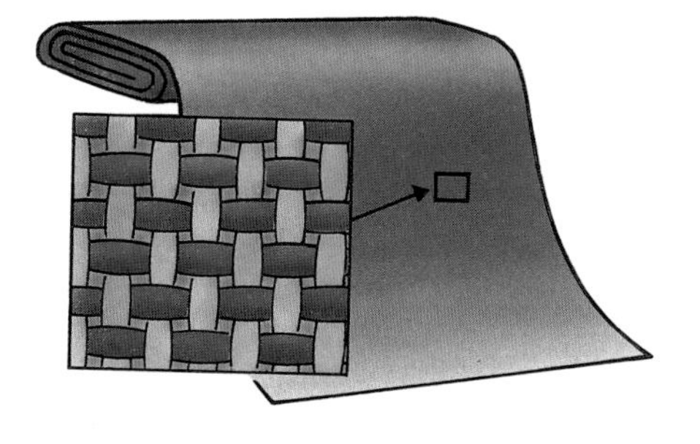

plain weave

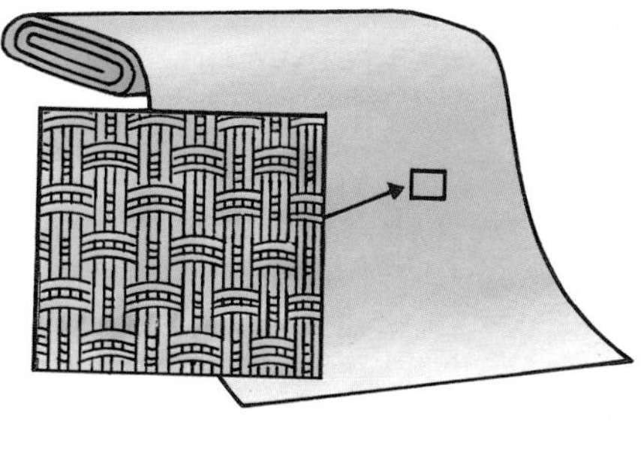

basket weave

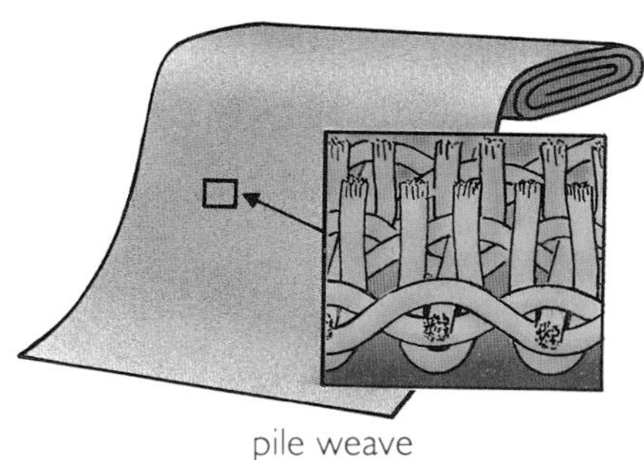

pile weave

LOOMS

In a small loom the heddles are moved up and down by treadles worked by the weaver's feet. The operation of separating the warp threads is called shedding. The shuttle is then 'thrown' by hand between the warp threads. The slay or batten is pushed away from the heddles in order to press each new weft thread tightly against the woven cloth.

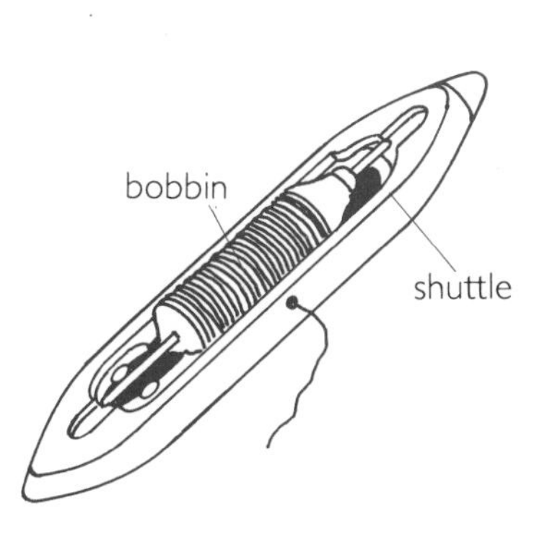

Oil Refining

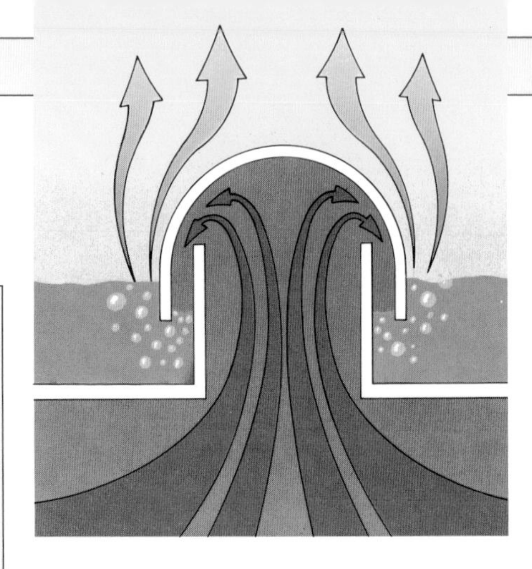

'Bubble caps' within a distillation tower direct rising vapours through liquids to separate out the various components or fractions of crude oil.

The crude oil that is pumped from underground (including under the sea-bed) is the remains of tiny plants and animals that lived millions of years ago. It is sometimes called 'black gold' because it can make a lucky prospector, or landowner who owns oil deposits, as rich as if it were gold.

Many useful substances, called petrochemicals, can be made from crude oil. Besides fuels like gasoline (petrol), engine oil, diesel fuel, paraffin, kerosene, etc., many plastics, drugs, paints, explosives and pesticides are made from substances extracted from oil.

The crude oil which comes from an oil well is a thick, black liquid. It is a mixture of many different hydrocarbons – chemicals made up of carbon and hydrogen combined. Crude oil must be refined before it can be used.

Distillation

The first step is to heat the crude oil to 350°C, causing it to give off gases. The gases pass into tall distillation columns, and as they rise up the column they pass through holes in trays set across the column. As it cools, a gas changes into a liquid and collects on a tray. Each tray collects a different liquid, called a 'fraction', which is drawn off through a pipe.

The lightest chemicals, such as butane and propane, are drawn off at the top of the column. Petrol and paraffin are produced lower down, and a heavy residue is produced at the bottom of the column.

Each fraction may need further refining. The residue at the base of the distillation column can be distilled a second time at reduced air pressure, a process called vacuum distillation. This produces diesel oil, asphalt, lubricating oil and paraffin wax.

Cracking and reforming

Heavy fractions, such as thick oils, can be changed into more valuable light fractions, such as petrol. They are heated under pressure in a large vessel containing a catalyst, which speeds up the breakdown of the heavy oils and waxes, turning them into petrol and gases such as ethene and ethylene. This process is called catalytic cracking. After use, the catalyst is pumped to a regenerator where carbon which accumulates on it during cracking is burned off so that it can be used again.

It is also possible to change light fractions into heavier ones using a catalyst. This process, called reforming, is used to increase the yield and improve the quality of petrol. The final step in producing petrol is to remove any strong-smelling sulphur compounds which would make car exhausts even more unpleasant.

Left: *Tanker ships unload crude oil at a refinery. Offshore, a drill rig bores through the sea-bed to tap oil from a well.*

The many uses of oil.

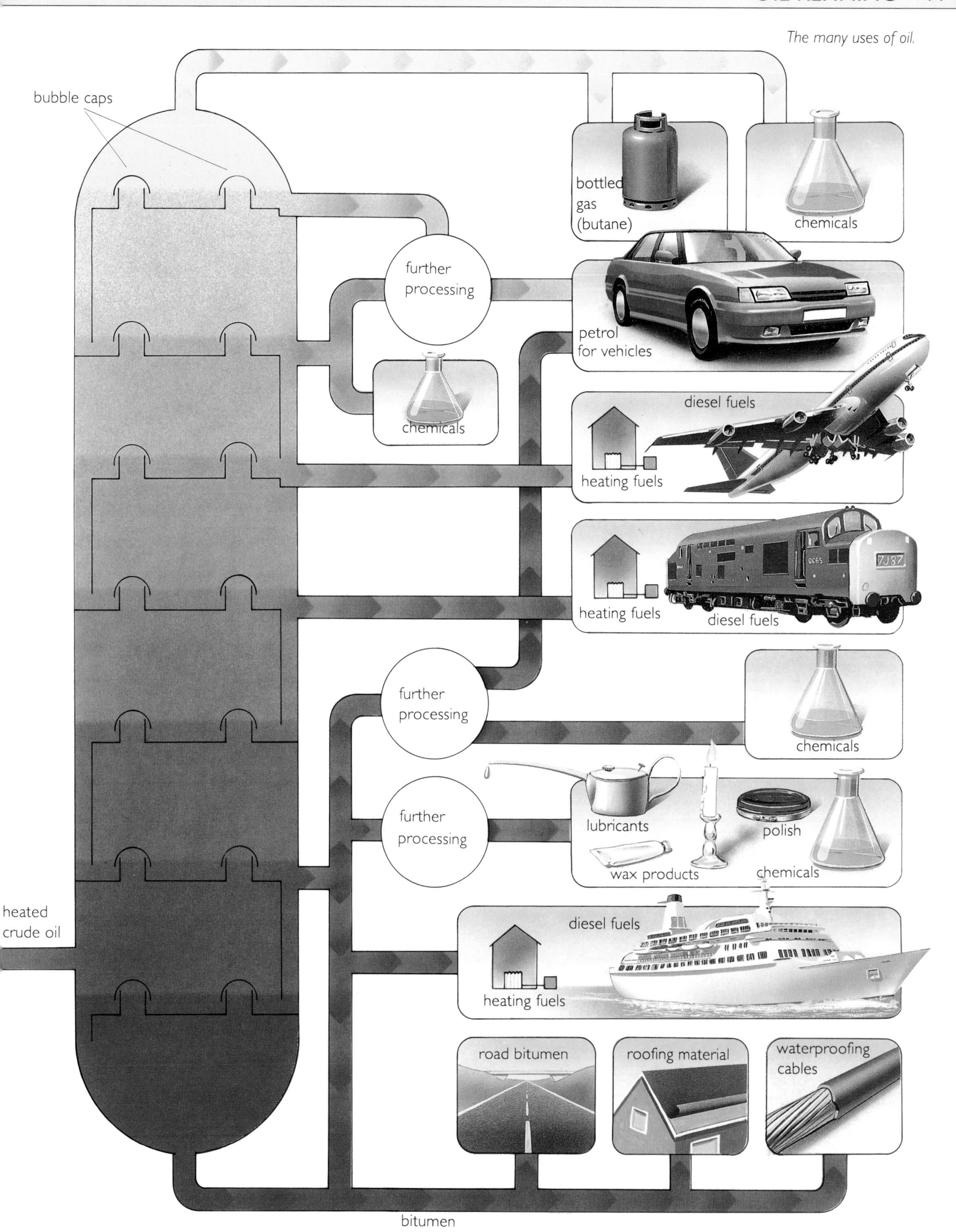

Plastics and Ceramics

The word plastic comes from a Greek word meaning 'able to be moulded'. One of the great advantages of plastics is that they can be easily made into any shape. Ceramics, which are made from clay or other earthy substances and baked hard in an oven, can also be shaped easily.

Plastics
Unlike ceramics, plastics are a modern invention. They were unknown before the nineteenth century. Plastics are materials made up of very long molecules containing carbon and hydrogen. The molecules of most plastics are chains built up of smaller molecules joined together. For instance, molecules of the plastic polyethylene (polythene) are made up of many ethylene molecules joined in a chain. The process which builds up these giant molecules is called polymerization, and plastics made in this way are called polymers. Names such as polyethylene, polystyrene, etc. show that these materials are polymers.

Thermoplastics become soft when heated, and when allowed to cool they are tough and flexible. They are used for such things as plastic bottles, shopping bags, and artificial fibres like nylon.

Thermosetting plastics, on the other hand, cannot be resoftened once hardened. They are hard but not flexible. Examples are melamine, Formica and Bakelite (one of the earliest mass-production plastics). Some of the quick-setting glues are based on thermo-setting plastics; they are also used in boat hulls and car bodies, and can be strengthened by adding glass or carbon fibres.

An injection-moulded plastic milk crate.

SHAPING PLASTIC

Plastics can be shaped in a number of ways. The first step in each process, though, is nearly always to heat the plastic in order to soften or melt it. In the extrusion process, the liquid plastic is then forced through a specially shaped nozzle. In blow moulding, the plastic is blown into a mould (as for plastic bottles). In injection moulding, the plastic is forced into a mould under pressure. In vacuum forming, air pressure is used to pull a soft plastic sheet around a mould; the plastic is then allowed to cool and harden. For thermosetting plastics, a doughy form of the plastic, called a resin, is squeezed into shape by a mould; after reheating, the resin sets hard.

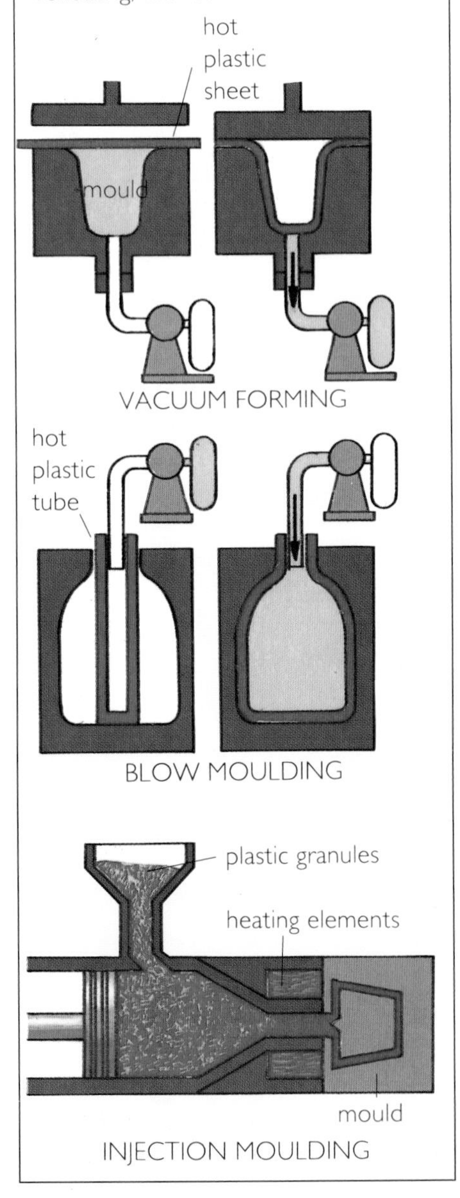

A variety of everyday objects made from plastics and ceramics or with plastic or ceramic components.

Ceramics

Ceramics are harder than most metals and plastics. They are not easily attacked by chemicals and they can stand very high temperatures. This explains why they are so widely used in crockery such as cups and saucers, cooker hobs, rocket nose cones, machine tools, abrasives, and nuclear fuel rods.

People were making simple ceramics in the Middle East over 8,000 years ago, and the potter's wheel was invented before the first civilizations arose. Simple clay ceramics such as bricks, roof tiles and sewer pipes are still made today, though a much bigger variety of materials is now available.

Ceramics made from minerals found in nature, such as magnesite and dolomite, are used to line the walls of steelmaking furnaces. The newer ceramics are made from pure compounds, such as barium titanate and zirconium boride. Alumina (aluminium oxide) is widely used in bearings, grinding powders and as an electrical insulator in spark plugs. Titania (titanium oxide) is made into permanent magnets, radio aerials and computer memories.

There are many ways of making ceramic articles. Bricks can be made by pressing clay into box-shaped lumps, or by extrusion, in which a column of soft clay is forced through a rectangular hole and then cut into short lengths. Cups and similar objects can be formed on a potter's wheel, much as they were in ancient times, or by casting. In casting, clay is pressed into a mould and the mould is removed when the clay has dried. Whatever the method, the finished object is fired in a kiln to harden it.

Glass

Glass was made by the Ancient Egyptians and it is still one of our most useful (and attractive) materials. It is cheap, because it is made mostly from sand. It is waterproof, easy to clean, not corroded by chemicals, transparent and very hard (though easily broken).

Glass is made by heating a mixture of sand, soda (sodium carbonate) and limestone (calcium carbonate) in a furnace to about 1,500°C. The mixture melts to form red-hot liquid glass. As it cools the liquid hardens into a transparent solid. This basic sodalime glass is suitable for bottles, windows and light bulbs.

Above: *Stained glass window made from small pieces of coloured glass held together with strips of lead.*

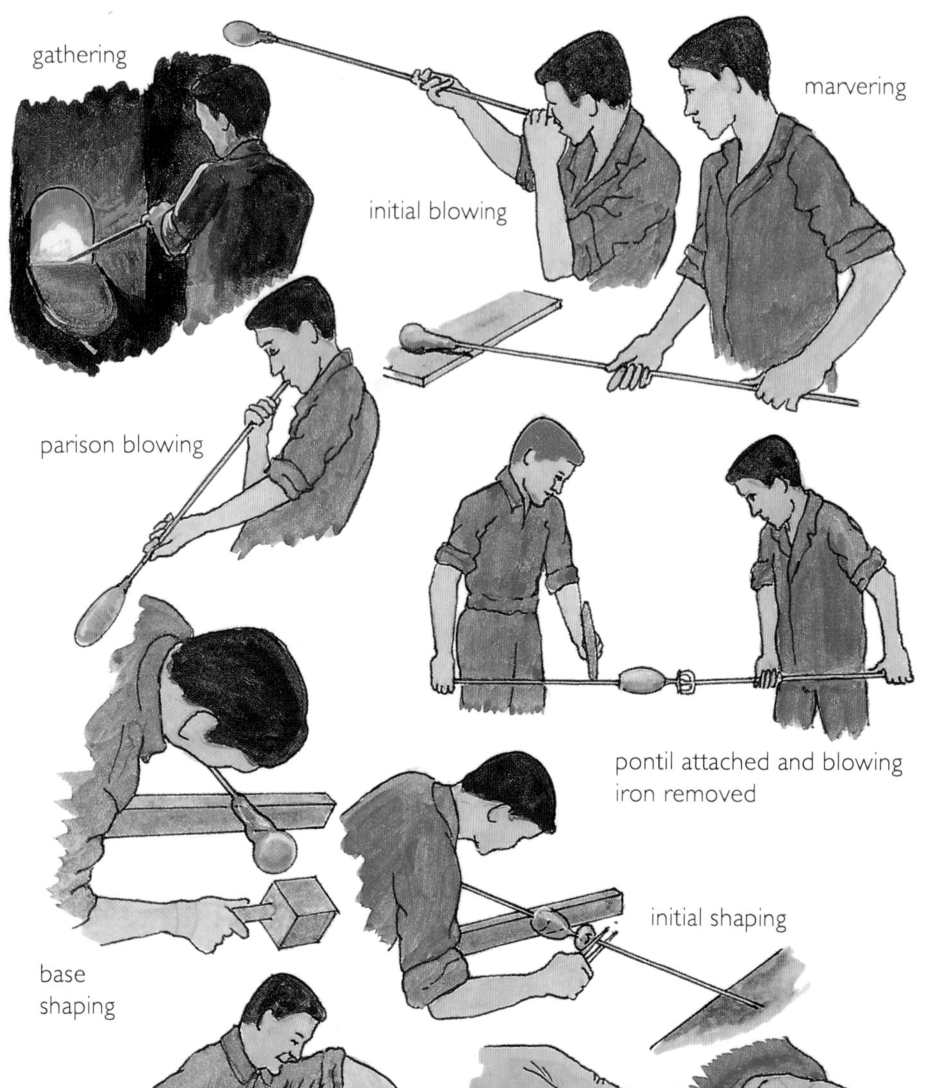

Left: *Stages in glass-blowing. Shaping of the glass vessel is carried out while the glass is still red-hot, several minutes after it is removed from the furnace.*

Making bottles

The traditional way of making bottles and other glass vessels is by blowing. The glass blower lifts a ball of sticky glass from the furnace on the end of a hollow tube called a pontil. He blows down the tube while turning it quickly, and the ball expands into a hollow sphere which is then shaped into bottle form.

Bottles are made by machines in factories in a similar way. A ball of molten glass is shaped into a cylinder by the pressure of metal moulds. A metal plunger then enters the cylinder from below and blows a puff of air which hollows out the bottle and forms the neck.

Manufacture of sheet glass by the drawing method (top left) *and the float glass method* (beneath).

Sheet glass

There are two methods of producing glass in sheets, for windows, patio doors, etc. In the drawing method a heated wire frame, the 'bait', is dropped on to the molten glass and draws it upwards between a pair of asbestos rollers. It emerges as a continuous sheet which is cracked off in suitable lengths, or fed to the lehr. The lehr is a tunnel in which the temperature is carefully controlled so that the glass cools very slowly. The slow cooling process, called annealing, ensures that the glass is as strong as possible. If glass is not annealed it may have weaknesses due to one side cooling faster than the other. Plate glass for shop windows is usually made by the drawing method.

In the float process molten glass flows on to a bath of molten tin. The floating glass is pulled across the surface of the tin until it forms a solid sheet. Float glass has a very smooth surface and does not need polishing. Most window glass is made by this process.

Special types of glass

Different kinds of glass can be made by melting different ingredients. A very strong glass can be made by adding boron compounds such as boron oxide. This borosilicate glass is used for cooking pots and laboratory flasks. Lead or crystal glass is made by adding lead oxide; it is very clear and is used to make lenses.

Glass can be coloured by adding metals like lead, which produces green glass. Cobalt gives a blue colour and copper a bright red. Metal can also be sandwiched between two sheets of glass before annealing.

Detergents, Dyes and Drugs

Before the Industrial Revolution began in Europe about 200 years ago, people depended on natural substances to get their skin clean, to dye their clothes, or to cure their illnesses. Today, the chemical industry has provided us with many alternatives. Detergents, for example, are artificial soaps – chemical 'cocktails' made from hydrocarbons extracted from crude oil, developed by scientists in laboratories.

Soaps and detergents

Soap was first made by boiling animal fat with wood ash. The ash contains an alkali which reacts with the fat to produce soap. The reaction is called 'saponification'. Modern soapmaking methods use different fats and oils, including tallow, coconut oil and olive oil, and as alkalis, caustic soda (sodium hydroxide) and potassium hydroxide. After saponification the soap is purified and processed into bars, flakes or powders.

Detergents are usually made from hydrocarbons extracted from crude oil. All detergents contain a substance called a 'surfactant'. The surfactant, like soap, helps water wet the object being washed. It is the water that cleans your hands; soap simply makes its job easier. A second important ingredient is the 'builder'. The builder helps keep dirt particles floating in the water after they have been removed by the surfactant. Detergents may also include bleaches, brighteners, and perfumes.

Spraying detergent on to an oil slick to break it up and disperse the oil.

Above: *Detergent molecules removing dirt particles from fabric.*
Below: *In colour photographic film, three dyes are used to create the full range of colours.*

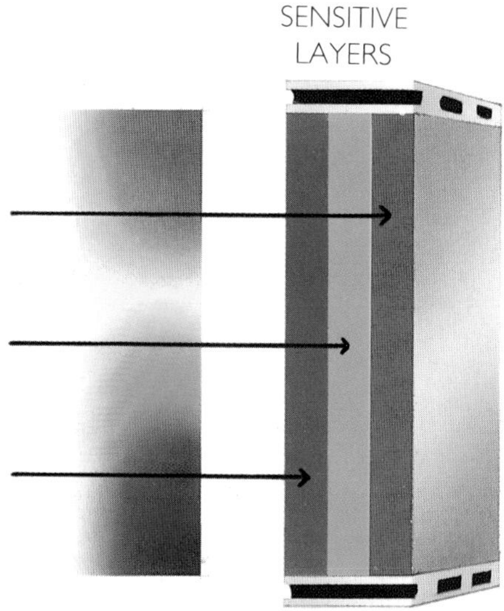

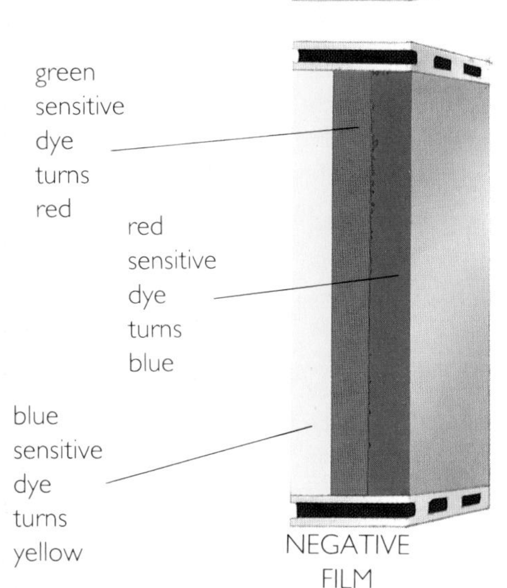

Dyes

The first colouring agents, or dyes, came from plants such as woad (blue) and madder (red). In 1855, the first artificial dye was made by William Perkin, from coal tar. The dye was a brilliant purple colour and was called mauvine. Spurred on by Perkin's success, chemists soon extracted many other dyes from coal tar. These were called aniline dyes. However, although these dyes were brilliantly coloured, they were easily washed out of cloth. This problem was solved by first treating the cloth with a chemical called a 'mordant'. The mordant makes the dye stick strongly to the cloth.

Dyes called azo dyes are the most common artificial dyes today. They are used for wool and cotton, as well as in colour photography. Indigo, used to dye blue jeans, belongs to another group of chemical dyes called vat dyes. Reactive dyes cannot be washed out because they join chemically with cloth fibres such as rayon.

Drugs

The first medicines were natural substances extracted from plants, as many still are. The widely used drug aspirin was first extracted from the bark of the willow tree. Painkillers such as morphine and codeine are obtained from the opium poppy.

However, most modern drugs were developed in chemical research laboratories and tested for many years before being used by doctors. They include anaesthetics such as procaine, which prevents pain during operations, and antibiotics such as penicillin, which kills harmful bacteria. Some drugs, such as insulin (used to treat diabetes), are produced from living organisms, usually bacteria. This is an example of the new science of 'genetic engineering'.

An assortment of drugs in tablet and capsule form.

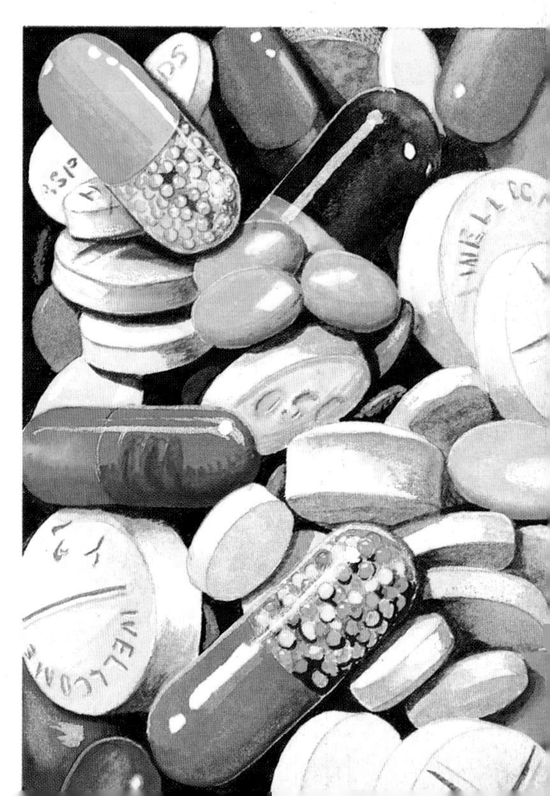

Rubber, Timber and Paper

The true importance of the world's forests has only recently been realized, as natural forests are unfortunately being destroyed faster than ever before. But trees have, for a long time, provided us with fuel as well as many other resources. In particular, trees provide rubber, timber and paper – three products which we use in huge amounts in many different forms and for many purposes.

Rubber

Natural rubber is a material obtained from the hevea tree, a native of Brazil, and certain other trees and shrubs. Rubber oozes out of the tree as a milk-like liquid called latex when the bark is cut. After collection, the latex is washed and treated with a chemical such as acetic acid (the acid in vinegar). The rubber forms in small crumbs, which are dried and pressed into sheets.

Chemically, rubber is made up of long, chain-like molecules of up to 65,000 carbon and hydrogen atoms. The molecule is normally twisted into a coil, but it can be stretched to four or five times its normal length. That is what gives rubber its stretchy, bouncy quality.

Artificial rubber can be made by 'polymerization', joining together molecules containing small chains of carbon and hydrogen. The material for car and truck tyres is made in this way. Another artificial rubber, neoprene, is used for conveyor belts because it is so strong.

Below: *Cross-ply and radial car tyres with steel inner cords and wires and rubber tread and covering.*

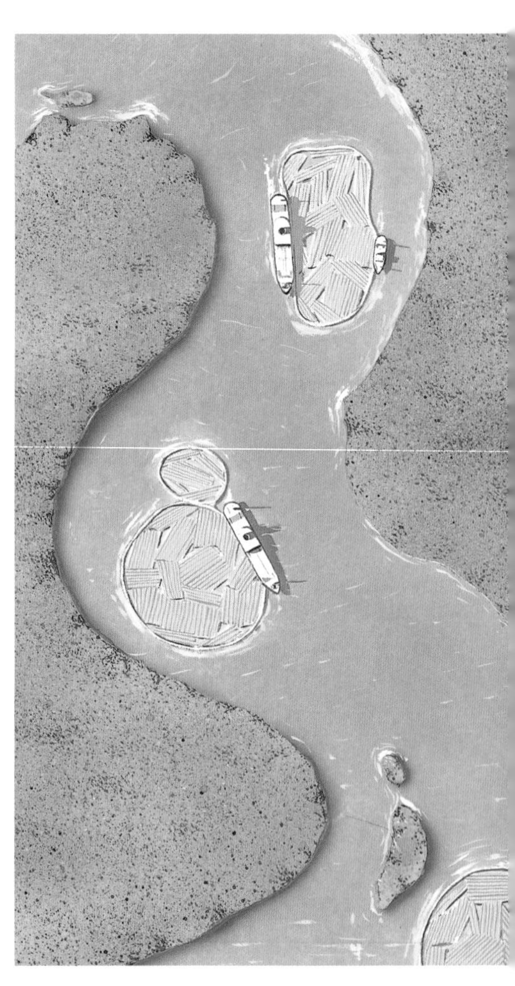

Above: *Boats transport logs from forests to sawmills as giant rafts.*

Timber

Timber is divided into hardwood and softwood. Most softwood trees are conifers with leaves like needles, whereas hardwoods mostly have broad, flat leaves. Common hardwoods are beech, ash, elm, eucalyptus, and mahogany. Common softwoods are pine and cedar.

The best timber is cut from the centre of the trunk (the heartwood). The outer layers (sapwood) are less durable and are used to make boxes and crates.

> ENERGY FROM TREES
>
> Wood was mankind's earliest fuel and is still the main fuel for cooking and heating in poor countries. It may become an important fuel of the future, as timber is a 'renewable resource' (unlike coal or oil), and fast-growing trees do well on even the poorest land.
>
> Modern wood stoves are efficient and cheap to run. In factories a new kind of burner (called a fluidized bed combustor) burns wood extremely efficiently even when wet. Wood can also be converted into alcohol, a power-packed liquid that could be used to fuel cars and other engines. Wood alcohol produces less pollution than gasoline (petrol) or diesel.

Making paper

Paper was first made by the Chinese about 2,000 years ago. They collected together old fish nets, rags, and bits of plants, which they boiled into a wet, soft pulp. A fine wire mesh was dipped into the pulp and removed with a layer of pulp on it. The layer of pulp was drained, pressed and dried to make paper.

Modern methods are similar in principle, but large machines (over 200m/660ft long) make the paper. The raw material is softwood from trees such as pine and spruce. It takes as many as twelve trees to make one tonne of paper.

The timber is first ground to pulp by stone grinders. The pulp is treated with chemicals and fed into a paper-making machine called a Fourdrinier, (named after its French inventor) where it is spread on a belt and dried, producing a continuous strip of paper. A modern paper-making machine produces 1,000m (over 3,000ft) of paper per minute. Fourdrinier machines are some of the longest machines in use today.

Below: *Stages in the manufacture of large rolls of printing paper from wood pulp.*

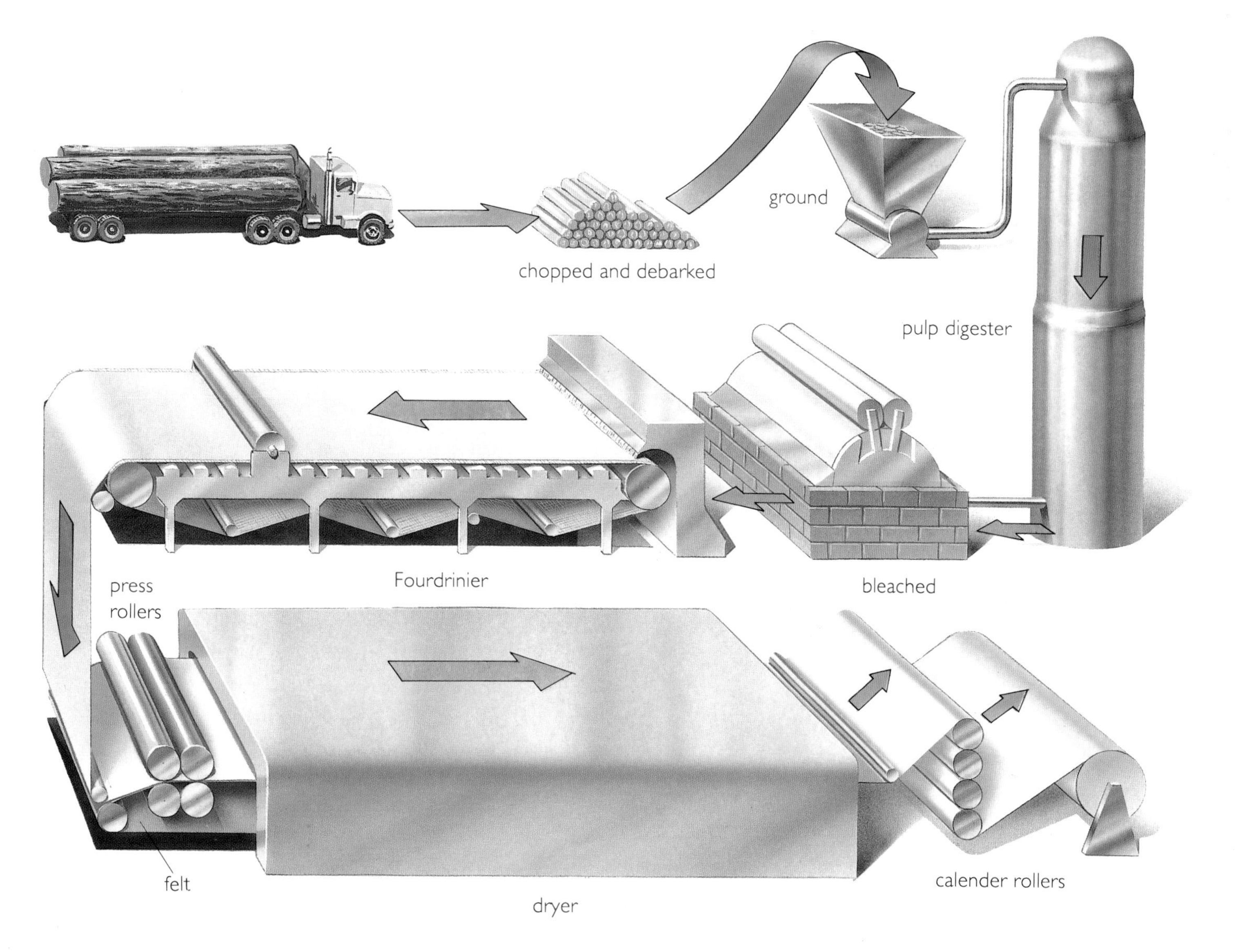

Explosives and Missiles

No one knows who invented gunpowder, the first explosive. Gunpowder is a mixture of saltpetre (potassium nitrate), charcoal (carbon) and sulphur. For about 400 years it did not change, but since the nineteenth century different types have been made by changing the ingredients or their proportions. The Chinese had gunpowder 1,000 years ago, but they used it only for fireworks and signals.

Blasting the base of a chimney stack to bring down the structure.

Guns

The first 'guns' appeared over 300 years later: they fired arrows from an iron pot. For a long time guns were almost as dangerous for those firing them as they were for those being fired at! However, new inventions and improvements made guns steadily more effective. One great advance was the invention of the cartridge, which made possible repeating or automatic guns, such as the machine-gun.

Modern explosives

There are two kinds of explosive. High explosives which are used for bombs and blasting produce a very violent explosion with an intense blast or shock wave. Low explosives, such as gunpowder, explode more slowly and are more easily controlled.

An explosion is simply the result of rapid burning, which produces a large quantity of heated gas that explodes outwards.

The first high explosive was nitro-glycerine, but it was very dangerous because it exploded so easily. In 1867, Alfred Nobel discovered that a safe explosive could be made by mixing nitro-glycerine with *kieselguhr*, a fine chalk-like material. The new high explosive was called dynamite. A number of other explosives are now in use. TNT (trinitrotoluene) is the most common. Military explosives are often based on the powerful cyclonite, or RDX. The most powerful explosives of all are based on RDX mixed with TNT and aluminium.

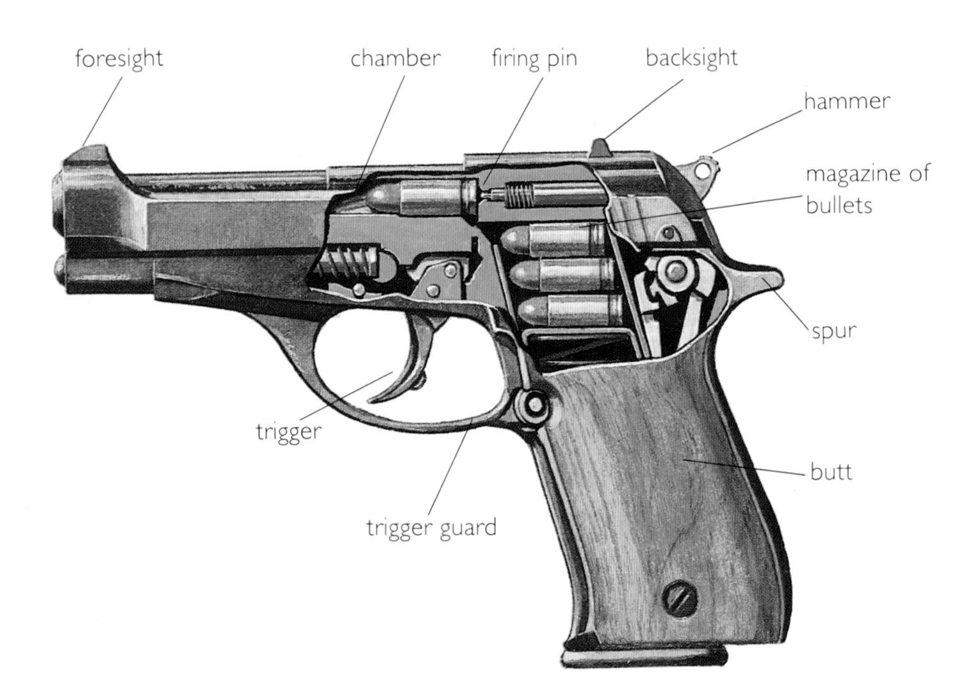

Left: *Cut-away of an automatic pistol.*
Below: *Rifle and mortar shells.*

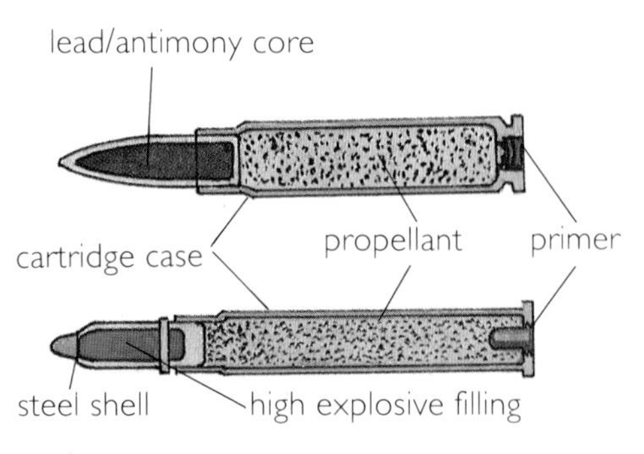

Missiles

Missiles are explosives with their own method of propulsion. Rockets are the oldest missiles. The Chinese had rockets in the thirteenth century.

Missiles are classified as surface-to-surface missiles (SSM), air-to-air missiles (AAM), surface-to-air missiles (SAM), or air-to-surface missiles (ASM). A strategic missile is a powerful long-range missile intended to be launched against an enemy's homeland. A tactical missile is a short-range missile for use on the battlefield. An intercontinental ballistic missile (ICBM), is a long-range missile that is launched into space and, when its rocket engine stops, falls in an arc on to its target.

How missiles work

The main parts of a missile are the propulsion unit or engine, the control system, and the warhead or bomb. Most missiles have rocket engines but a few have jet engines.

The control system consists of the guidance system and the autopilot. The autopilot contains gyroscopes that steady the rocket in flight. The guidance system, which tells the missile where to go, consists of radar and computers, either in the missile or on the ground. These track the missile and calculate the correct direction and distance it must travel to hit its target. Some small missiles have heat-seeking devices fitted to their noses which home in on the engines of enemy aircraft. Others are guided by signals sent along wires that trail behind the missile in flight. Laser-guided missiles home in on a laser beam which is reflected from the target.

The warhead or payload in a missile is the actual explosive. It may be a nuclear bomb. Some missiles have more than one warhead, each directed to a different target.

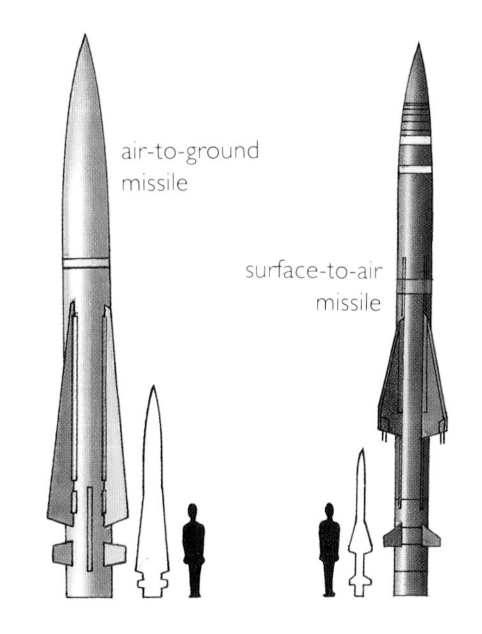

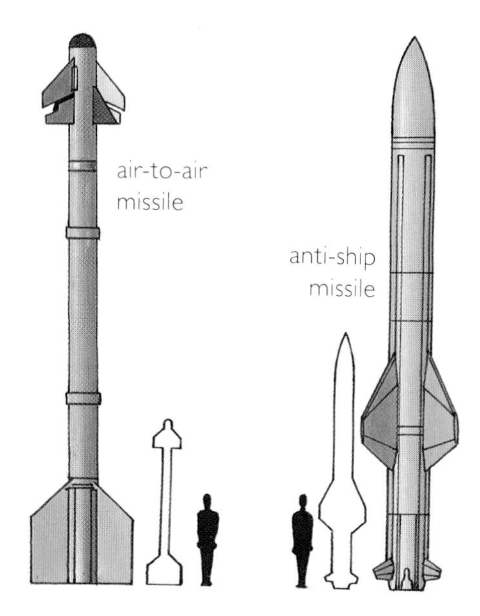

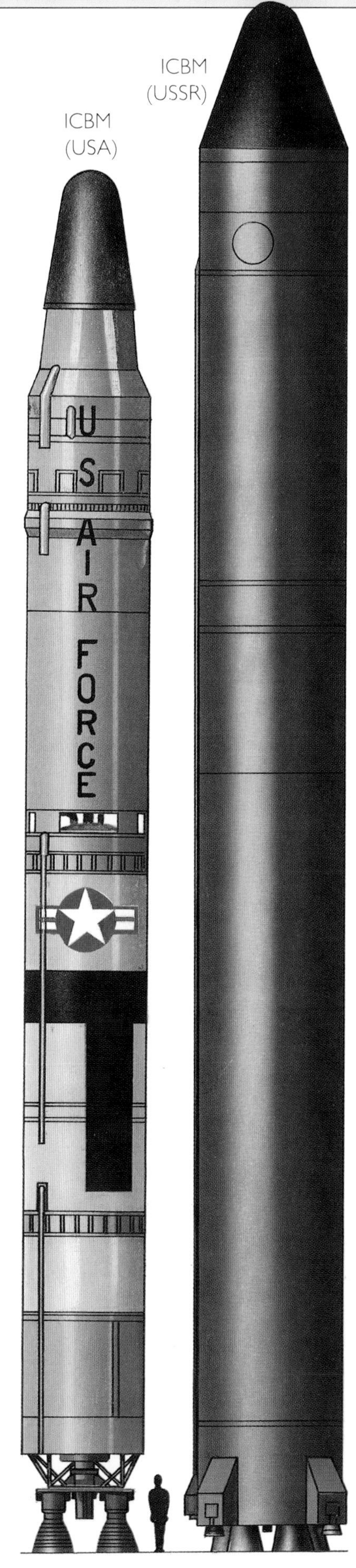

A range of tactical and strategic missiles including rockets with nuclear warheads.

References

Alkali A soluble substance that can react with an acid to produce water and neutralize the acid.

Alloy A mixture of two or more metals; for example, brass is an alloy of copper and zinc.

Aniline Oily liquid used in making dyes (most 'aniline dyes' today do not contain aniline).

Artificial intelligence (AI) The ability of a computer to perform tasks which might be expected from human intelligence, such as reasoning, and learning from experience.

Automation The control of manufacturing processes without direct involvement of people or human action. Much of car production, for example, is automatic, being under the control of computer systems.

Barium A silver metallic element used to give a green colour to fireworks. A 'barium meal' (actually barium sulphate) is given to hospital patients before their stomachs are X-rayed because it shows up well inside the body.

Blast furnace Large tower, lined with fire-proof bricks, in which metal ores are heated to high temperatures to separate the metal from impurities.

Boron A yellow, powdery or crystalline element, used in hardening steel, in nuclear reactors, and in electronic components such as silicon chips.

Carbon A very common chemical element: coal, diamonds and graphite are all different kinds of carbon, and carbon in some form is found in all plants and animals.

Casting Running molten metal or pressing a soft material into a mould to give it a certain shape and form.

Catalyst A substance which speeds up a chemical change without being changed itself.

Cellulose A tough material found in all plants, from which rayon and some plastics are made.

Cobalt A grey metal used to make strong magnets and stainless steel. Cobalt compounds provide the blue colouring for ceramics.

Coke The fuel made by heating coal to a high temperature without burning. It is mostly carbon and is a much better fuel than coal for blast furnaces etc.

Detergent Chemical usually used for cleaning materials, extracted and refined from crude oil. Detergents include some bleaches, brightners used in washing powders, and perfumes.

Distillation A method for purifying or separating liquids. The mixture is heated until vaporized, and the vapour is then condensed. As different liquids have different boiling points, they can be separated by this method.

Drug Any chemical compound with medicinal qualities. Some drugs, such as morphine and penicillin, are natural, being extracted from plants or produced by fungi. Others, such as procaine, a pain-killer, are man-made.

Ethylene A colourless gas with a sweet taste and smell, made by cracking petroleum gases. Used in the manufacture of many plastics.

Genes The substances found in all animals and plants that determine how closely an offspring resembles its parents.

Genetic engineering Techniques of using living organisms, such as bacteria, to produce useful substances by changing the genes of the organism.

Hydrocarbon A chemical compound that contains carbon and hydrogen. Examples are petroleum and natural gas.

Hydrogen A colourless gas which burns easily and is lighter than air. It is the simplest chemical element.

Limestone A common hard rock formed from the remains of microscopic sea animals that settled on the sea bed millions of years ago.

Mould A container in which a liquid is put to set into shape, such as a jelly mould.

Nobel, Alfred (1833–96) Swedish chemist and industrialist who invented dynamite in 1867. He left his great wealth to give international prizes – the Nobel Prizes – each year for outstanding work in science, literature, and the promotion of peace.

Ore A rock or mineral from which a metal can be extracted.

Oxygen A colourless, tasteless gas that is found in air. Oxygen is a chemical element; it is essential for all forms of life, and for burning.

Perkin, William (1838–1907) English chemist who discovered the first artificial dye, mauvine, in 1856. His discovery was accidental: he had been trying to make an artificial form of the drug quinine.

Petrochemical A substance made from crude oil (petroleum) or natural gas, such as plastics, detergents and fertilizers.

Pneumatics A system that uses high-pressure liquid or gas to control machines.

Polymer A material that is made up of very large chainlike molecules. Plastics such as nylon are polymers.

Resin A substance used as an adhesive which softens when heated; the sap which drips from pine trees is a natural resin; plastics are artificial resins.

Textile Any woven or knitted cloth.

Titanium A strong, white metal, used to make light corrosion-resistant alloys for aircraft, missiles and ships.

Vacuum An empty space that contains no air or other material; a perfect vacuum is practically impossible on Earth.

Zirconium A greyish metal resembling titanium used in alloys, in nuclear reactors (as a neutron absorber), and for other industrial purposes.

Sky and the Cosmos

The Atmosphere

Without an atmosphere rich in oxygen life on Earth could not exist and the Earth would be as dead and dusty as the moon. The atmosphere is prevented from leaking away into space by the Earth's gravitational field, the same force that holds us down on the ground.

Gravity gets steadily weaker farther away from the Earth, so the atmosphere gets thinner. In fact, atmospheric pressure drops by a factor of 1.250 for every kilometre in height. That is why mountaineers find breathing more difficult as they climb higher and why airliners have to be pressurized with their own air supply.

Wind and rain

All the clouds, snow and rain in the atmosphere come from water evaporating from the Earth's oceans. The water vapour is carried upwards by rising air currents until it meets colder air and condenses into clouds, which may produce rain or snow.

The air masses over the poles and tropical regions are in constant conflict. They meet over the oceans, giving rise to constantly changing weather patterns which are blown by the prevailing winds across the water towards the land. The winds themselves are caused by air rushing from areas of high pressure to fill areas of low pressure.

The layers of the atmosphere

The atmosphere is divided into several layers. The lowest, the troposphere, contains most of the material in the atmosphere and most of the weather systems. It extends to 18km (11 miles) above the equator, but only 6km (4 miles) above the poles.

Between about 60km (37 miles) and 1,000km (612 miles) above the Earth, there is also a region called the ionosphere. Because it is rich in electrons, the ionosphere reflects most radio waves back to Earth. It is essential for relaying radio communications around the world. Radio communications between the Earth and a spacecraft must use very high frequency radio waves, which can pass through the ionosphere.

Hot and cold

The atmosphere is warmed by radiation from the Sun, but it is not at an even temperature from top to bottom. Neither does the temperature rise or fall smoothly with height. At the Earth's surface, the warm ground heats the atmosphere directly above it. Temperature falls with height, reaching about -60°C at the top of the troposphere. Above this, the temperature begins to rise again, because ozone in the stratosphere absorbs solar energy. At 50km (30 miles) above the Earth, the temperature has risen to 0°C. In the mesosphere temperatures fall again, to -100°C, before rising once more to 1,500°C in the outer fringes of the thermosphere.

There is no sharp division between the atmosphere and space. The atmosphere extends for thousands of kilometres, growing thinner all the time, but space is officially said to begin at a height of 100km (62 miles).

Right: *A satellite picture of a tropical storm which shows the still centre or 'eye' of the hurricane.*

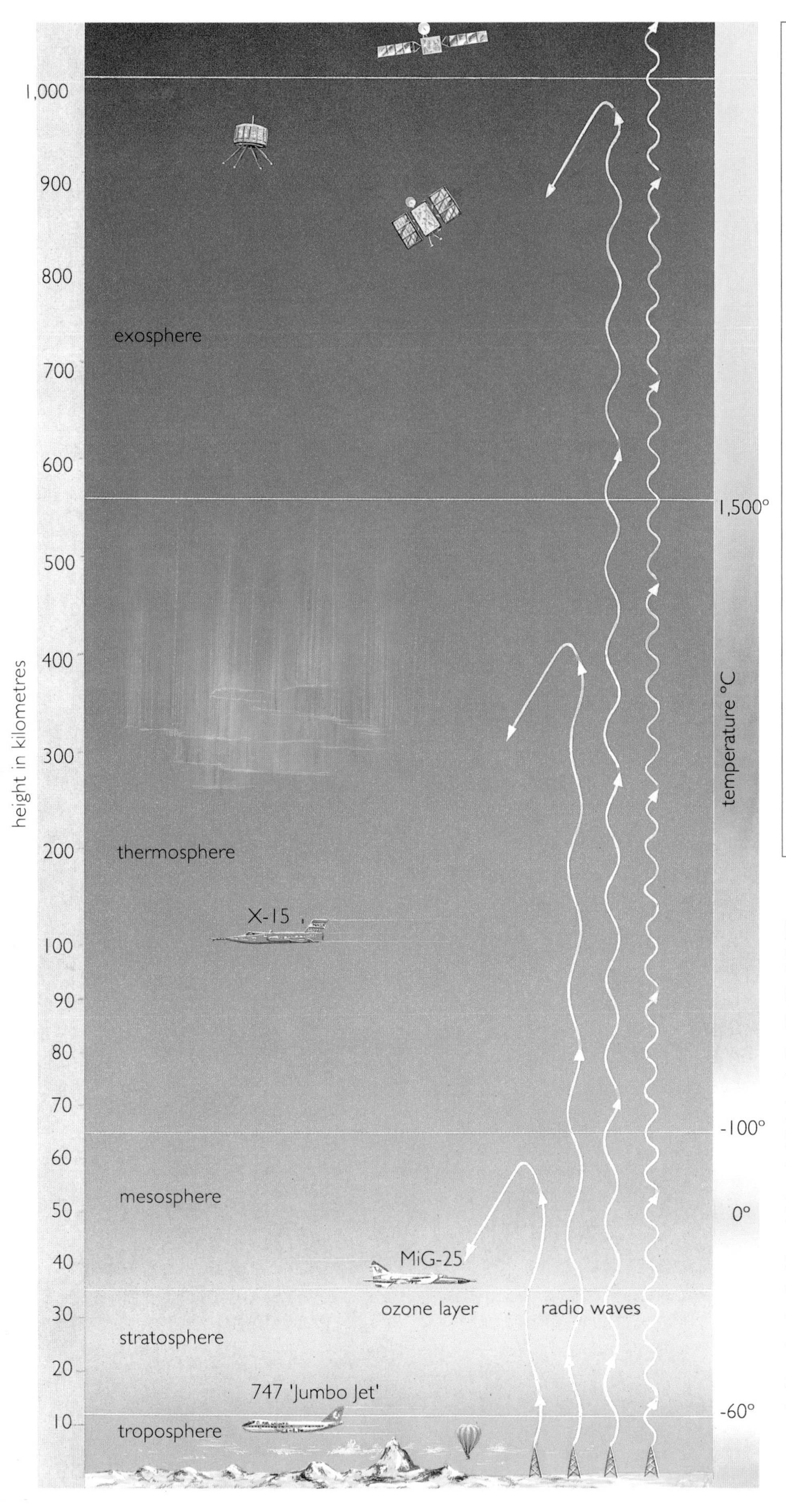

THE GREENHOUSE EFFECT

The atmosphere contains mainly nitrogen (78 per cent) and oxygen (21 per cent). The remaining one per cent is composed of gases such as argon and carbon dioxide. Despite the tiny amount of carbon dioxide, it has important effects.

Sunlight passes through the atmosphere and heats the Earth. The Earth tries to send the Sun's energy back into space as heat, but carbon dioxide and water vapour in the atmosphere will not let the heat pass through. It is trapped in the atmosphere and warms the Earth as if it were inside a greenhouse. This is called the 'greenhouse effect'.

The amount of carbon dioxide in the atmosphere is increased by burning fuels such as wood, coal and oil. Although plants help to reduce it, forests (especially the great rain-forests) are being cut down. The greenhouse effect is therefore increasing, and may have disastrous results. As the Earth grows warmer, polar ice may melt, which will make sea levels rise, causing serious flooding in many parts of the world.

How high can you fly? Balloons, gliders and most aircraft fly within the troposphere. A Jumbo Jet, for example, flies at up to about 13km (8 miles). A Soviet MiG-25 fighter reached 37.6km (23 miles) in 1977. In 1963 an X-15 experimental rocket plane, launched from a B-52 bomber in flight, reached a height of 107km (66.5 miles). The X-15 pilots were awarded astronauts' wings because they had flown to such great heights – they were virtually in space.

Left: *The layers of the atmosphere.*

Telescopes

Including the Earth there are nine planets in the solar system and most of them have moons. There are millions of stars, like our Sun, in the universe, but most are so far away that we are unable to see them.

Telescopes enable us to see the planets and their moons in more detail; to study more stars than we can see normally; and to examine stars by other means than visible light.

One of the first scientists to use a telescope was Galileo, who began to make his own instruments in 1609, and made many discoveries, including the rings of Saturn. His instruments were based on the invention of a Dutch maker of spectacles, Jan Lippershey, who put two lenses together by accident.

A large radio telescope.

Refractors and reflectors
There are two types of telescope: refractors and reflectors. A simple refractor (like Galileo's) is a tube with a glass lens at each end. Light from a star enters the telescope through the object lens. This bends the light rays together and forms an image at the other end of the tube. The image is viewed through the second lens, the eyepiece. The object is seen many times larger than with the naked eye, but upside down.

Isaac Newton made the first reflector telescope in the 1660s. Light enters the open end of a tube and travels down it to a curved mirror at the other end. This reflects the light back up the tube and bends the rays together to form an image. A small flat mirror about half way along the tube reflects the image through a hole in the side of the telescope, where it is viewed through an eyepiece lens.

New astronomy
When we look at the stars, with our eyes or through a telescope, we are seeing the evidence of visible light. But stars (and other objects), give out other kinds of rays besides light rays. New types of astronomy study *all* the radiation given out by objects: gamma rays, X-rays, ultraviolet, infra-red and radio waves. These radiations, invisible to the human eye, *can* be detected by electronic instruments. However, the Earth's atmosphere absorbs most of the radiation from space and stops it reaching the Earth's surface. Instruments that can detect this radiation must be lifted above the atmosphere by rockets. There is one exception, radio waves, which *can* be received on the Earth's surface.

Light paths inside refractor and reflector telescopes.

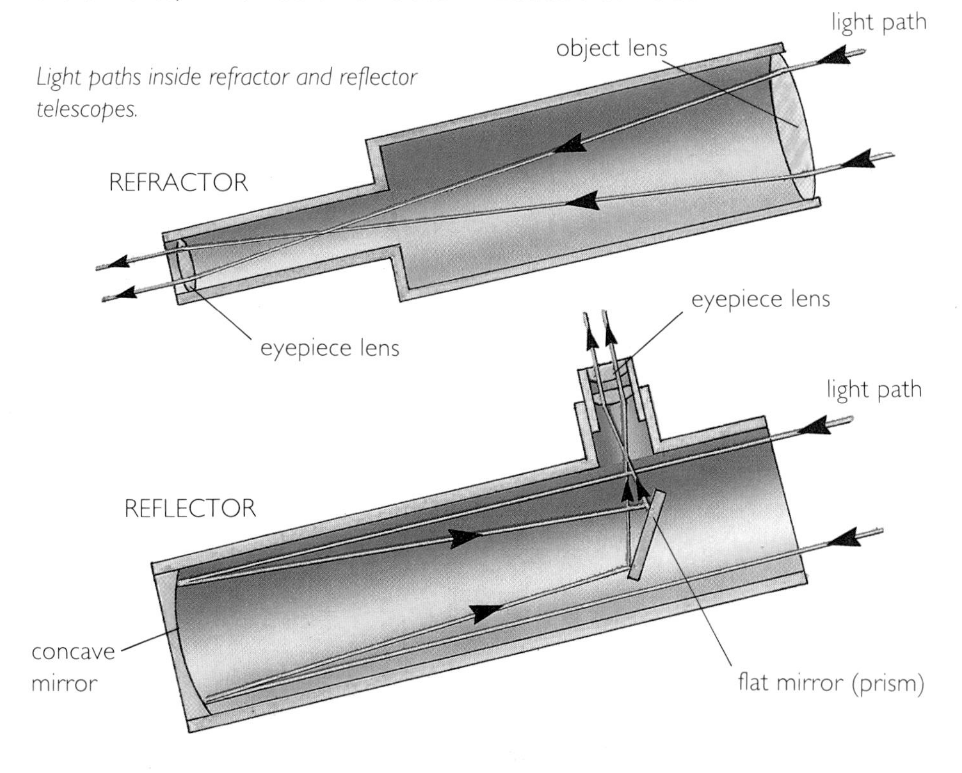

Above and left: *The Hale reflector telescope and dome at Palomar Observatory, California.*

Radio astronomy
Radio waves from distant stars are received by radio telescopes. Most are metal dishes shaped to reflect the radio waves and bring them together at a receiver suspended above the dish.

The largest radio telescope in the world is a wire-mesh dish 305m (about 1,000ft) across in Puerto Rico. The largest steerable radio telescope, which can be moved to face any point in the sky, is the 100m (330ft) dish at Effelsberg, Germany. The radio signals received by these telescopes are transformed into television pictures by computers.

HUBBLE SPACE TELESCOPE

Light from distant stars is refracted (bent) as it travels through the Earth's atmosphere. The atmosphere is a swirling mass of air and water vapour with continually changing regions of different temperature and pressure. Starlight is bent by different amounts in different parts of the atmosphere. It is this that makes stars appear to twinkle.

Atmospheric effects make it difficult to study very distant, faint stars from the Earth's surface. The ideal solution is to place a telescope above the atmosphere. The Hubble telescope, named in honour of the US astronomer Edwin Hubble and launched into space from the space shuttle in 1990, is just such an instrument. It is a reflector with a mirror 2.4m (8ft) across. Several reflectors on Earth are larger than that, but the Hubble telescope's position above the atmosphere should enable it to see details ten times finer than the larger, Earth-based telescopes.

Unfortunately, the mirror proved faulty after the telescope was launched. Astronauts hope to correct it in 1992.

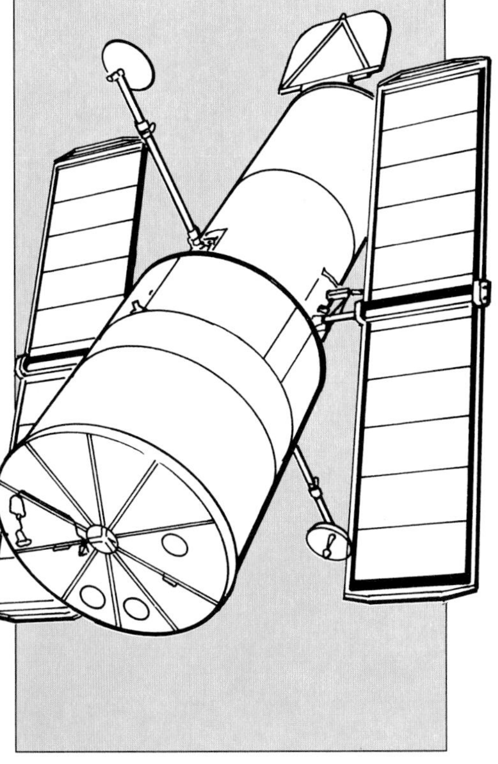

The Sun and its Neighbours

The Sun, the planets that circle around it and everything within their orbits is known as the solar system (solar means 'of the Sun'). The Sun is a star. It was formed from a contracting cloud of gas and dust about 4.5 billion years ago. Material that was not sucked into the Sun was locked in orbit around it; it formed into lumps which grew in size over millions of years to become the planets.

Right: *The Solar System, with the planets and their moons illustrated to scale and in ascending order of their distance from the Sun – Mercury, Venus, Earth, Mars, Jupiter, Saturn, Uranus, Neptune and Pluto.*

The Sun

The Sun dominates the solar system. Its mass is about one thousand times greater than the mass of everything else in the solar system put together. Its hugely strong gravitational field controls the movements of everything else. Without the Sun's rays, the Earth would be pitch dark, icy cold and completely lifeless.

The Sun is a great fire, which is burning itself up. It consumes 4 million tonnes of its own matter every second to produce heat and light equivalent to billions of hydrogen bombs. But the Sun is so huge that it will continue to burn for another 5 billion years before it runs out of fuel.

Like any great bonfire, the Sun does not burn steadily. Vast disturbances, which scientists cannot fully explain, take place. Black spots (sunspots) often appear on the Sun's surface. They may measure up to 100,000km (62,000 miles) across and last for a few hours or several months. They mark regions where powerful magnetic fields break through the surface and prevent some heat and light escaping. Although they appear black, they are in fact as bright as a full moon. Because they are slightly cooler than their surroundings, they appear darker. For unknown reasons, sunspots seem to follow a regular cycle, coming in bursts every eleven years.

Magnetic disturbances in the Sun's outer layers can cause violent storms and explosions that throw material out into space. These fiery fingers projecting from the Sun's surface are called solar flares. Two days after flare activity on the Sun, the effects reach Earth. Particles from the flares interact with the Earth's magnetic field, especially near the poles, and cause a brilliant display of shimmering colours in the sky. In the north these displays are called the aurora borealis ('northern lights'); in the south the aurora australis ('southern lights').

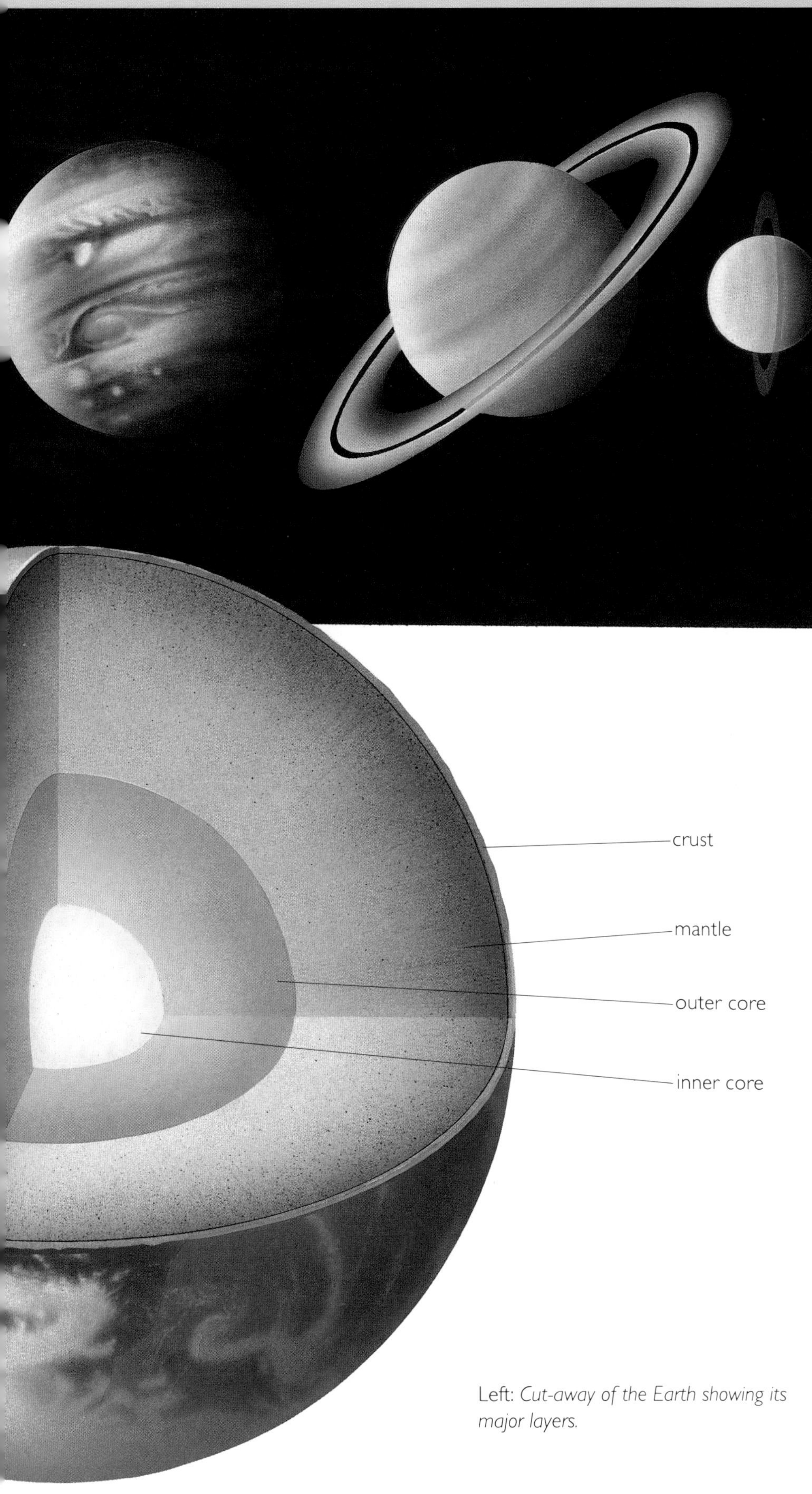

Left: *Cut-away of the Earth showing its major layers.*

The Earth

The Earth, the largest of the inner planets, is the only body in the solar system known to support life. No one can say exactly when life began, but fossil remains have been found of plants and animals that lived about 3 billion years ago.

The Earth has a solid inner core, over 3,000km (about 1,800 miles) across, of iron and nickel. Around it is an outer core, a liquid layer of the same material 1,800km (1,100 miles) thick. Currents in this liquid, metallic layer are probably responsible for the Earth's magnetic field. A dense, rocky layer called the mantle, 3,000km thick, floats on the outer core, and it is covered with a thin outer layer, the crust, of lighter rocks at the surface.

The Planets

The planets, which are named after gods of Ancient Rome, can be divided into two groups. The inner planets, closest to the Sun, are mostly small, rocky worlds. The outer planets are giant globes of gas and liquid. Between the inner and outer planets is the asteroid belt. Asteroids are large rocks, some big enough to be called minor planets.

The inner planets
Mercury is an airless, waterless world, whose orbit is only 58 million kilometres (36 million miles) from the searing heat of the Sun. To avoid being sucked into the Sun, it must race around its orbit at 176,000kph (109,000 mph). Mercury seems to have a huge iron core with a rocky covering, or mantle, about 600km (370 miles) deep.

Venus is similar in size to the Earth, but is very different. Its surface, hidden by sulphuric acid clouds in a carbon dioxide atmosphere, is very hostile, the temperature reaching almost 500°C. Venus turns very slowly, and its day (243 Earth days) is longer than its year (225 Earth days)!

Mars was once thought to be inhabited, but the two US Viking spacecraft that landed on it in 1975 found no traces. They sent back photographs revealing that Mars is covered by a fine, red dust, which explains its red appearance. Mars has volcanoes, some twice as high as Mt Everest, and deep canyons, where water may once have flowed.

The outer planets
Jupiter is the largest planet. Its mass is twice as great as the mass of all the other planets and moons put together. It is made up mostly of liquid hydrogen and helium. Its famous Great Red Spot, visible through telescopes, is a storm which covers an area larger than the Earth and has been raging for over 300 years.

The other three giants are Saturn, mostly liquid hydrogen; Uranus, whose methane atmosphere gives it a green colour; and Neptune, never visible to the naked eye. Pluto, farthest from the Sun and only discovered in 1930, is small, about half the size of the Earth.

Below: *Phases of the Earth's moon – as lit by the Sun and as viewed from Earth.*

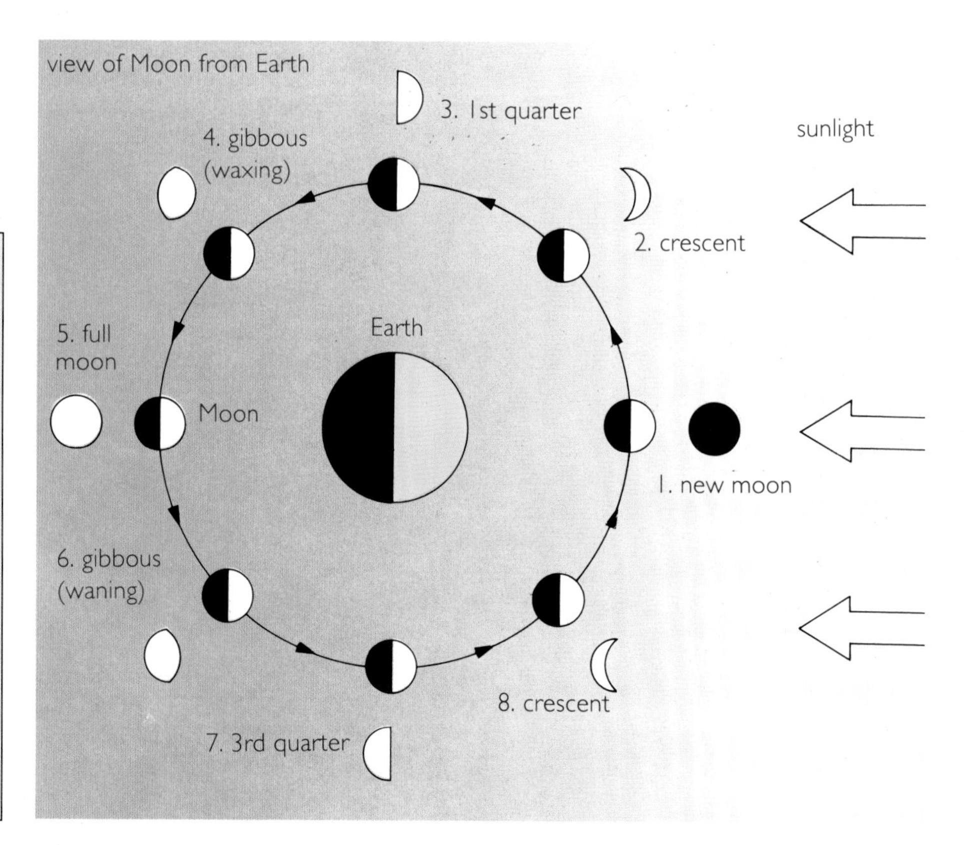

MOONS

The Earth's moon turns on its axis in the same time as it takes to orbit the Earth, so we always see the same side. It is the only body in space that people have visited. Mars has 2 moons, Mercury and Venus none, but the outer planets have many: Jupiter has 16, Saturn at least 23, Uranus 15 and Neptune 8, though Pluto has only 1. Neptune's largest moon, Triton, is the most interesting. It has a magnetic field and an atmosphere, and it orbits Neptune in the opposite direction from all the other moons and planets in the system.

RINGS AROUND PLANETS

The famous rings of Saturn are made up of material left over from the planet's formation. Each ring is actually thousands of separate ringlets, some of them intertwined. Some rings are made up of microscopic particles, others of objects up to 10m (33ft) across. Since spacecraft visited them in the 1970s, we now know that Jupiter, Uranus and Neptune also have rings.

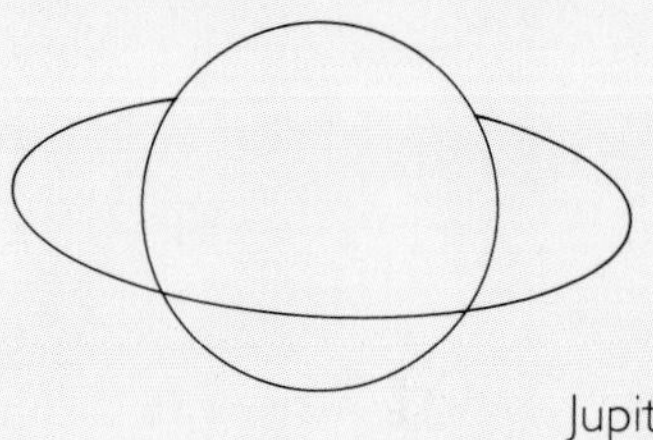

Jupiter

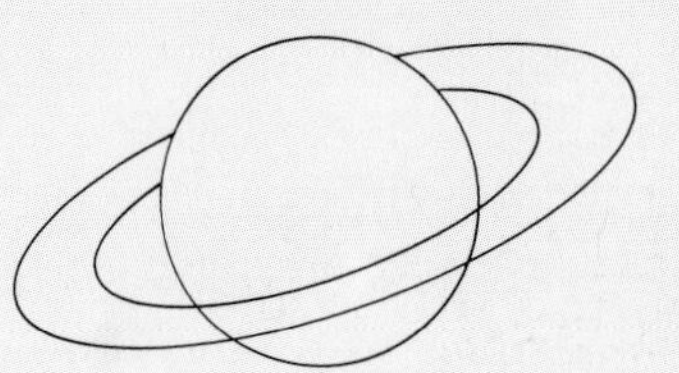

Saturn

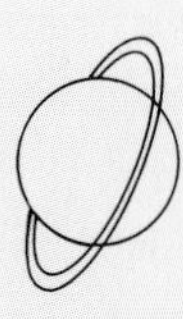

Uranus

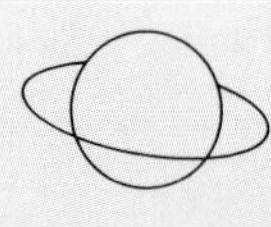

Neptune

METEORS AND COMETS

Other objects are flying around the solar system. Meteors are lumps of rock left over from the creation of the planets. When they enter the Earth's atmosphere they appear in the night sky as streaks of light ('shooting stars'). Most of them burn up, but sometimes a large one reaches the ground.

Comets are made up of ice and dust. When they come close to the Sun, they often have a visible 'tail' of light. Some follow a regular path. The most famous, Halley's Comet, appears every 76 years (it is next due in 2062).

Below: *Halley's Comet as seen from the spacecraft Giotto launched in 1985.*

The Stars

A star is a luminous sphere of gas, held together by its own gravitational field. Stars were once thought to be objects which never changed. Certainly their life-span is long – billions of years – but they are born, go through a series of stages, and finally die, like everything else in the universe. By observing many stars in different stages of their development, astronomers have learned how the life of a star progresses from beginning to end.

Birth of a star

Stars begin in the clouds of dust and gas, called nebulae, that drift through space. The material in nebulae is the remains of older stars that have exploded or blown their outer regions of matter away. If a nebula passes close to a galaxy, or experiences the shock wave of an exploding star, it may be compressed. The particles of matter then begin to move closer to each other. The gravitational field of each growing clump of matter holds it together and attracts more material. The ball of matter contracts, due to its own gravity, and its temperature rises. This primitive lump of material is called a protostar. The core of the protostar contracts more rapidly than the outer 'envelope'. When its temperature reaches 10 million ℃, hydrogen in the core begins to burn, in the process called nuclear fusion.

Right: *The stages in the life of a star such as the Earth's Sun.*

Hydrogen atoms combine to form helium, releasing huge amounts of energy in the form of heat and light, and the core stops contracting. The dark protostar has changed into a shining star. It may take up to 100 million years for a star to light up in this way.

Main sequence

Stars are continually being born in our galaxy. Once it begins shining, a star is said to have entered its 'main sequence'. The Sun is an example of a main sequence star.

Giants and dwarfs

When there is no hydrogen fuel left in the star's core, gravity takes over and the core contracts again. It heats up and ignites hydrogen in the matter surrounding it. This material expands and the star grows enormously. Its red glow gives rise to its name – a red giant. The core continues contracting and heating up until it is hot enough (about 100 million ℃) to ignite the helium of which it is composed. This produces carbon and oxygen. Up to half of the star's envelope may be blown away into space during this stage by the turbulent currents raging through the envelope. When the core's helium is exhausted, it contracts again, heating up and igniting the helium in the envelope. At this stage, the rapidly expanding envelope may be blown away into space at around 70,000kph (about 43,000mph). The core cannot contract any further.

Burning ends and the star becomes a white dwarf. Eventually it cools, ceases to give out any light and disappears from sight.

Black holes and neutron stars
A star that is more than about five times the mass of our Sun ends its days in a different way. It continues contracting, igniting and producing new materials, until the core is composed of iron. Burning ceases and the core collapses violently, setting off an explosion that blasts the star's outer layers into space. This is a supernova – possibly the most spectacular event in the universe.

The exploding star may be brighter than an entire galaxy. The material thrown out into space will eventually help to form new stars and planets. The heaviest elements in the universe, such as gold and uranium, were all made by supernovae. The star's core may survive a supernova explosion as a tiny, dark, dense body called a neutron star or sometimes as a 'black hole'. The matter in a neutron star is packed so tightly that one cubic centimetre of it would weigh thousands of millions of tonnes.

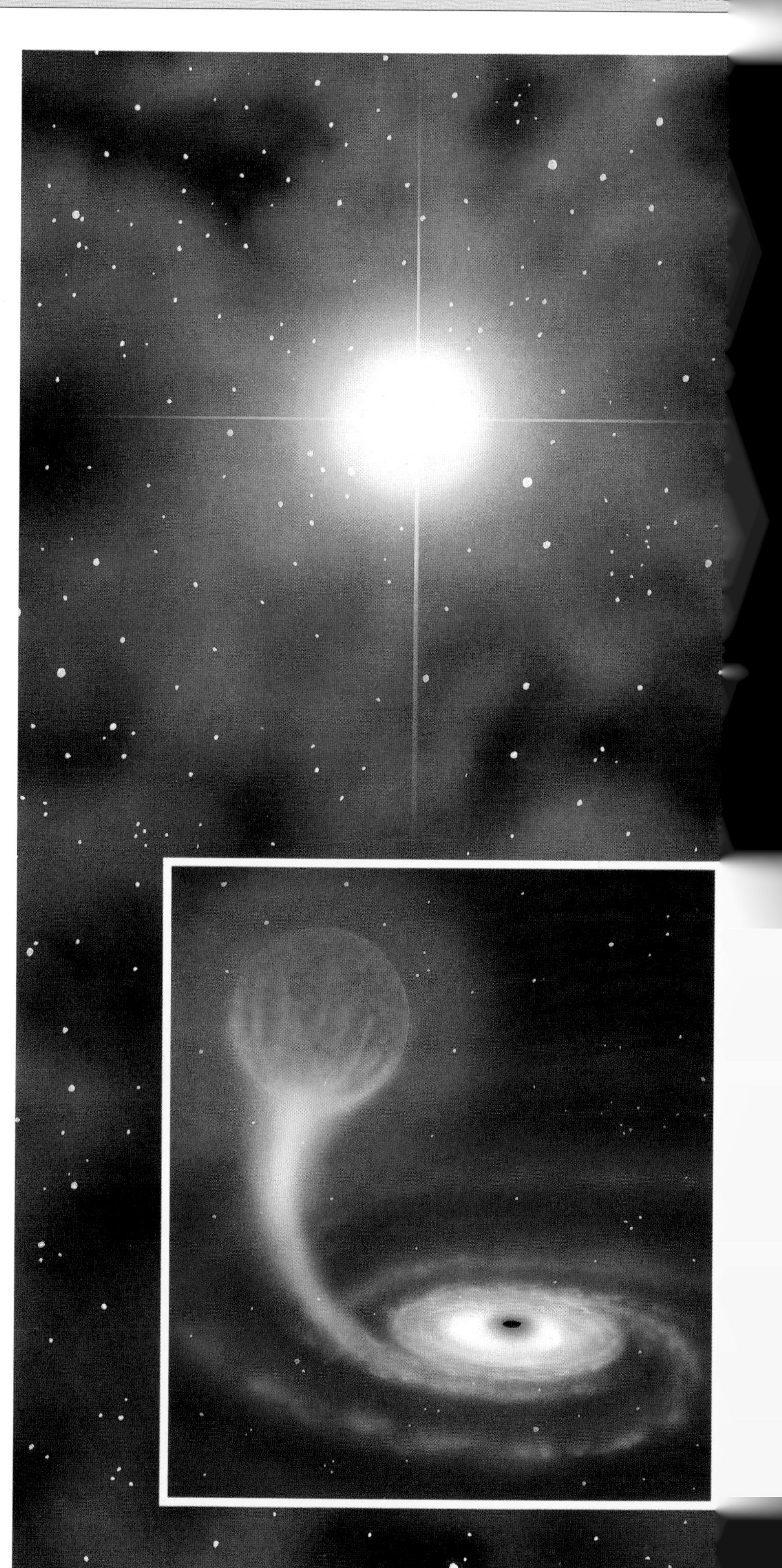

Top: *A supernova, the death of a giant star.* Inset: *The gravitational field of a black hole is so strong that it can strip material from a neighbouring star. The hole is black because nothing, not even light, can escape from its surface.*

Galaxies and Beyond

The Sun is one of 100 billion stars that travel through space together, forming the galaxy we call the Milky Way. A spacecraft travelling as fast as light would take 100,000 years to cross the Milky Way from one side to the other. The solar system is situated on one of the spiral arms of the galaxy about 30,000 light years from its centre. The whole galaxy is spinning, and the solar system takes about 200 million years to make one orbit of the galactic centre.

Quasars

The most extreme example of an active galaxy is a quasar, short for quasi-stellar ('star-like') object, because when quasars were first observed, in 1963, they were thought to be stars. In fact, they are the most distant objects in the universe. We can see them only because they are so bright. They pack the energy of 100 galaxies into an object the size of the solar system.

Types of galaxies

The universe contains about 100 billion galaxies. There are three basic types: spiral, elliptical and irregular. Spiral galaxies like the Milky Way have a central ball of older stars surrounded by spiral arms containing dust, gas and younger stars. Elliptical galaxies have already used up all their dust and gas in forming stars; they appear as smooth balls of large red stars. Irregular galaxies are loose collections of stars with no particular shape.

Some galaxies exist on their own, but most belong to clusters, which travel through space together. The Milky Way belongs to a cluster of more than 20 galaxies called the Local Group, which in turn is part of the Virgo supercluster.

Active galaxies

All galaxies send out radio signals, which can be received on Earth. Some galaxies are classified as 'active' because they produce surprisingly large amounts of radio energy, or because they have an unusually bright core.

The major types of galaxy as observed from the Earth.

Above: *Our own galaxy, the Milky Way. The Solar System lies in one of the spiral arms far from the centre.*
Below right: *An impression of the Big Bang, the birth of the universe.*

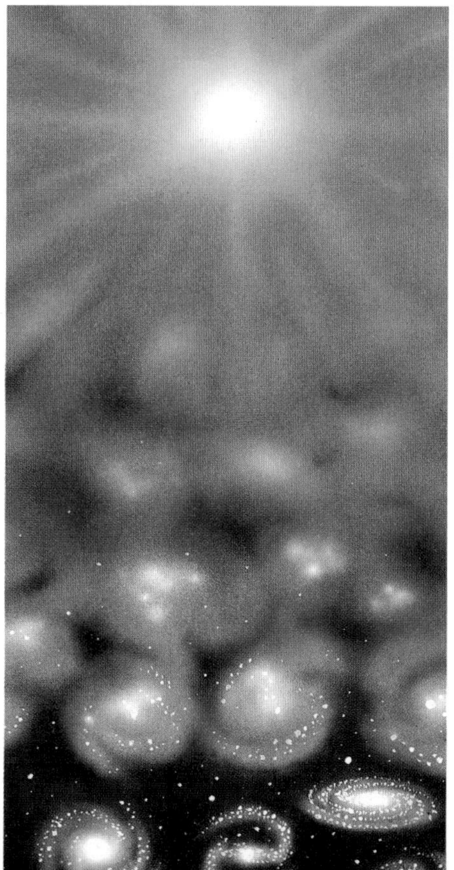

THE BIGGEST BANG EVER

Mosts scientists believe that the universe began between 10 and 20 billion years ago with an event called the Big Bang. The universe and everything in it existed then at a single point. At the beginning of time there was an explosion – the Big Bang. The universe began to expand and it is still expanding. The matter in the universe then was mostly hydrogen and helium. In some places, particles of matter began to stick together and draw more particles towards them by gravity. The huge gas clouds began to condense into lumps of more dense material – the beginning of the galaxies.

The future of the universe
Scientists disagree about how the universe will behave in the distant future. Perhaps the universe will continue expanding, as it is now, and the galaxies will continue to race away from each other for ever. The stars will cool and the universe will grow dark.

According to a different theory, gravitational attraction between the galaxies will slow down and eventually stop the expansion of the universe. The universe will then begin to contract, and may eventually collapse in on itself.

Rockets and Satellites

The Space Age began on 4 October 1957 when the Soviet Union launched the first artificial satellite, Sputnik 1. Before then, astronomers had no way of testing their theories. Since 1957, satellites carrying cameras and scientific instruments have landed on or flown near every planet in the solar system except Pluto. The universe still holds many mysteries, but astronomy has advanced enormously.

Right: *Liquid oxygen and hydrogen fuel tanks and rockets inside a Saturn V launcher used by the Apollo moon missions.* Above: *The Lunar Lander carried by Saturn V.*

Rocket engines

Aeroplane engines will not work in space because they need oxygen to burn their fuel. But rocket engines are powered by a propellant which contains both fuel and an oxidizer. They are mixed in the rocket's combustion chamber where they burn furiously and expand rapidly: hot gases rush out of the rocket's exhaust nozzle. Some rocket engines have movable nozzles to help steer them.

Rocket engines may have either liquid or solid propellants. The US space shuttle uses liquid hydrogen (fuel) and liquid oxygen (oxidizer). They have to be kept very cold, in pressurized tanks. As fuel and oxidizer are stored separately, the engine can be turned on and off, and thrust can be controlled by the rate at which the propellant enters the engine. Solid-fuel rockets cannot be turned off.

Big rockets usually have two or three stages, which are really separate rockets. The first stage launches the rocket, and when it has used all its fuel it separates and falls away. The second stage then takes over, followed by the third. The reason for this arrangement is that no useless weight, such as empty fuel tanks, has to be carried.

Gravity

In order to send spacecraft on the correct flight path, or to put satellites in orbit, the effect of the Earth's gravity must be calculated.

Gravity gets weaker as distance from the Earth increases. At the surface, objects are pulled towards the centre of the Earth at a rate of 9.8m (32ft) per second every

SPEED VOYAGERS

In 1977, two US spacecraft called Voyager 1 and 2 were launched on the longest space mission ever. As a result of a rare alignment of the planets, it was calculated that a spacecraft could use the gravitational pull of each planet to help it on its way to the next.

Most spacecraft have solar panels to convert sunlight into electricity, but the Voyagers were going too far from the Sun, so they were powered by small nuclear generators. They were the fastest man-made objects that ever left Earth, travelling at 52,000kph (over 32,000mph) in space. They reached the moon in less than ten hours. (Apollo spacecraft on moon flights took three days.)

Voyager 1 reached Saturn in 1980; Voyager 2 reached Neptune in 1989. Both then left the solar system.

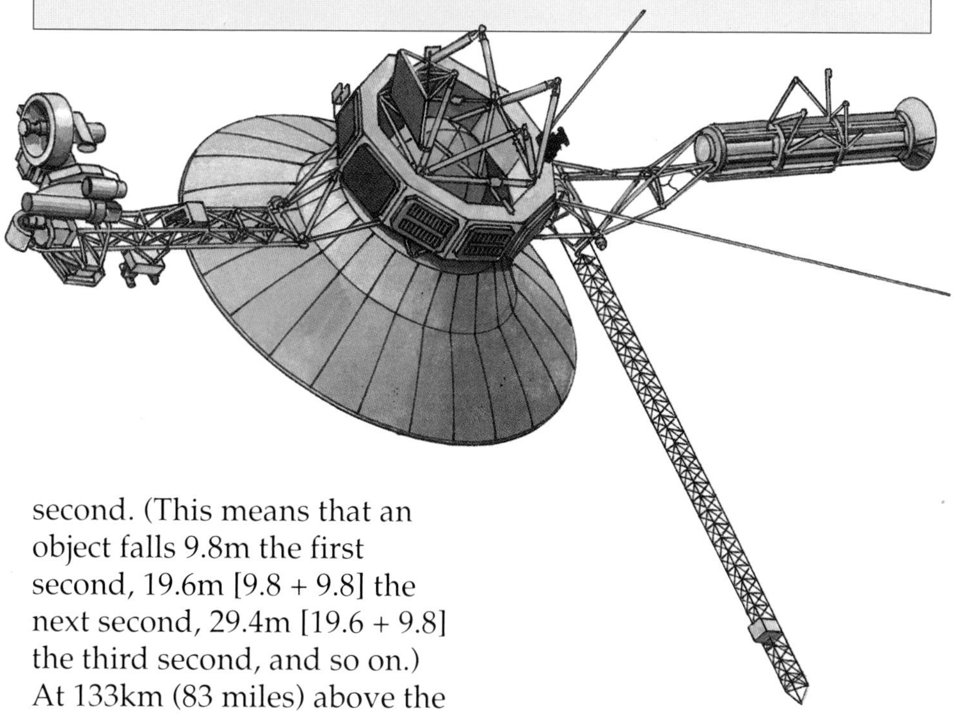

second. (This means that an object falls 9.8m the first second, 19.6m [9.8 + 9.8] the next second, 29.4m [19.6 + 9.8] the third second, and so on.) At 133km (83 miles) above the surface, the acceleration rate due to gravity is only 4.9m (16ft) per second. The curve of the Earth means that if something travelled on a horizontal line above the surface, it would be 4.9m further away for every 8km it travelled. So, if a satellite is boosted to a speed of 8 kilometres per second at a height of 133km, gravity will pull it down by 4.9m in every 8km, which matches the curve of the Earth. The satellite continually falls towards the surface of the Earth, but never gets any closer.

Choosing an orbit

Satellites designed to observe the Earth are placed in orbit over the poles. As the Earth turns beneath them, they eventually 'see' every point on the Earth's surface.

Polar orbits are not suitable for communications satellites. They must stay in the same position to keep contact with ground transmitters and receivers. A satellite orbiting at a height of 36,000km (22,369 miles) completes one orbit in the same time as it takes the Earth to revolve once. It therefore stays above the same point on the Earth. This is called a geostationary or geosynchronous orbit.

Below: *Different orbits for satellites used for aerial surveys of Earth and communications links.*

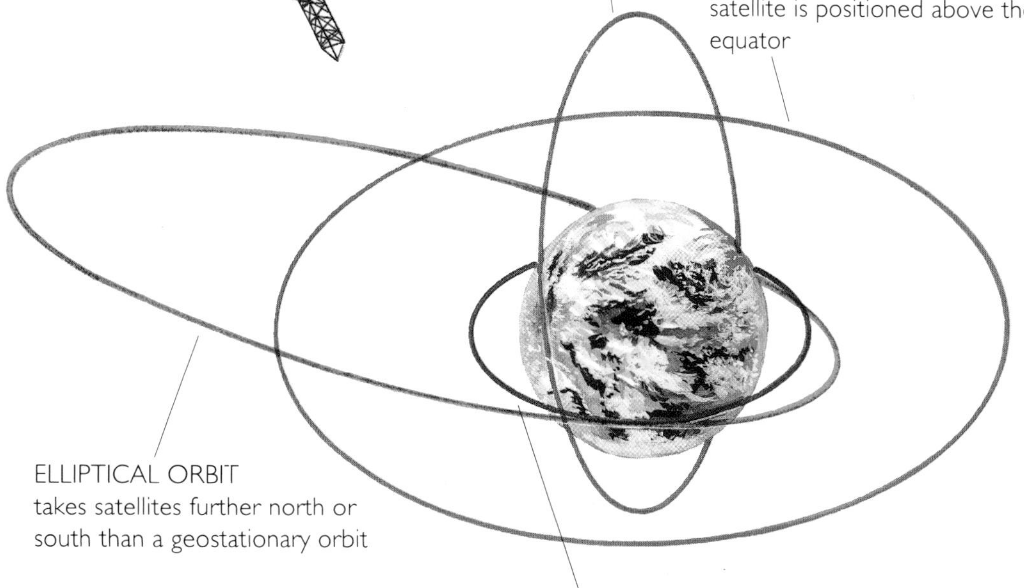

POLAR ORBIT
satellite flies above the poles

GEOSTATIONARY ORBIT
satellite is positioned above the equator

ELLIPTICAL ORBIT
takes satellites further north or south than a geostationary orbit

LOW EARTH ORBIT
used by manned space craft

The Uses of Space

Since 1957 the Sun, the stars and planets and the Earth itself have been studied with the help of artificial satellites. The most famous projects have been the manned flights to the Moon and the probes of spacecraft such as the Pioneer and Voyager series to the outer planets. But a far greater number of satellites are in orbit around the Earth. They photograph its surface, record its weather patterns and relay telephone calls, television pictures and computer data to different centres around the world.

Although scientific space exploration still continues, there is now a large and growing space industry which serves the needs of businesses and governments.

Earth observation
The many satellites that survey the Earth provide valuable services. They can show how crops are growing, predict how much food will be produced and give early warning of shortages. Plant diseases also show up in photographs taken from space. Satellites help in the battle against pollution by detecting spillages of oil or chemicals into the sea. Monitoring the sea also reveals concentrations of plankton, and therefore of the fish that feed on it, so satellites can direct fishermen to the best fishing grounds.

Factories in space
Small space stations, such as the US Skylab, the European Spacelab and the Soviet Salyut and Mir stations, have experimented with industrial processes in Earth orbits. Some metals and drugs, for example, can be manufactured in a very pure state in the weightless conditions. Studying the structure of protein molecules found in the human body may help to develop new drugs to fight diseases.

Skylab, launched in 1973 and manned for a total of 171 days, returned to Earth in 1979.

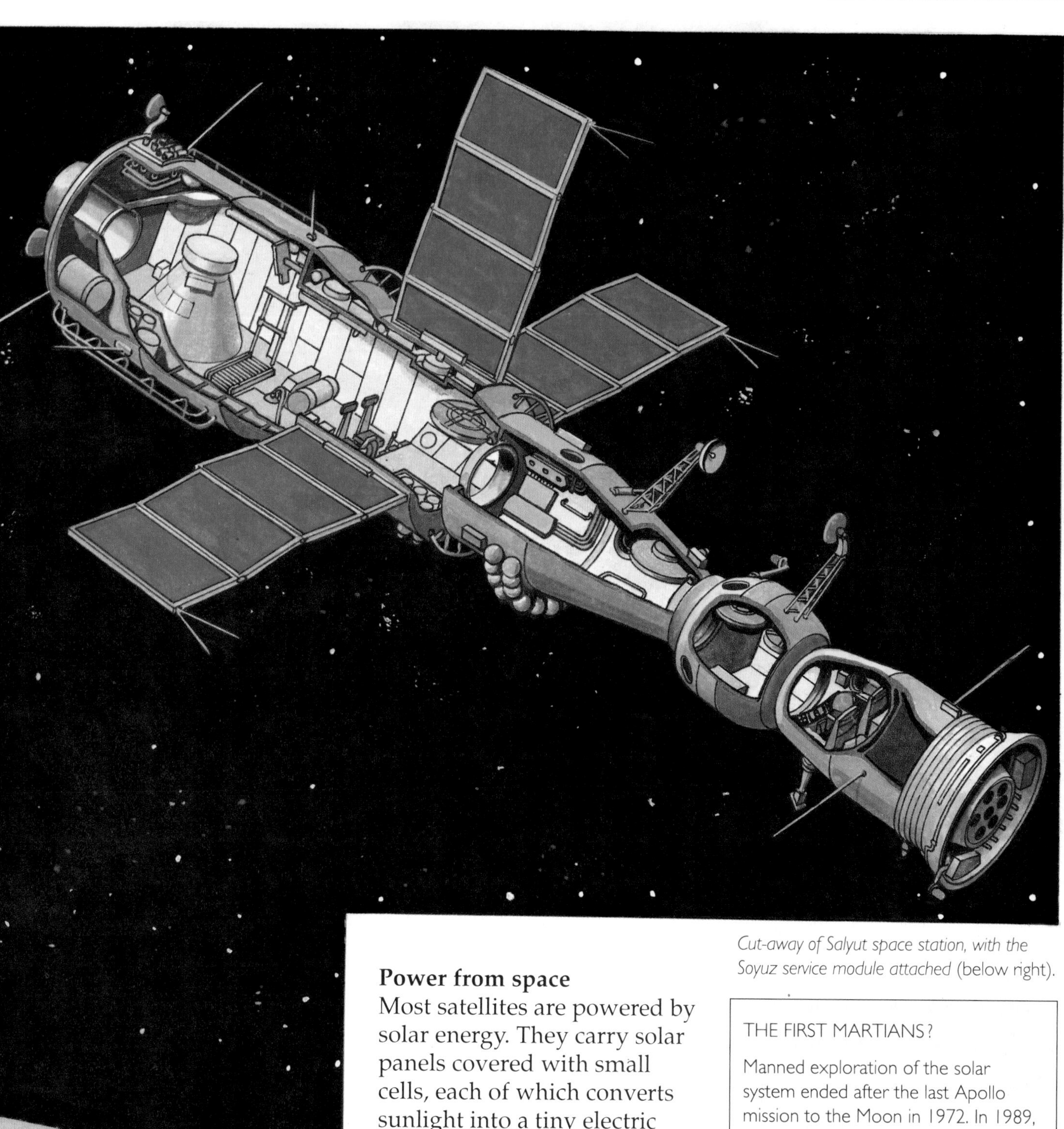

Cut-away of Salyut space station, with the Soyuz service module attached (below right).

Power from space

Most satellites are powered by solar energy. They carry solar panels covered with small cells, each of which converts sunlight into a tiny electric current. Thousands of cells acting together can provide the power necessary for all the satellite's equipment. It is possible that satellites could collect solar energy and transmit it to Earth, perhaps as laser beams or high-power radio signals, to be converted into electrical power.

THE FIRST MARTIANS?

Manned exploration of the solar system ended after the last Apollo mission to the Moon in 1972. In 1989, US President Bush announced that astronauts would be returning to the Moon and travelling to Mars in the next century.

A new space station in orbit will act as a staging post for the Martian journey. From there spacecraft will ferry crews and supplies to a permanent base on the Moon, where the long journey to Mars will begin. It will take over six months to get there.

References

Aphelion The point in an elliptical orbit around the Sun that is farthest from the Sun.

Apogee The point in an elliptical orbit around the Earth that is farthest from the Earth.

Astronaut A person trained to travel at an altitude greater than 100km (62 miles) above the Earth; a cosmonaut in the Soviet Union.

Astronomical unit (AU) The average distance between the Earth and the Sun (149.6 million km or 93 million miles), used as a measure of distance in the solar system.

Aurora A display of coloured lights in the sky near the poles produced by interaction of the solar wind with the Earth's magnetic field.

Big Bang The explosion of matter that is thought to have marked the beginning of the universe.

Binary star One of a pair of stars orbiting each other.

Black hole An object believed to be produced when a very massive star comes to the end of its life and collapses. The gravitational field of the collapsed core is so strong that not even light can escape.

Comet A chunk of ice and rock orbiting the Sun. As it nears the Sun, a fuzzy 'coma' appears around its head and it develops a long, bright tail pointing away from the Sun.

Corona The Sun's 'atmosphere', a layer of gas usually only visible during an eclipse.

Eclipse An interruption of the light travelling from a bright object to a dark object. When the Moon passes between the Earth and the Sun, a shadow is cast on the Earth. This is a solar eclipse. When the Earth passes between the Sun and the Moon, the Earth's shadow blocks out the Moon. This is a lunar eclipse.

Ellipse A flattened circle. The orbits of all of the planets are ellipses.

Equator An imaginary line around a planet mid-way between the poles.

Escape velocity The minimum speed necessary for an object to escape from the gravitational field of a planet. For spacecraft leaving Earth it is 11.2kps (7mps).

Flare An explosion on the Sun's surface, sending material into space.

Galaxy A system of billions of stars held together by their gravitational field.

Galileo Galilei (1564–1642) Italian scientist who made many discoveries, made his own telescopes, and proved that the Earth moves around the Sun.

Halley, Edmund (1656–1742) English astronomer who predicted the movements of Halley's Comet.

Ionosphere A region of the atmosphere rich in radio-reflective, charged particles that extends from 60km (37 miles) upwards, vital for bouncing radio waves around the world.

Kepler, Johannes (1571–1630) German astronomer whose laws of planetary motion described the paths of the planets.

Light year The distance a ray of light travels in one year, equivalent to 9.46 million million km (5.87 million million miles), used to measure astronomical distances.

Magnitude The apparent brightness of a star: the smaller the magnitude number, the brighter the star.

Main sequence A stage in the life of a star when its light is produced by nuclear reactions in its core. Most stars, including the Sun, are main sequence stars.

Meteor A lump of rock, possibly the remains of a comet, which enters the Earth's atmosphere.

Meteorite A meteor that does not burn up in the atmosphere and reaches the Earth's surface.

Nebula A cloud of gas and dust in space.

Neutron star The dense, dark, collapsed core of a star left after a supernova explosion.

Orbit The circular or elliptical path of an object as it travels around a star or planet.

Parsec A unit of distance in astronomy, equivalent to 3.26 light years or 30 million million km.

Perigee The point in an elliptical orbit around the Earth that is closest to the Earth.

Perihelion The point in an elliptical orbit around the Sun that is closest to the Sun.

Propellant The substance or substances used in rocket engines to generate the gas that provides thrust.

Pulsar A neutron star that emits pulsating radio waves.

Quasar A quasi-stellar object, the most distant, fastest-moving object in the universe.

Red giant A fairly cool star with helium burning in its core and hydrogen burning around the core.

Red shift The shift of the spectrum of light from a star or galaxy towards the red end of the spectrum, indicating that the object is moving away from the observer.

Satellite A small body which revolves around a planet, such as the Moon, and including man-made devices in orbit around the Earth.

Solar wind A stream of charged particles thrown out from the Sun. *See also* **Aurora**.

Supernova A star that explodes as a result of the sudden gravitational collapse that happens when its nuclear fuel is finished.

Telemetry The use of radio signals to send information from spacecraft back to Earth.

Van Allen belts Two doughnut-shaped belts of charged particles encircling the Earth, trapped by the Earth's magnetic field, named after the US scientist, James van Allen.

White dwarf A small, dim star near the end of its life.

Measuring and Analysis

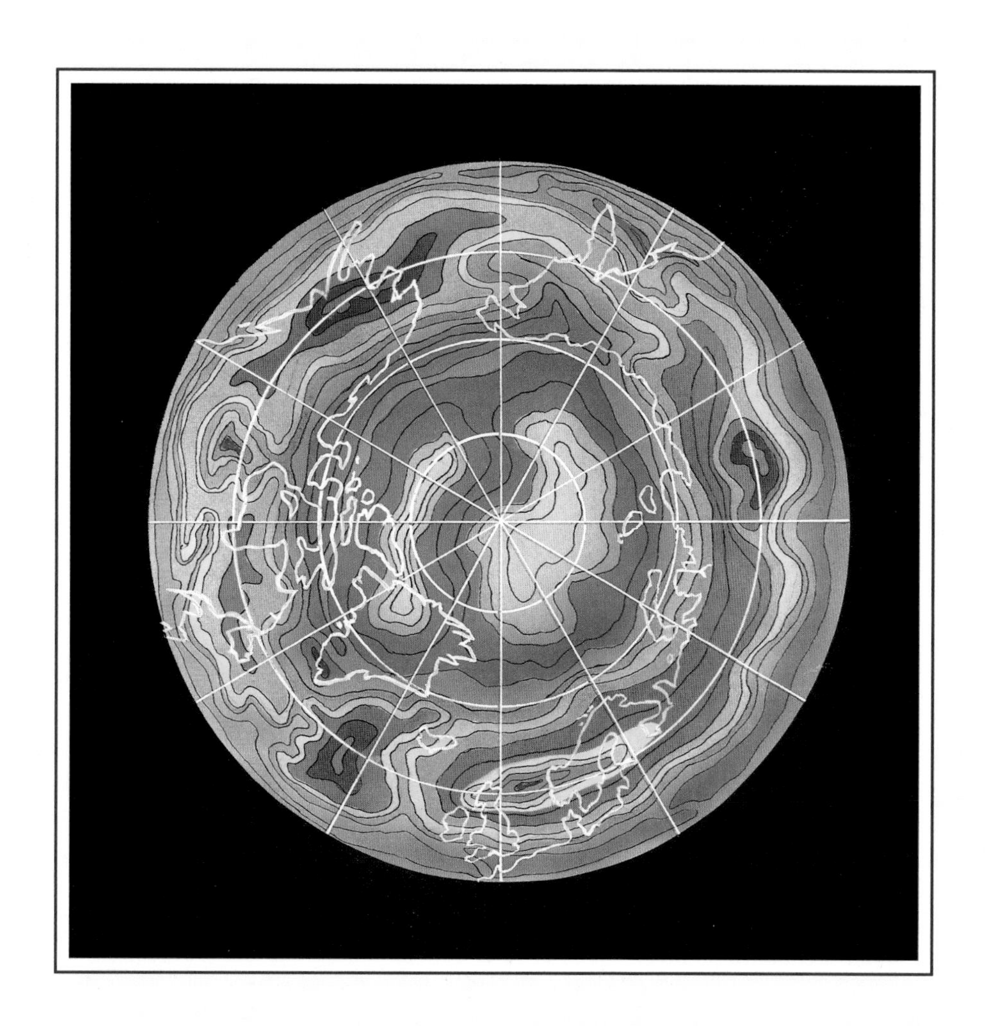

Timekeeping and Navigation

Before the 19th century, people had little need to know the exact time. They worked by the Sun. The earliest clocks also worked by the Sun. They were sundials in which an upright stick, the gnomon, casts a shadow on a scale which is marked off in hours. As the Sun travels across the sky the shadow moves round the scale. Sundials can be quite accurate, but they are no good when the Sun is not shining.

More reliable were waterclocks, in which water dripped through a small hole to fill up a basin with the hours marked in a scale on the side.

Mechanical clocks

Mechanical clocks were invented in the 12th century. They were not very accurate until the spring was invented in the 15th century: the force of the uncoiling spring turns a toothed wheel.

Alternatively, the turning force could be provided by a weight. It was difficult to regulate the mechanism so that the wheel turned at a constant speed, and a great advance was the invention of the pendulum in the 17th century. Its regular swing produced much more accurate clocks and by the late 18th century, spring-driven watches (you can't have a pendulum in a watch!) were equally accurate.

Electronic and atomic clocks

In mechanical clocks, a system of gears transmits the motion of the wheel to the hands, but most modern clocks do not use the complicated clockwork mechanism.

An electric clock is driven by power from a battery.

PENDULUM CLOCK

In this pendulum clock, a curved arm bearing a pair of prongs is linked to the top of a weighted, swinging rod (the pendulum). The prongs regulate a rotating toothed wheel, allowing it to turn by only one tooth for each swing of the pendulum. The wheel is driven by a descending weight (or a spring), which jolts the pendulum as it moves and keeps it swinging. The time the pendulum takes to swing from side to side depends on the length of the rod.

Electronic clocks and watches measure time through the vibrations of a quartz crystal. The power from a battery sets the crystal vibrating.

The most accurate clocks are atomic clocks, which depend on the natural vibrations of atoms of the element caesium. They are accurate to within one second in 1,000 years.

ATOMIC CLOCK

In an atomic clock, caesium metal is heated in an oven to produce a stream of atoms. The outermost electrons in each atom constantly switch from one energy state to another, and as they do so they emit, or absorb, some energy. A fixed number of changes takes place in one second – the number is 9,129,631,770.

Navigational instruments

The earliest navigational instrument was the compass, still used today. Because the Earth acts like a giant magnet, it attracts the points of the compass needle north and south (actually, the compass points to magnetic north, which is not the same as true north, though fairly close).

Sailors have used many instruments to find their position at sea with the aid of the stars or the Sun. The most efficient is a sextant. It consists of a telescope through which light from the Sun or a star can be seen at the same time as the horizon, by adjusting the angle of a mirror. A pointer

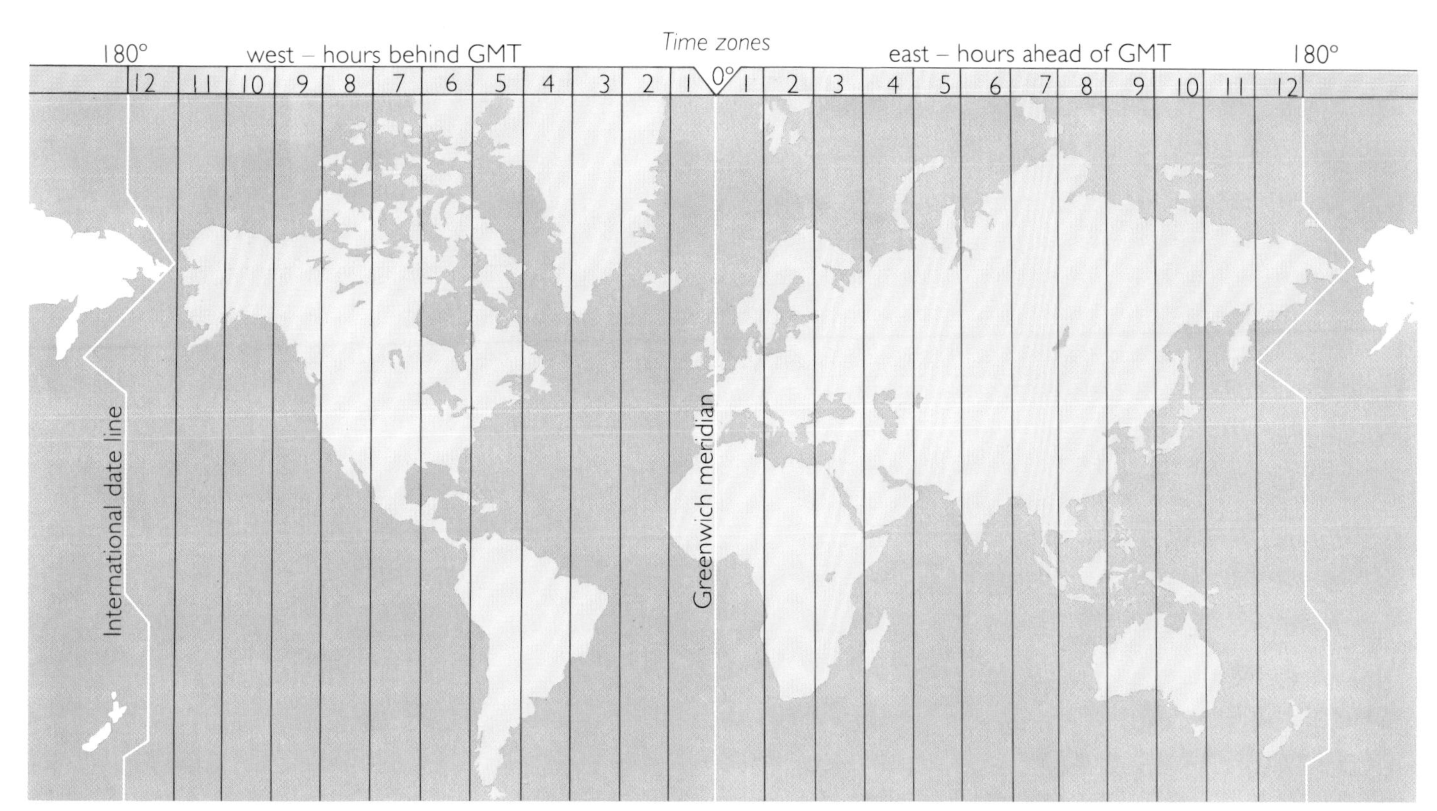

connected to the mirror indicates latitude.

Most aircraft and submarines navigate by gyroscope systems. A simple gyroscope consists of a rapidly spinning, heavy wheel which always stays pointing in the same direction whatever movements the frame supporting it may make. In a gyrocompass three wheels are used, one pointing north-south, one east-west, and one vertical. The latest gyroscopes have two moving laser beams instead of a spinning wheel.

Electronic systems

Most ships and aircraft now navigate with the help of a worldwide system of radio transmitters and receivers. Radio waves normally travel in straight lines and at a constant speed, so that both the position of the ship and its speed of travel can be worked out.

LONGITUDE AND LATITUDE

Any point on the Earth's surface can be located from the imaginary grid consisting of lines of latitude (running east-west) and longitude (north-south). The equator is the line of 0° latitude, and 0° longitude runs through Greenwich in London, England. On a map the position of any place can be given in degrees and minutes (60 minutes = 1 degree) of latitude and longitude.

TIME ZONES

Because the Earth is turning while it orbits the Sun, one side is light while the other is dark. To make the time shown on the clock correspond with the actual time of day, the world is divided artificially into time zones. Greenwich time is taken as the standard: places east of the Greenwich meridian (0° longitude) are ahead of Greenwich mean time, by one hour for each zone; places west are behind.

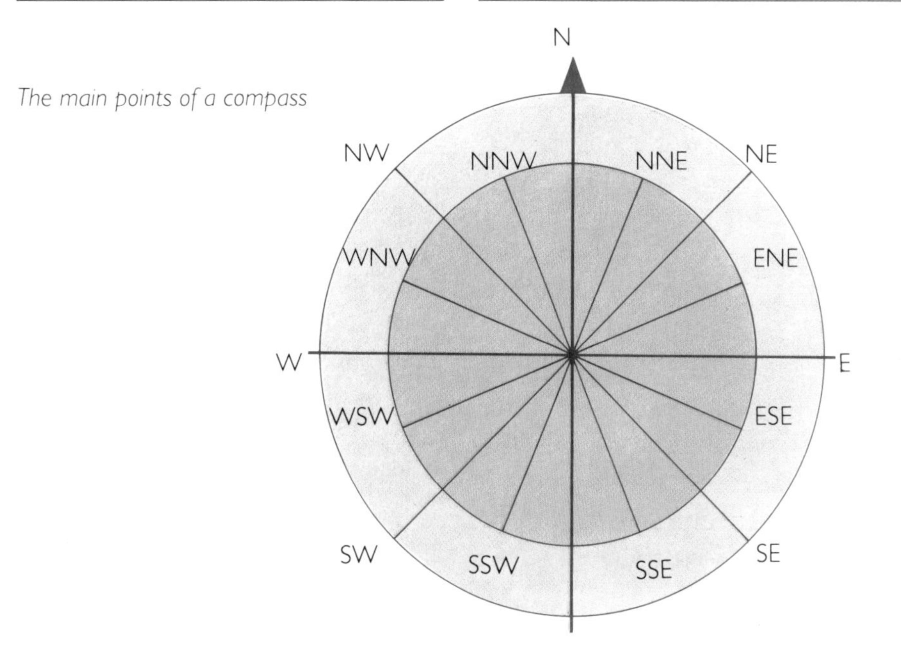

The main points of a compass

Balances and Thermometers

In order to measure, for example, the size and weight of this book, we compare the unknown quantities with known quantities, such as a metre rule and a kilogram weight. All measurements involve comparisons with 'standards' and with the units we derive from them (for example, centimetres, millimetres, grams and milligrams).

There are internationally accepted standards for all forms of measurement. The standard kilogram, for instance, is a tube about 40mm long and 40mm wide, made of 90 per cent platinum and 10 per cent iridium, which weighs the same as a litre of pure water at 4°C. It is kept at Sèvres, in France.

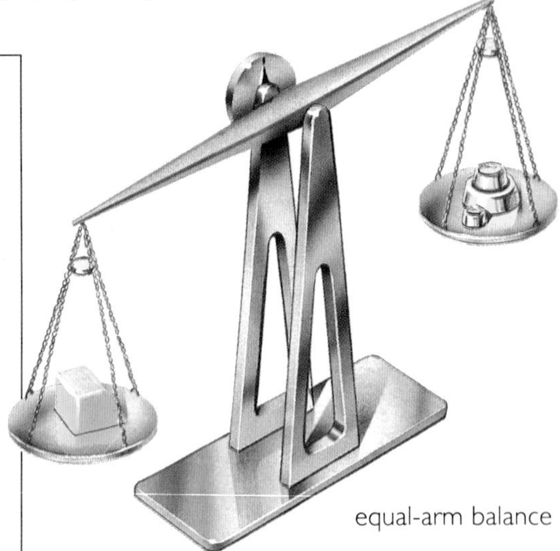
equal-arm balance

Balances and strain gauges
One of the first, and the simplest, instruments for measuring weight is the equal-arm balance. A beam rests on a central pivot and weighing pans are suspended from each end of the beam. The object to be weighed is placed in one pan and known weights are added to the other pan until the beam comes to rest perfectly level.

A variation on the beam balance is the weighing machine used by doctors. The platform is connected to the beam close to the pivot. It is counterbalanced by small weights suspended at the opposite end, a long way from the pivot.

Beam balances in fact measure mass not weight. To measure the weight of an object, a spring balance is used. This consists of a spring from which the object is hung. The spring expands and the weight is shown on a scale.

The most sensitive balances are known as strain gauges. These are electrical devices, as used in most shops. A ribbon of metal changes its electrical resistance when stretched, and the change in length indicates the weight of the object.

Four main types of balance – three mechanical and one (below right) *electrical.*

weighing machine

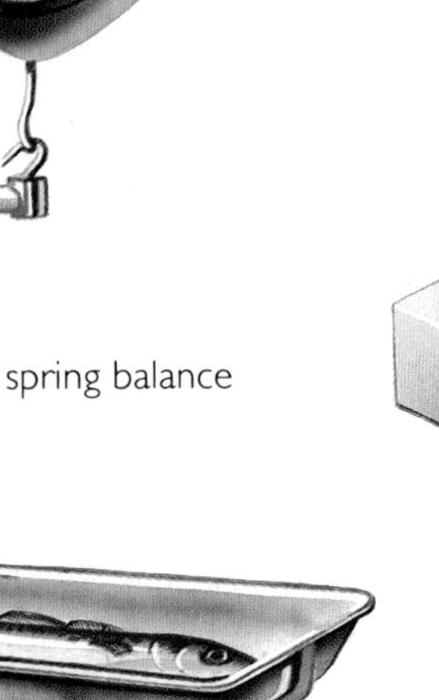
spring balance

strain gauge

Temperatures
Temperature is measured with a thermometer and is defined in units called degrees. It is not possible to compare directly two temperatures as you can compare, say, two lengths. Instead, temperature is related to two standard values, such as the freezing point and boiling point of water (0° and 100° on the Celsius scale).

A simple thermometer consists of a glass bulb and thin tube containing a liquid, usually mercury or alcohol. When the temperature rises, the liquid expands and moves up the tube. Alongside the tube is a temperature scale marked in degrees.

The standard thermometer with which all others are compared is the gas thermometer. It works on the principle that the pressure of a gas kept at constant volume increases evenly with temperature. The pressure of the gas exerted on a movable column of mercury is interpreted as a temperature reading. Other types of thermometer use the colour of light or the change in electrical resistance of metals with temperature. These are much more accurate than the liquid in glass thermometers and can measure temperatures up to many thousands of degrees Celsius.

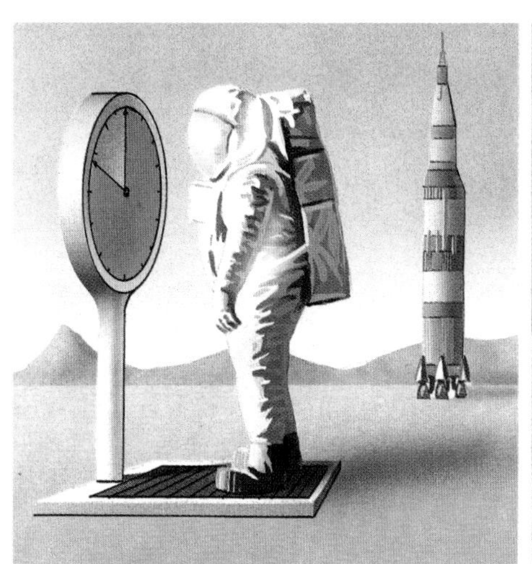

An astronaut measuring his weight on Earth and on the Moon will notice a sixfold difference due to the corresponding difference in gravitational pulls.

Mass and weight
Say your mass is 30kg (66lbs). This will remain the same wherever you are. But your weight can change. On Earth, at sea level, your weight is also 30kg (66lbs). But if you were to journey into space, your weight would decrease the further you get from the Earth's surface. This is because the Earth's pull of gravity gets weaker the higher you go.

Astronauts orbiting the Earth experience complete weightlessness. On the Moon, where the force of gravity is one-sixth that of the Earth's, you would weigh only 5kg (11lbs).

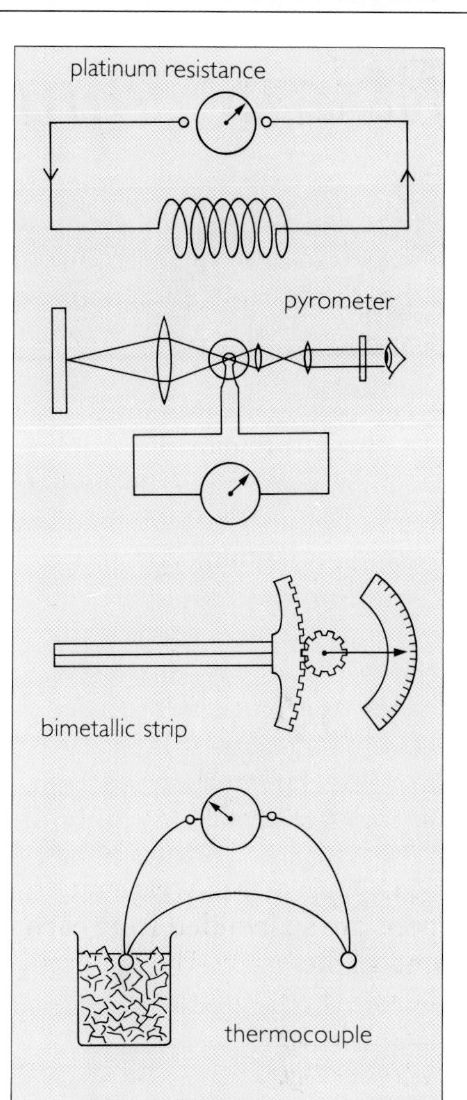

TYPES OF THERMOMETER

A platinum resistance thermometer contains a coil of platinum wire whose electrical resistance changes with temperature.

Pyrometers ('fire measurers') are used for measuring very high temperatures in, for example, furnaces. An optical pyrometer compares and matches the colour and brightness of light from the hot object with that from an electric wire heated to a known temperature.

A bimetallic strip consists of two strips of different metals joined together. When heated, the metals expand at different rates, causing the strip to bend and move a needle over the temperature scale.

A thermocouple makes use of the fact that a junction between two different metals produces an electric current when heated.

Microscopy and Spectroscopy

How much silver or gold is there in a coin? What chemicals are present in tap water? How are the cells of a leaf arranged? Research of this type requires microscopes, chromatographs and spectroscopes.

The invisible world
A microscope makes it possible to study things too small to be seen with the naked eye. Optical microscopes, such as you might use at home or in school, have glass or perspex lenses and work by ordinary, visible light. The specimen must be thin and translucent so that light can shine through it. Optical microscopes magnify the size of the specimen up to about 1,000 times. This is sufficient to see, for example, the cellular structure of blood. For greater clarity, it is sometimes necessary to stain specimens with coloured dyes. Unfortunately, if the specimen is a live one, the staining process will kill it.

Greater detail can be seen with an electron microscope. This uses an electron beam rather than light, which is focused by electromagnets on to a fluorescent viewing screen. Electron microscopes magnify up to about 2 million times, and scanning electron microscopes, in which the electron beam moves rapidly to and fro over the specimen in a pattern of lines, can build up three-dimensional images. But live material cannot be studied.

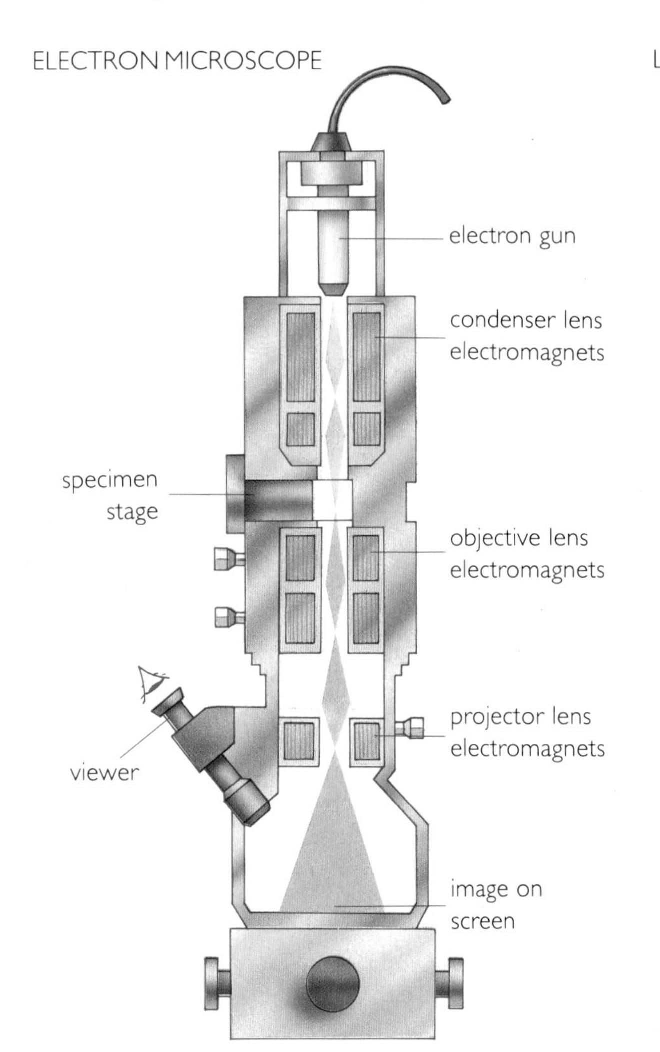

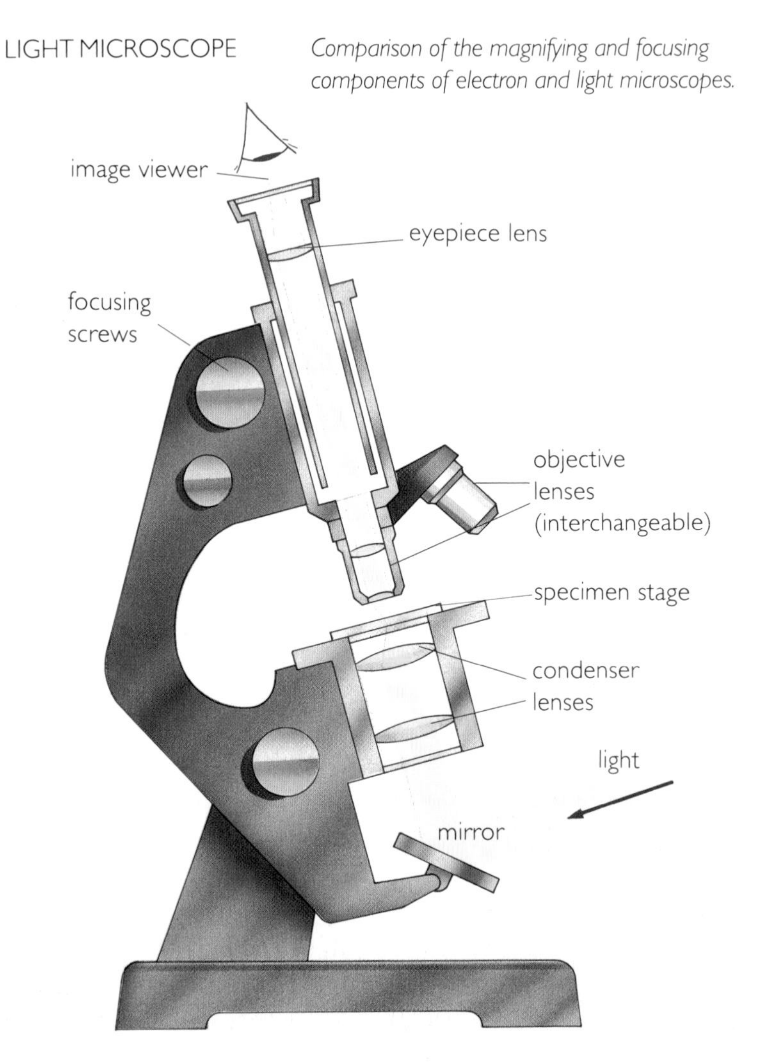

Comparison of the magnifying and focusing components of electron and light microscopes.

Since about 1980 other types of scanning microscopes have been developed. Tunnelling microscopes are so sensitive that they enable the atomic structure of objects to be studied. Emission microscopes are used for studying the structures of minerals, rocks and metals. The object is made to emit electrons by being heated or electrically charged, and the electrons are focused with electromagnets on to a screen.

LIGHT AND ELECTRON MICROSCOPES

The object to be viewed in a light microscope is mounted on a glass slide which is placed on the microscope stage. The position of the mirror is adjusted so that light is directed up through the slide. To focus the object clearly, the distance of the objective lens from the slide is adjusted by screws.

Transmission electron microscopes are used in a similar fashion: the electron beam passes through the specimen. With a scanning electron microscope the object to be viewed must first be coated with a fine layer of chemicals that will reflect the electron beam.

Spectrometry

Ordinary 'white' light is made up of light of a spectrum of many different colours.

Atoms and molecules of all objects form a spectrum of visible light rays, X-rays, microwaves and other types of radiation when they are heated or placed in an electrical or magnetic field. These spectra can be investigated with a spectrometer. By observing the lines in spectra, scientists can tell, for example, the temperature on the surface of a star, what chemical elements the star contains, and how fast the star is travelling.

Mass spectrometers are particularly sensitive and are able to detect chemicals which are present only as one part in 100 million.

Chromatography

Chromatography is a means of separating and identifying substances on the basis of solubility (how readily they dissolve in a liquid), adsorption (how well they attach themselves to a solid, such as charcoal), and volatility (how quickly they turn to a gas when heated).

The simplest method is paper chromatography. In this process a tiny drop of the sample liquid, for instance blood plasma, is placed at the bottom of a long thin strip of blotting-type paper. The strip is dipped in a suitable dissolving liquid. As the dissolving liquid is drawn up the paper strip, the various substances in the plasma are washed out at different levels.

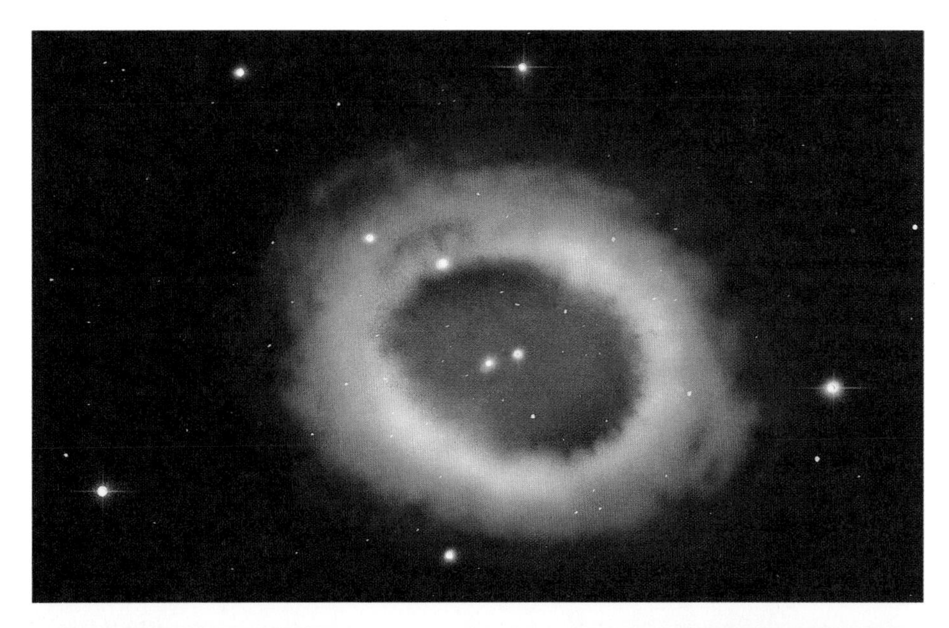

A direct and spectral image of a star, the latter revealing the chemistry of the star.

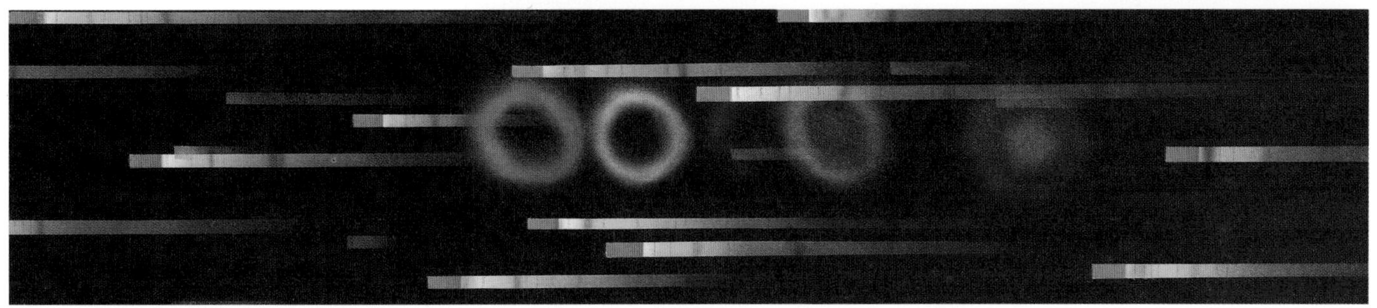

Meters and Displays

The term 'meter' means any instrument which measures accurately. A barometer, for example, measures air pressure.

A display is any device that shows the results of measurements, such as a computer monitor, a dial and pointer, or a written or drawn record (known as a gram).

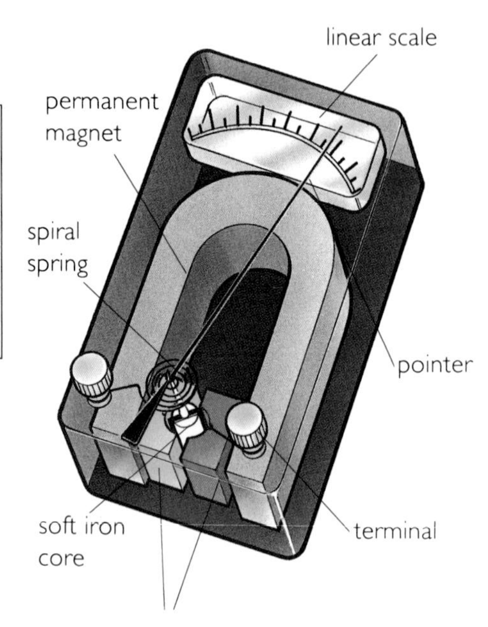

Above: *An electric meter comprises a movable coil set between the North and South poles of a permanent magnet.*

Electric meters

A typical electric meter consists of a U-shaped magnet with an iron core fixed between the arms of the magnet so that it can rotate. A metal wire is wrapped around the core. As current flows through the wire the core is forced to turn, and this action tightens a coiled spring. A pointer attached to the coil moves across the meter dial by an amount proportional to the strength of the current.

The light meter on a camera contains a photoelectric cell. Light rays falling on the photoelectric cell create an electric current. This current moves a pointer across the dial. The brighter the light, the stronger the current and the further the pointer moves.

A pressure meter measures the changes in electrical resistance of carbon grains, as they become more (or less) tightly packed together by the pressure.

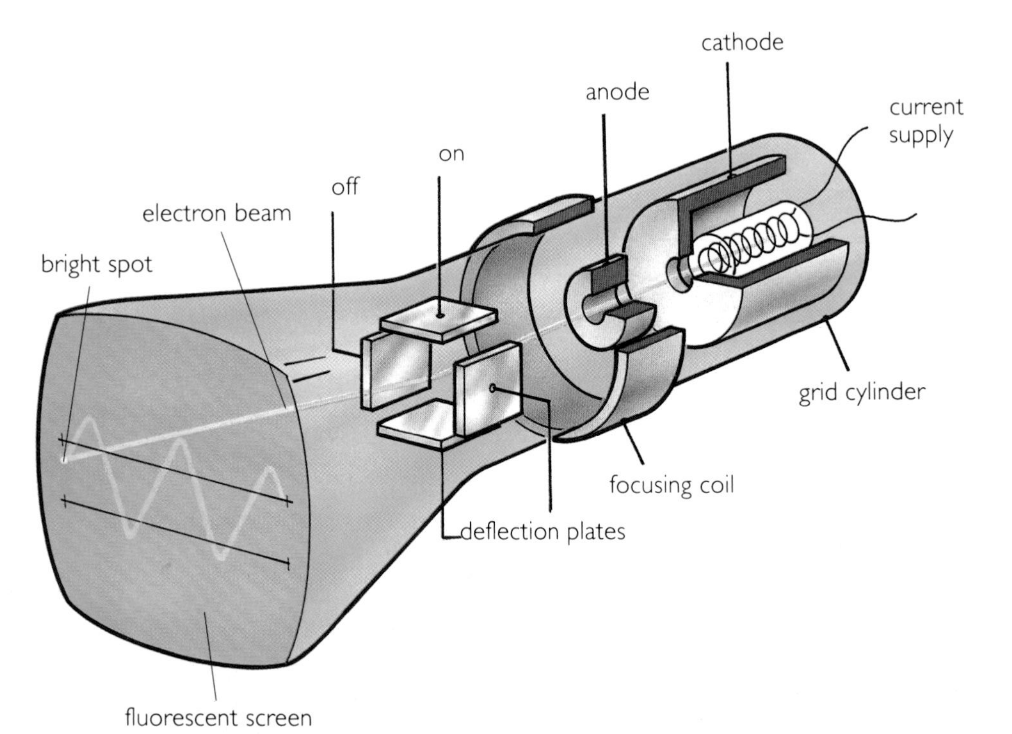

Above: *The electron generating and focusing elements inside an oscilloscope tube.*

Most modern scientific instruments work on similar electromagnetic principles. In an oscilloscope, which makes an electric current visible, the changing strength of the current moves a beam of electrons across a television-type screen. The movement is seen as a wavy line moving across the screen. The current itself is often the output from a microphone, which converts sound waves into electrical signals.

A medical ultrasound scanner, which is used to examine an unborn child, also measures the strength of sounds. Harmless sound waves are reflected from the embryo in the mother's womb and converted into electrical signals which are recorded on a TV screen as a series of spots of varying brightness.

Displays

Television-type screens and small 'windows' like those on pocket calculators are the most common forms of displays. As in an oscilloscope or a TV receiver, the image on the screen is created by beams of electrons scanning across the surface.

Window-type displays employ the changing optical properties of liquid crystals or silicon chip devices. Long, thin, but tiny packets of crystals or chips are joined end to end to create letter and number shapes.

Liquid-Crystal Displays (LCDs) use a substance that flows like a liquid but consists of molecules arranged into a neat pattern, as in a solid crystal. The pattern changes when the substance is heated or when an electric current or magnetic field is applied. When heated, the crystals change colour. Plastic-strip thermometers, which you can place on your forehead to tell your body temperature, work in this way. With electromagnetic signals, the crystals change from transparent to opaque.

Light-Emitting Diode (LED) displays convert electrical energy into visible light. Electrical signals boost electrons from a low to a high-energy state. As the electrons fall back again into the lower energy state, they give off their surplus energy as light. LEDs are used in instruments in which a luminous display is needed, such as station clocks.

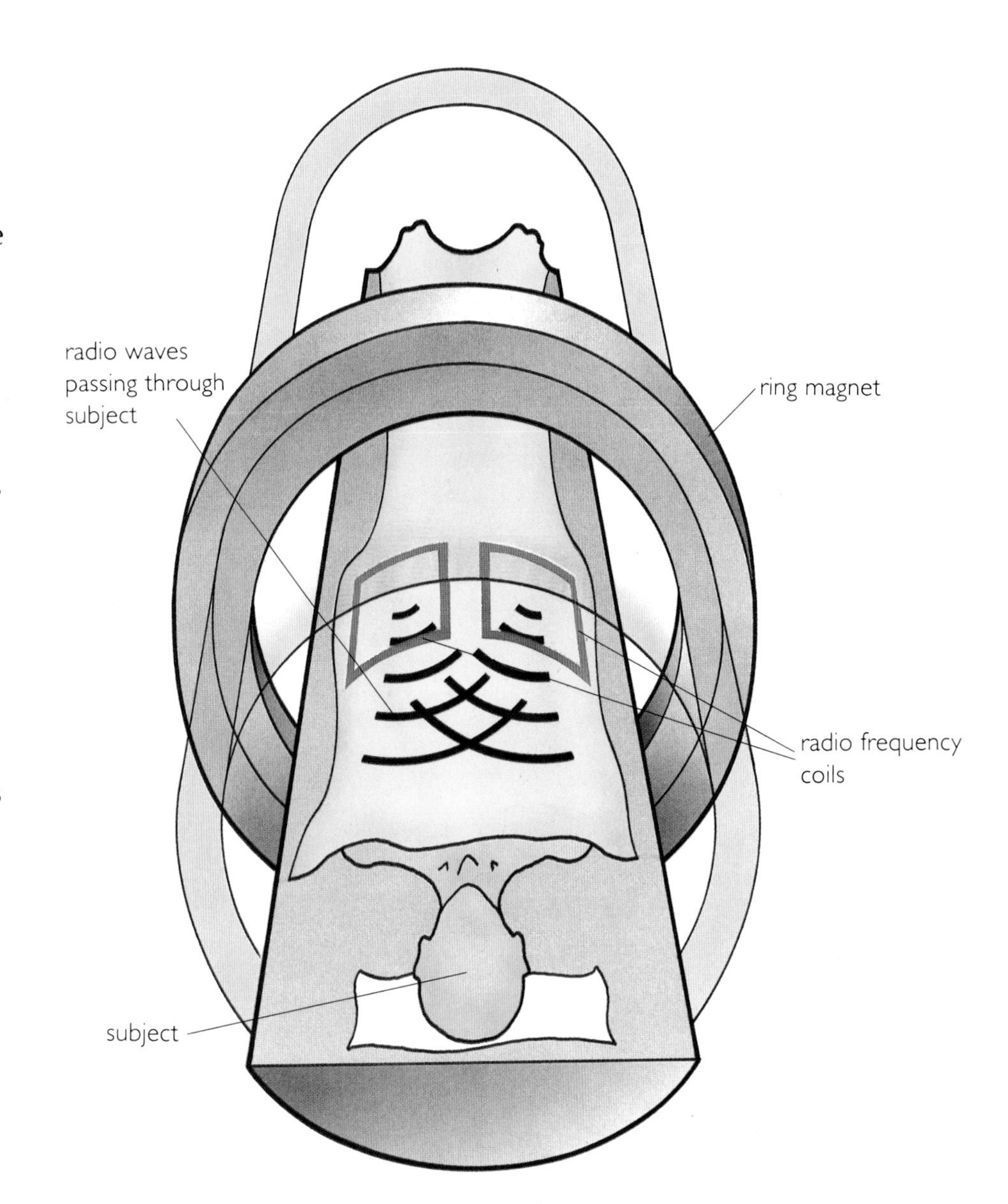

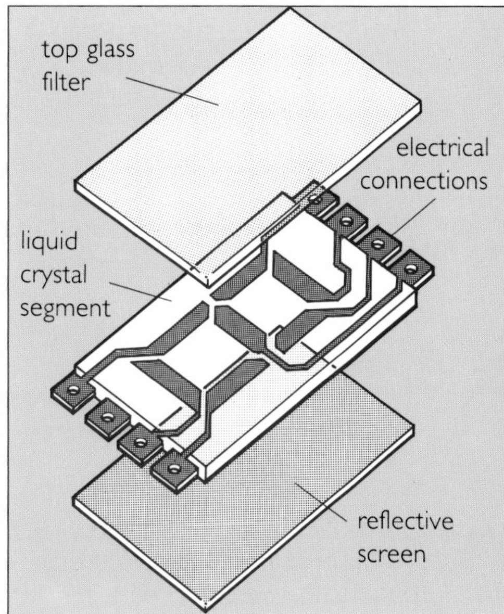

LCD

In an LCD a film of liquid crystal is sandwiched between two glass sheets that are each coated with a thin, transparent layer of metal. An electric current can flow from the metal of one sheet to the other through the liquid crystals. Normally, the crystals direct light rays passing through the sandwich so that the display is completely transparent. When a current flows, some of the crystal molecules change position, preventing light from passing through. The corresponding numbers or letters in the window become opaque and therefore visible.

References

Ampère, André Marie (1775–1836) French scientist who was the first to establish the relationship between magnetism and an electric current and gave his name to the unit for measuring current.

Balance A weighing machine which works on the principle of the lever in the same way as a see-saw. The weighing pans rest on or hang from a beam that pivots about a central point.

Calibrate To make a scale on a measuring device so that the device can be used to measure quantities in particular units; for example, a ruler is calibrated in centimetres, millimetres and inches.

Cathode-ray tube The picture tube used in TV sets, oscilloscopes, radar viewers etc. It consists of a glass tube, narrow at one end and broad at the other, from which all air has been removed. A beam of electrons or cathode rays is directed at the broad end, producing spots of light on a fluorescent screen.

Cell The smallest unit or 'building block' of living things. Most cells are about 0.03mm across and can be seen only through a microscope.

Celsius The temperature scale using ice at 0° and steam at 100° as the lower and upper fixed points, also called the centigrade scale. A degree Celsius is written as °C. It is named after the Swedish astronomer Anders Celsius (1701–44), who devised this type of scale in 1742.

Cryogenics The study and uses of very low temperatures. Objects are usually greatly cooled by placing them in a bath of liquid oxygen (at -180°C) or the even colder liquid helium (at -269°C).

Electrocardiogram, electroencephalogram Medical instruments used to measure the electrical activity of the heart and brain respectively.

Fraunhofer, Joseph (1787–1826) German physicist who in 1814 discovered that a glass prism splits sunlight into a spectrum of colours crossed by large numbers of dark lines – the basis of spectroscopy.

Gauge A graduated instrument used for accurate measurements, such as a thermometer, ruler and speedometer.

Geiger counter An instrument for detecting and measuring atomic radiation. It consists of a tube containing a gas such as argon, which is electrically charged. As an atomic particle enters the tube it produces a pulse of electricity which triggers a counter or a tiny loudspeaker which emits a chattering noise.

Gyroscope An instrument for navigation, commonly comprising a rapidly spinning heavy wheel that always stays pointing in the same direction no matter how much its supporting frame twists and turns.

Image processing The use of computers to modify pictures and highlight details not normally visible. Pictures of planets and stars are often coloured with this.

Kelvin A unit of measurement of temperature. It is the same size as a degree Celsius, but on the Kelvin scale, 0°K is absolute zero (the lowest possible temperature, -273.15°C). It is named after the British physicist, Lord Kelvin (1824–1907).

Leeuwenhoek, Antonie van (1632–1723) Dutch merchant who, about 1670, developed a simple but high-quality microscope and became the first scientist to investigate individual living cells.

Logarithmic scale A scale of measurement in which an increase of one unit represents an increase of ten times in the quantity measured. For instance, as the scale increases 1, 2, 3, 4 and so on, the quantity increases 1, 10, 100, 1,000 times, and so on.

Magnification The number of times the diameter of an object appears enlarged compared with its real size.

Micrometer gauge A device for measuring very small thicknesses and diameters. It consists of a G-shaped clamp in which the gap between the measuring faces is adjusted by a graduated screw.

Quartz A crystalline form of a very common compound, silicon dioxide. Sand grains are tiny particles of quartz.

Sabine, Sir Edward (1788–1883) British astronomer who plotted the Earth's magnetic field and recorded how its fluctuations were related to the activity of the Sun.

Scale A set of quantities rising from a low to a high value; for example, a length scale might be in centimetres, from 0 to 100.

Seebeck, Johann (1770–1831) German physicist who established the principle that electricity is produced by the direct conversion of heat into an electric current. This is the basis of the thermocouple used to measure high temperatures.

SI system (from *Systéme International d'Unités*) The units of measurement used in science and, more and more, in everyday life. It is based on a standard metre, kilogram, second, ampere and degree Kelvin.

Torricelli, Evangelista (1608–47) Italian inventor of the barometer.

Weight The force by which an object is attracted by gravity. Weight is defined as the mass of an object multiplied by acceleration due to the pull of gravity. Mass and weight are often used as one and the same thing, but they are not. Mass is usually measured in kilograms and weight in newtons.

Zeiss, Carl (1816–88) German maker of optical instruments, who made great advances in microscopy and production of lenses.

Communications

Printing

Printing as we know it began in Europe in the fifteenth century, with the invention of movable type – individual letters carved on small blocks which could be put together to make up a page.

The Chinese had invented printing about 1,000 years before, carving a wooden board so that the characters (letters) stood out. The raised surface was then covered with ink and pressed against a sheet of paper. Movable type was not practical in Chinese, because the language has thousands of different characters. But the European alphabet contained only 23 (now 26) characters.

Type is no longer put together by hand. The text is composed on computers, and typesetting machines produce photographic film of it, from which a printing plate is made.

There are three main printing methods today: letterpress, gravure and lithography.

Letterpress

In letterpress, or 'hot metal' printing, small slugs of metal, each with a character moulded back to front, on one end, are lined up to form the text. Next, a papier-mâché sheet is pressed against the type. It takes up the shape of the type and from it a metal printing plate, which is usually in the form of a cylinder, is cast. The plate is inked and pressed against the paper, transferring the characters on to the paper. They appear, of course, the right way round.

Gravure

In a sense, gravure is the opposite of letterpress, because instead of standing out from the printing plate, the letters are etched into it by acid. The plate is inked and then polished to remove ink from the flat surface. When it is pressed against the paper, the ink trapped in the etched hollows is transferred to the paper. Gravure is especially suitable for colour printing.

Lithography

Lithography relies on the fact that water and grease will not mix. If the image to be printed is drawn in grease on the printing plate, a watery solution washed over the plate will be thrown off by the grease. When greasy ink is applied, it sticks to the image but not to the watery surface.

Lithography plates were originally flat stones (*lithos* is Greek for 'stone'), but most modern presses use a system called offset litho. A cylindrical plate is coated with watery gum and then inked. The image on the plate is then transferred to a rubber cylinder which prints the image on to the paper.

Three different methods of transferring ink from printing plate to paper – from left to right, letterpress, gravure and lithography.

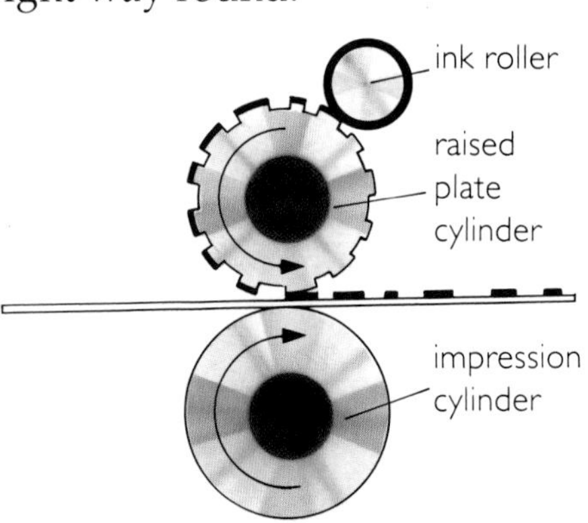

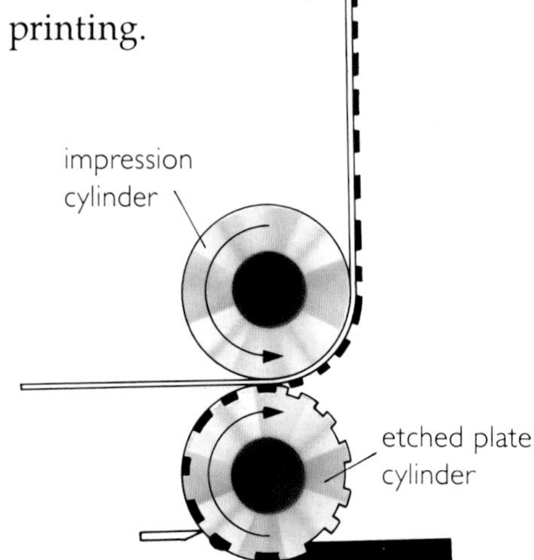

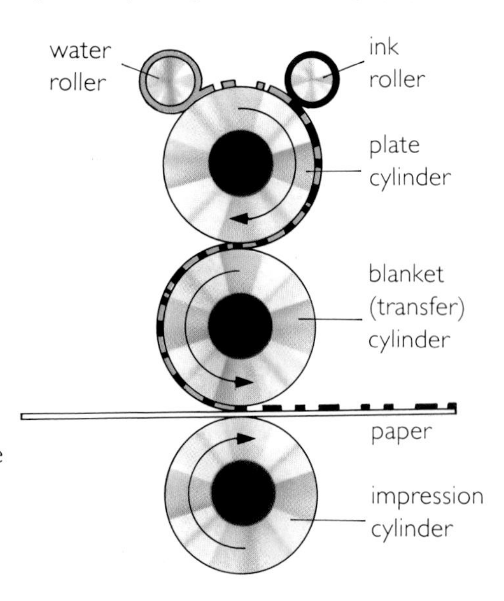

Colour printing

Colour pictures are built up from four separate images on four different printing plates, printing in yellow, cyan (blue), magenta (red) and black. Separating the colours for separate printing was a long and difficult task, but today it is much quicker and easier thanks to computers and lasers. The picture is scanned by a laser, assessed electronically and transferred to light-sensitive, aluminium printing plates, all under computer control.

Four-colour printing process with the original image laser-scanned and made into four separate printing plate films.

DESK-TOP PUBLISHING

Computers and lasers have made the work of the publisher much easier and cheaper. It is now possible for very small companies, even individuals, to become printers and publishers using 'desk-top publishing' systems. A typical system would include a general purpose computer for entering text and graphics (line drawings, etc.), perhaps a scanner for taking in photographs, and a laser printer for producing high quality printed material. The most important part of the system is the software, a computer program that tells the computer what to do with text, graphics and photographs. The operator can design the pages and control the way they are printed, jobs which used to require several specialist workers.

Photography

Photography has become an important part of modern life. Everyone sees photographs of some sort every day. Besides providing entertainment and a way of storing visual information, photography has many uses in science, medicine and industry. For example, most people have had an X-ray, which is a kind of photograph.

Early photographs

The word photography comes from Greek words meaning 'light', and 'writing' – writing with light.

Early photographs were made on glass plates covered with light-sensitive chemicals, usually salts of silver. The glass plate was placed in a light-proof box called a camera. A lens focused an image of the outside world on the plate. Where light fell on the plate, the silver salts were changed into metallic silver. The plate was developed by washing away any unchanged chemicals that had not been exposed to light and 'fixing' the metallic silver that formed the image. The image was then transferred on to a sheet of light-sensitive paper as a print.

The camera

In the 1880s the glass plate was replaced by a roll of flexible celluloid film coated with light-sensitive chemicals and the first Kodak cameras were sold already loaded with film which could be developed in a lab. Photographers no longer needed to handle fragile glass plates or to understand the chemical processes in photography.

When you take a photograph today, you press a button to release the shutter. In a fraction of a second, billions of light-sensitive crystals in the film emulsion are struck by light from the image focused by the camera lens. If a crystal absorbs enough energy from the light, the silver salts trapped in it are transformed into metallic silver. Despite all the advances in both cameras and film, the basic principle has not changed in the past hundred years.

Colour photographs

Early photographs could only be made in black and white; the first successful colour plates appeared in 1906. Modern colour film contains three layers of emulsion. The first layer is sensitive to blue light, the second to green light, and the third to red. When the film is developed and printed, colours produced in the three layers combine to reproduce the original colours in the image.

There are two types of colour film. Negative film produces a negative image when it is developed; it is used for positive prints. Reversal film produces a positive image called a transparency, which can be mounted as a slide and projected on a screen.

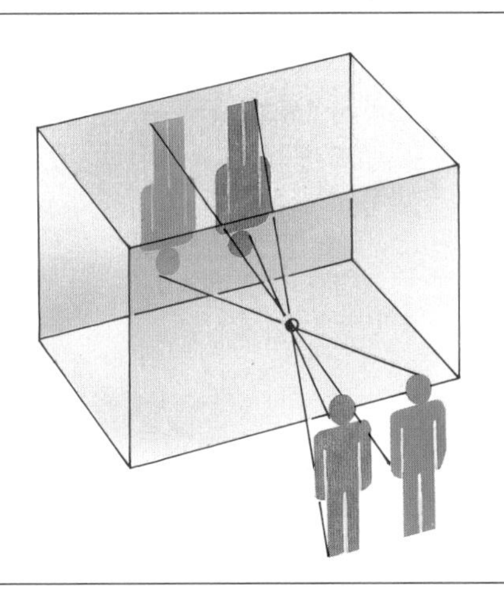

A PIN-HOLE CAMERA

A pin-hole camera consists of a box sealed so that light cannot enter except at a small hole at one end. The other end of the box is covered with semi-transparent paper. When the pin hole is pointed at a bright object, an upside-down image of the object appears on the paper. The image is upside-down because light rays from the object travel through the hole in straight lines.

DIY CAMERAS

In 1947 Edwin Land invented the polaroid camera that develops its own pictures. After a photograph was taken, it was pulled out, passing between rollers that spread the processing chemicals over the film emulsion. In two minutes the picture was fully developed.

Most modern instant cameras use integral film: the photograph is automatically ejected after the photograph is taken, and the picture develops after a few seconds in daylight.

SPECIAL PHOTOGRAPHIC TECHNIQUES

Some uses for photography rely on special films. For example, infra-red film is more sensitive to heat than light. It can reveal how heat leaks out of buildings by detecting 'hot spots' on the outside of the building.

Thermal images of another country's airfields taken by 'spy' cameras in high-altitude aircraft can reveal useful information. Aircraft on the ground with hot engines (because they have been flown recently) stand out clearly from others which have been parked on the ground for days. Warm patches of ground where aircraft and other vehicles recently stood are visible in a thermal image. Spy satellites also use thermal imaging, but because of the problems of returning film from space to Earth, they use video cameras instead of photographic film.

It is often vital for the safety of a structure (such as an oil rig) that the joints between its metal parts are welded properly. Small cracks in a welded joint can spread and eventually make the joint break apart. Welds can be checked by placing photographic film on one side of the joint and a source of X-rays on the other side. X-rays pass through the joint and strike the film, revealing the internal structure of the joint. This is also called non-destructive testing (NDT), because the joint is not damaged by the test.

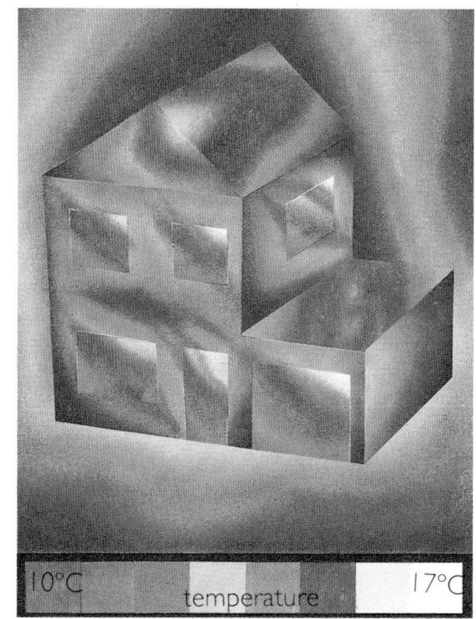

Infra-red image of a house and garage. The 'hot spots' appear white and yellow, indicating heat loss (through the roof and windows) while the 'cold spots', from where little heat is lost, appear blue.

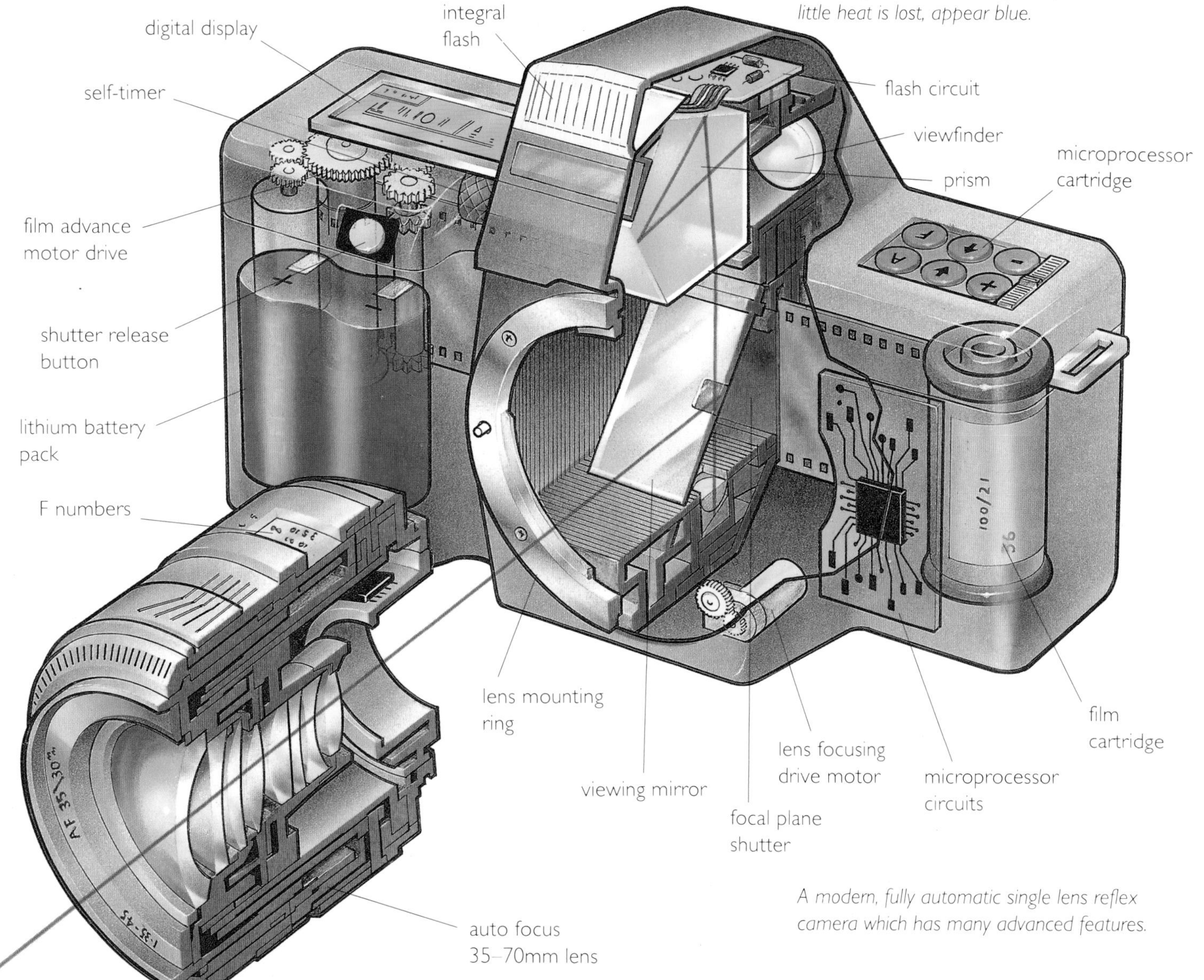

A modern, fully automatic single lens reflex camera which has many advanced features.

Photography and Motion Pictures

The craft of making motion pictures, or cinematography, includes two aspects – taking the picture, with a camera, and showing it, with a projector.

History of movie making
People have tried to make moving pictures for as long as they have tried to make still photographs – in fact longer. The zoetrope was one example of a device dating from before the age of photography which gave an illusion of movement.

The first movie was made in 1887. It was silent, black and white, fuzzy, jerky – and lasted just 13 seconds! Yet the first film which told a story and was shown in a public cinema was made less than ten years later. Sound was introduced in 1926, and the first feature film in 'technicolor' was produced the same year. Although the basic principles are still the same, many technical improvements have been made since. The challenge of television in the 1950s resulted in many new processes, such as CinemaScope or VistaVision, which made use of a variety of film sizes and types of sound.

A huge number of 'special effects' can be used by the modern film-maker. To make a dramatic scene such as this, a model of the craft is first filmed against a blank (normally blue) background and the true background, separately filmed, is superimposed.

Before each 'take' in making a film, a slate is held up in front of the cameras. This shows the film editor all the necessary information concerning the scene about to be filmed. When the film crew have the lighting and sound recording equipment ready, the slate's arm is clicked down and the cameras start.

Cameras

A movie camera takes still pictures, like any other camera, but it takes them automatically and at high speed, generally at the rate of 24 per second. A shutter stops light reaching the film while it is moving between frames. To make sure that the picture is sharp and clear, the camera must be sturdy and silent, with no vibration. It is driven by an electric motor and sometimes mounted on a cart called a crab dolly. Modern cameras, however, are extremely light and easily carried, which makes filming 'on location', rather than in a studio on a stage set, much easier. Modern film-makers can choose from a huge variety of lenses, together with filters, screens and other devices. Generally, a scene is filmed by several cameras and from different viewpoints, at the same time. Most commercial films are made on 35mm film (the width of each frame), which is supplied in rolls and cut into strips 300m (900ft) long.

The zoetrope was a popular device in the nineteenth century. When you look through a slit at pictures revolving in a drum, an illusion of movement is created.

Sound

Sound may be recorded at the same time as filming, or separately, in which case it is 'dubbed' in during the editing of the film. For background music, which may be provided by a large orchestra, the film is projected on an extra-large screen, which can be seen by all the musicians while they are playing.

THE PROJECTOR

The film is shown on a screen by a projector. The film, stored on a reel, passes over a magnetic sound head and between a light and the lens. The film is projected at the same speed at which it was filmed, but the shutter on the projector is designed so that each frame is actually shown three times. This helps to reduce flickering.

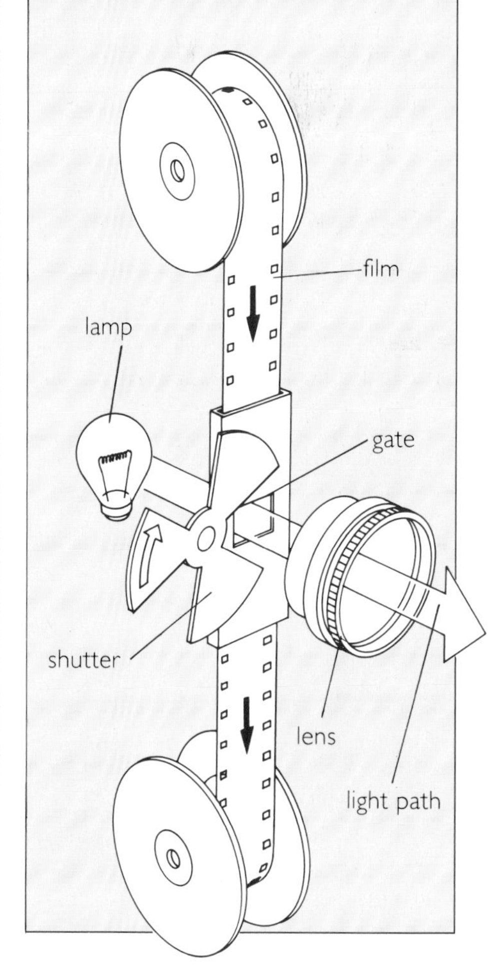

Audio and Video

Before the twentieth century, there was no television or radio. Even the phonograph (ancestor of the record player), the first device to reproduce sound, was only invented in the 1870s.

Recording sound

Most of the programmes on television and radio today are recorded before they are broadcast. Before sounds can be recorded, a microphone changes them into electric signals. These signals change the strength of the magnetic field produced by a record/play head in a tape recorder. As the tape passes the head, the changing magnetic field affects magnetic particles in the tape. The particles move to line up with the field. When the tape is wound back and played, the changing patterns of magnetic particles in the tape pass in front of the record/play head again. This time they produce tiny electrical signals in the head. They are amplified and changed back into sounds by a loudspeaker.

Television pictures

Television pictures can also be recorded on magnetic tape. Because a television picture contains much more information than the sounds that go with it, a different recording method is needed. Inside a video recorder, at least two record/play heads are fixed to a metal drum that can spin at high speed. The tape travels in one direction. The drum, set at an angle to the tape, spins in the opposite direction. Making recordings at an angle across the width of the tape in this way enables much more information to be stored on the tape. Sound and pictures are recorded together on the same tape.

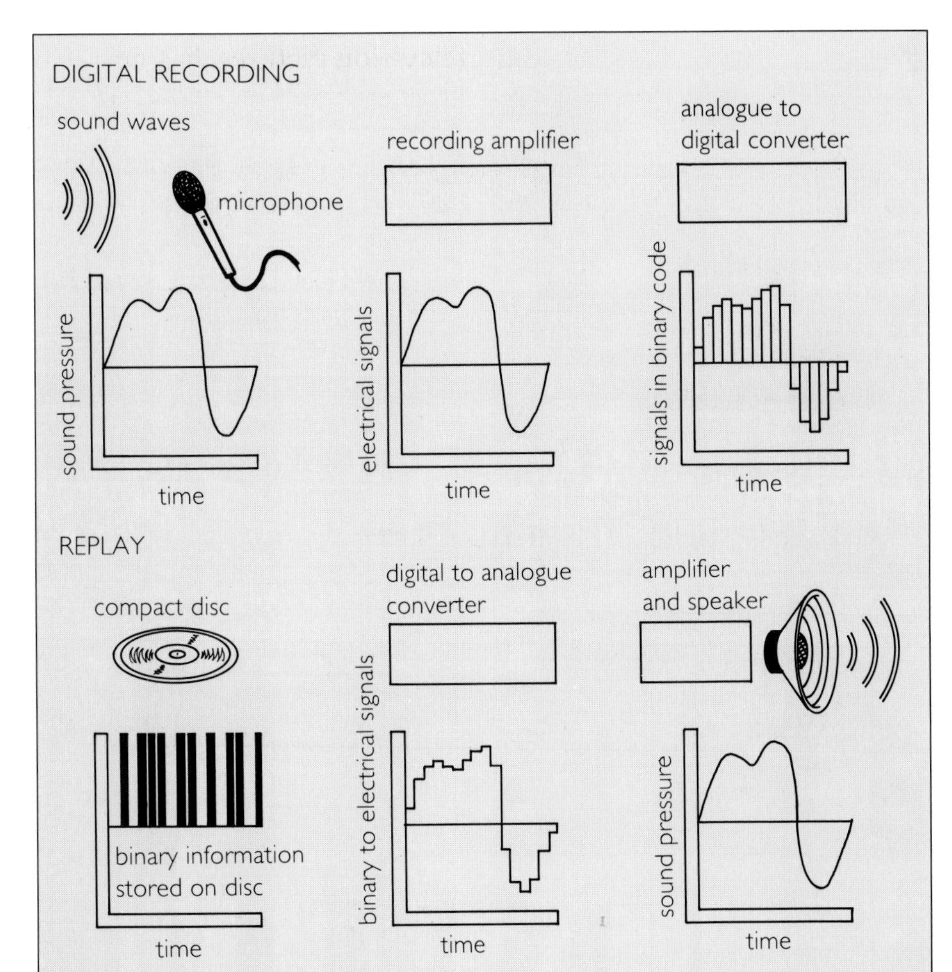

HOW A LOUDSPEAKER WORKS

We cannot hear electric currents, so we need a way of changing the electric signals inside radios, television sets and tape players into sounds that we *can* hear. This is done by a loudspeaker.

Electric currents from a radio (for example) are fed into a coil of wire inside a loudspeaker. The coil is positioned inside a magnet at the back of the loudspeaker. When the strength of the current flowing through the coil changes, the magnetic field surrounding it makes the coil move. The coil is attached to a cone made from paper or plastic. The vibrating coil makes the cone vibrate too, and this in turn makes the air vibrate. The pressure waves produced in this way travel out from the cone and vibrate the ear drums of the listener. The vibrations in the ear drums are registered by the brain as sound.

Left: *How analogue sound signals are converted to digital electrical signals and back again in a hi-fi sound system.*

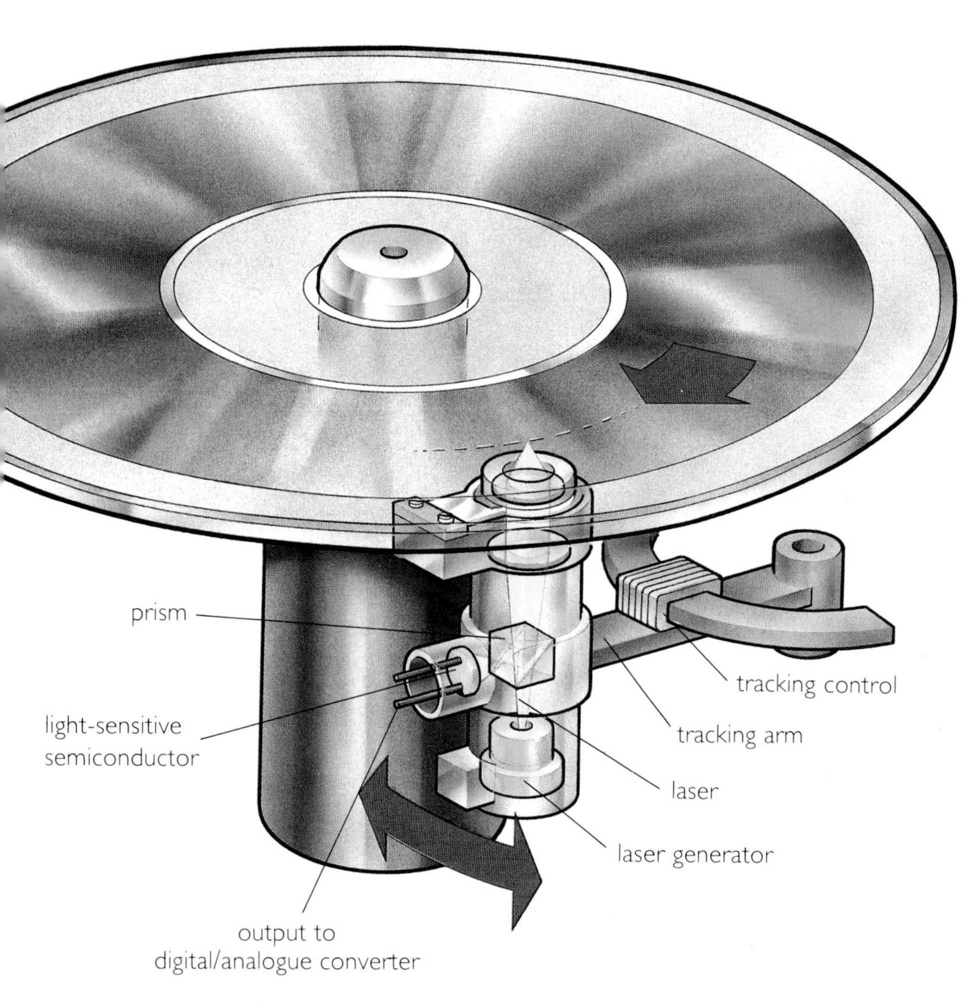

Above: *The playback laser unit on a compact disc player. The playing surface is on the underside of the disc.*

Below: *A carrier radio wave and television signals and how they are combined to form modulated waves.*

Records and discs

Sounds and pictures can also be recorded on discs or records. When making an LP (long-playing record), electrical signals from a microphone make a stylus vibrate on the surface of a rotating wax disc as it cuts a groove. The wax 'master' disc is coated with metal to strengthen it, and thousands of copies can then be made from it by pressing it into a blank disc of plastic. When the disc is played, a stylus resting in the groove vibrates as the disc turns. Its movements are changed into an electric current, which is amplified and changed into sounds by a loudspeaker.

A newer type of disc, which can record sound *and* television pictures, has no grooves at all. Instead of a stylus, it has a tiny laser. The invisible infra-red beam of the laser is reflected by the disc's metallic coating, and the reflections recreate the sounds and pictures stored on the disc.

Broadcasting

When a recorded programme is to be broadcast, the electrical signals on the tape are transmitted along with a high-frequency radio signal called a carrier wave. This enables programmes to be broadcast to radio and television receivers over a wide area (depending on the power of the transmitter).

Sound waves need air to carry them (if you shout in a vacuum, no one will hear you), but radio waves can travel through empty space. Radio is therefore used to communicate with spacecraft.

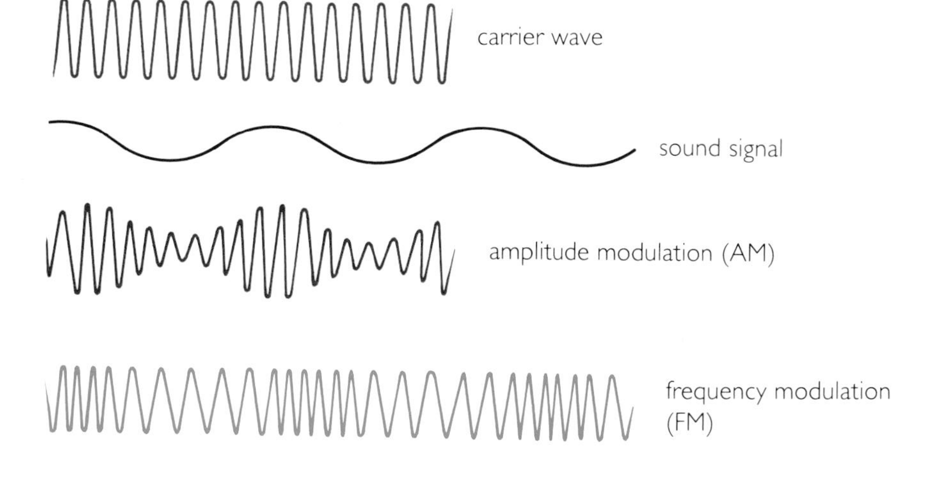

THE IMPOSSIBLE RADIO SIGNAL

Radio waves were unknown 100 years ago, although they had been predicted by a famous scientist, James Clerk Maxwell, in 1864. No one managed to generate and transmit such waves until 1886, when Heinrich Hertz showed that they obeyed the same laws as light. He couldn't think of any use for them, however!

The Italian, Marconi, was one of the first to transmit messages (in Morse code) by radio waves, in about 1895. Progress was rapid. In 1901 Marconi successfully transmitted a radio signal across the Atlantic Ocean. This was, in theory, impossible, because if radio waves behaved like light waves they should not follow the curve of the Earth but continue on a straight line into space. The answer was the ionization layer, which reflects radio waves back to Earth. This was suspected, but not finally proved until the 1920s.

Wavelengths

Invisible radio and television signals stream around us all the time – not only radio and television programmes, but also police radio messages, signals from satellites in space and many others. We decide which signals we want to receive by our choice of aerial and receiver.

A radio signal is, like visible light, a wave-like combination of electric and magnetic fields, called an electromagnetic wave. Different radio and television signals have waves of different sizes (different wavelengths). If a metal aerial is held in the path of a radio signal, the signal's electrical and magnetic fields are strong enough to move electrons in the rod. If the length of the aerial is chosen to match the size of the waves, this effect is strengthened. The electrical changes in the aerial vary in step with the radio signal causing them. They are amplified in the receiver, which also selects the precise signals required and converts them into sounds and pictures.

Below: *Micro- and short-wave radio signals can travel furthest through the Earth's atmosphere.*

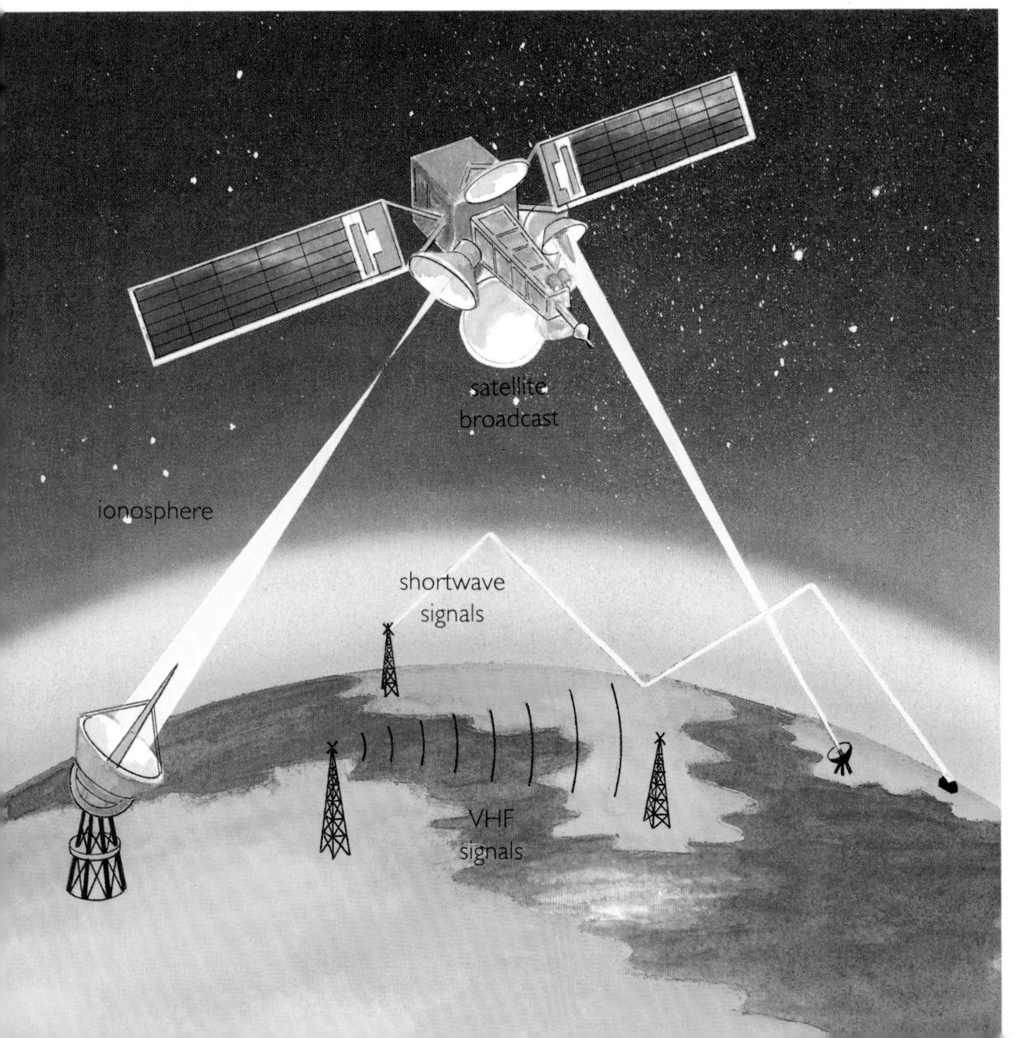

Inside a television set

When a television signal is routed into a television receiver, the sound and picture parts of the signal are separated. The sound signal is amplified and converted into sound again by a loudspeaker. The picture signal activates three electron guns at the back of the tube. They fire electrons at the front of the tube, the screen. The electron beams move down the screen, while also sweeping from side to side. At the bottom, they flip up to the top and start again. This happens 50 times a second producing 25 pictures every second.

The screen is covered with fine vertical stripes of three different chemicals called phosphors. When struck by electrons, they glow in three different colours: red, green and blue. By varying the strength of the electron beams, the brightness of the picture is controlled. By changing the mixture of red-, green- and blue-glowing phosphors, the colour of the picture is altered.

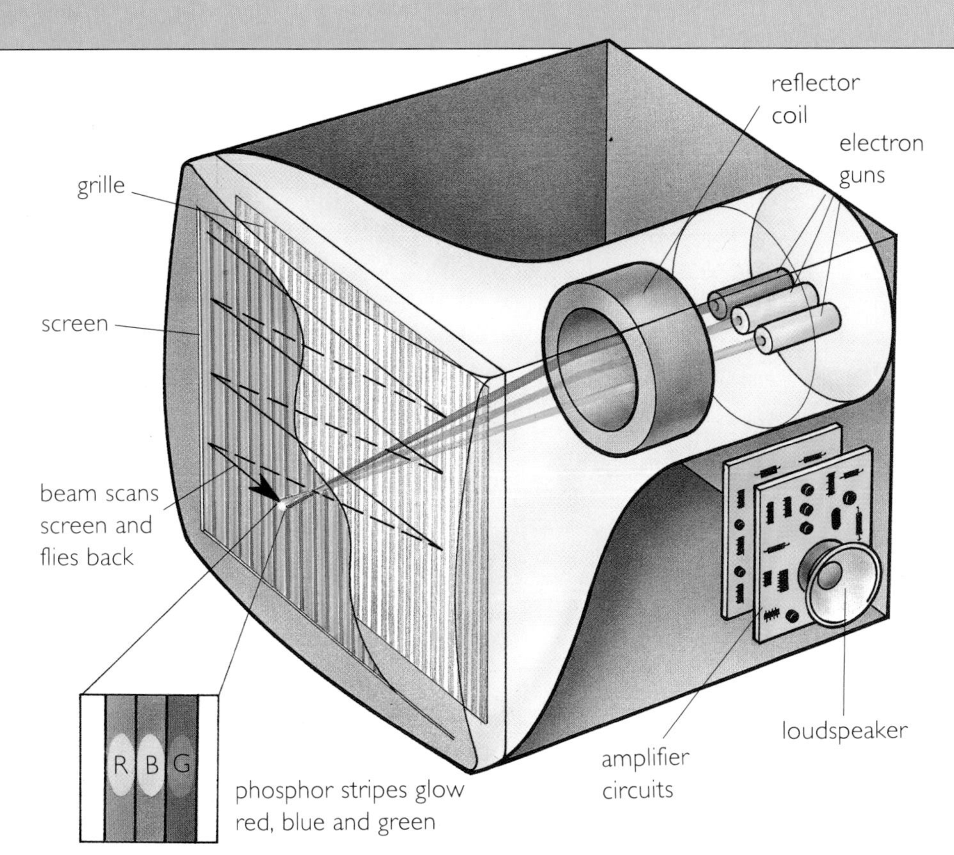

Above: *Inside a colour television tube showing the electron guns which make red, blue and green dots on the phosphor screen.*

Home video

When a video tape is played in a home video recorder, the recorder produces signals very like the signals from a television transmitter. This enables the programme recorded on the tape to be shown on an ordinary television set.

Home video equipment is being refined all the time. A few years ago video cameras and recorders were large, heavy, instruments. Today they are combined in a single, lightweight machine called a camcorder (from *cam*era-re*corder*).

Below: *Inside a camcorder showing the optical and magnetic recording systems.*

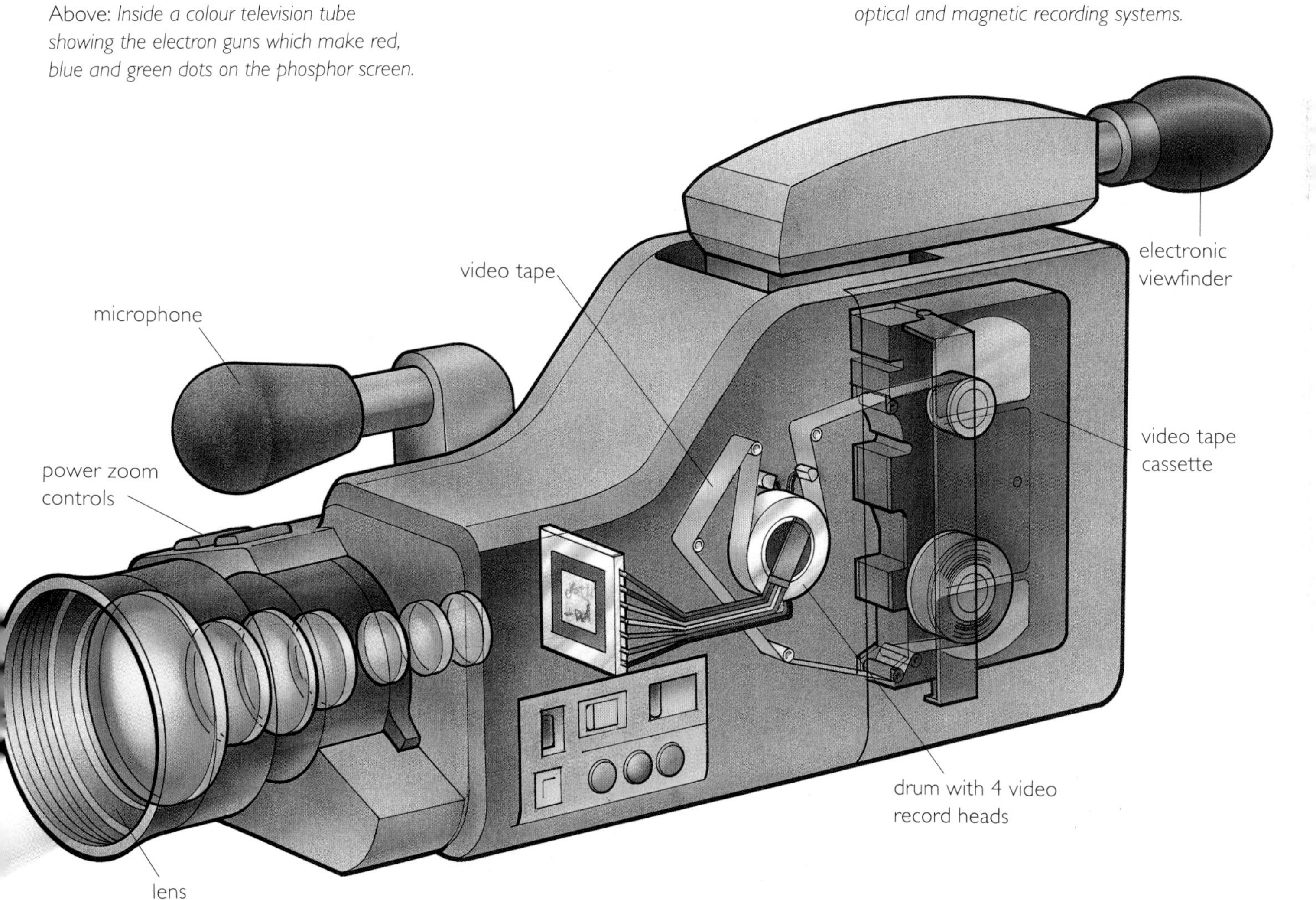

Telephone and Telex

The telephone has transformed our world since it was invented in 1876 by Alexander Graham Bell. Without the instant communication between people and businesses that the telephone network permits, life would be very different.

In its early years, the telephone enabled only a few people to talk to each other over long distances. Cables laid across the Atlantic Ocean provided a few dozen telephone circuits between Britain and the USA. Satellites have provided many thousands more circuits and now anyone can make a telephone call to almost anywhere else in the world.

Digital networks

Computers and digital switching equipment control the worldwide communications network. Telephone calls are still transmitted as 'analogue' waves, but the digital system is taking over in many countries. Digital signals consist of a series of pulses, which can be handled easily by digital equipment (such as computers). Any signal that is to be sent by digital telephone link must be converted into the same form by a process called digitization. To digitize a human voice, for example, 8,000 samples of the voice are taken every second. Each sample is given a number. The voice becomes a series of numbers and then a series of electrical pulses which computers can handle. These are sent along the telephone line and converted back to a voice at the other end. Digital transmission is more reliable than analogue. It also enables different forms of information to be transmitted through the same network, including human voices, music, computer data, telex, telegraph, television and radio.

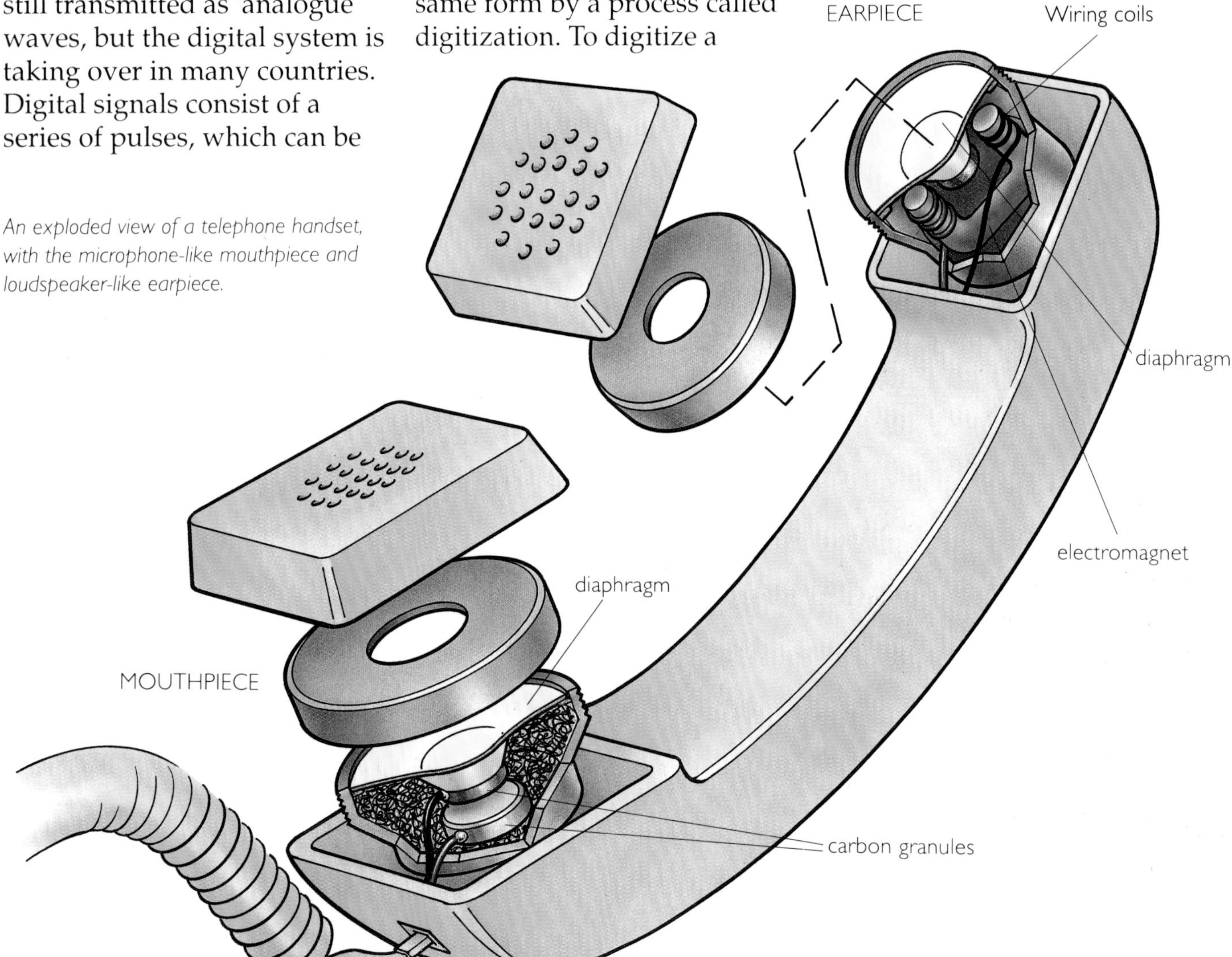

An exploded view of a telephone handset, with the microphone-like mouthpiece and loudspeaker-like earpiece.

MOBILE TELEPHONES

As modern telephones use the same digital electronics as computers, they benefit from the same improvements, especially in miniaturization, as computers. Very small radio transmitters and receivers can now also be made, and when they are combined, the result is a mobile telephone.

One type of mobile phone can be used only within a few metres of its base station, allowing the user to move about a house or office while carrying on a conversation.

A second is self-contained and has a more powerful radio transmitter. It relies on a nationwide network of transmitters and receivers called cell stations. During a call, the mobile telephone is connected with the network by a short-range radio link to the nearest cell station. If the caller moves out of that station's range, the next cell station takes over. This is particularly useful for people making calls from cars.

There is a third type of mobile telephone, even smaller than the last because it uses a very low-power transmitter. A caller has to find one of the thousands of base stations that are situated in public places; calls can only be made within 100m (about 300ft) of a base station.

A mobile telephone has a push-button keypad for selecting numbers and an aerial to pick up the radio signals.

Telex and 'fax'

The telex service, which began in 1932, provides a way of sending written messages quickly and reliably by telephone. The message is typed into a telex terminal which looks like a bulky typewriter. The telex number of the receiver is dialled and the message transmitted. At its destination the message is printed.

Although telex is still very popular it is being replaced by other services, such as facsimile transmission or 'fax'. A fax machine can convert any written or printed material into a code that is transmitted by telephone. Pictures, drawings, text and even handwritten messages can all be sent by fax.

Right: *Facsimile (fax) machines transmit and receive written or printed information via ordinary telephone lines.*

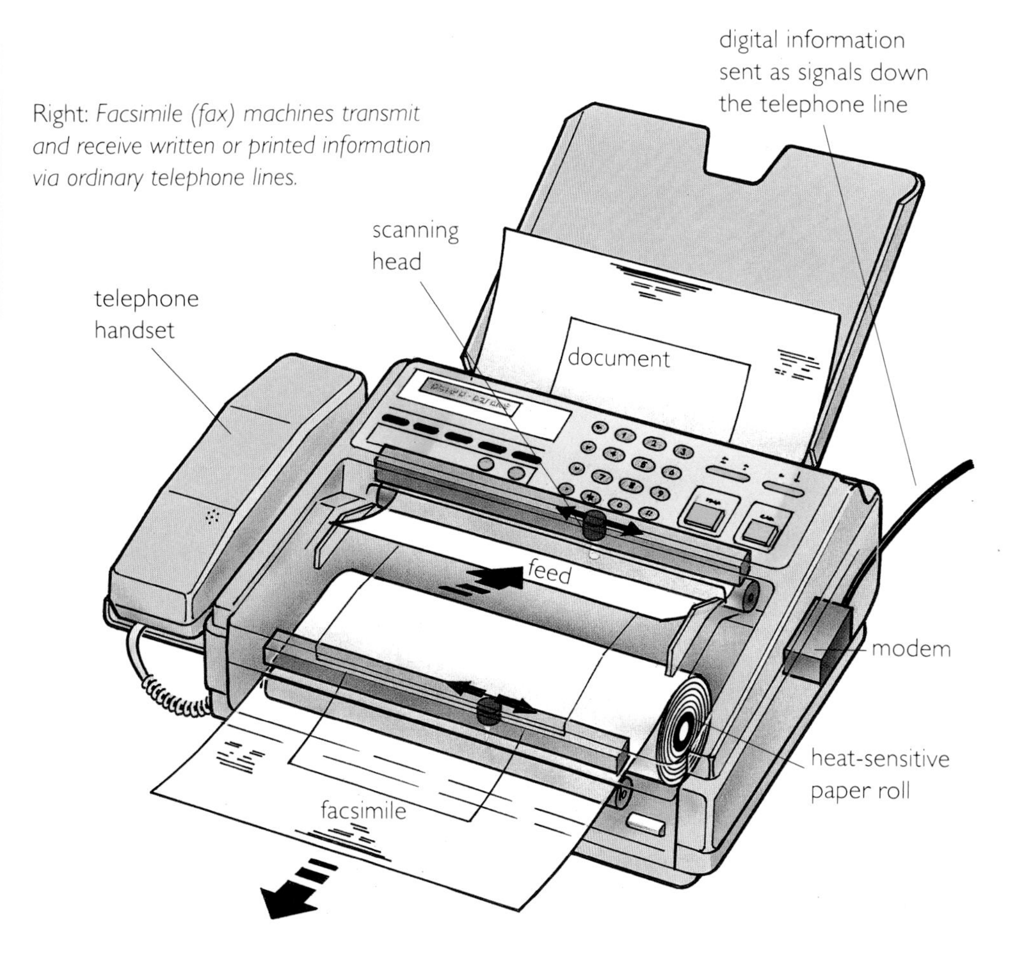

Optical fibres

Telephone cable used to be made from metal wire, but that is being replaced by strands of glass called optical fibres. Voices and computer data are converted to flashing beams of intense light from a tiny laser, which travel along the glass fibres. An optical fibre as thin as a hair can carry many more telephone calls (and more reliably) than a thick metal wire.

Chips and Computers

Computers affect almost every aspect of our society. Among many other things, computers store details of our education and employment records, help to predict the weather, control some car engines and household appliances such as washing machines and video recorders, and control robots that make other machines.

A computer is a machine that takes in information, stores it in its memory, processes it according to a set of instructions called a program and then sends the results to an output device such as a television screen or a printer. The machine itself is called hardware and the programs that make it do things are called software. Each is useless without the other.

Mechanical computers with motorized shafts and gear wheels were built in the 1930s to speed up arithmetic calculations. They were replaced by the first electronic computers, using components called valves – large glass bulbs similar to light bulbs. The valves controlled electric currents flowing through the computer from input to output.

Transistors and chips

A major breakthrough in computer design came with the invention of the transistor in 1948 and, later, the miniaturization of electronic components.

Complete electronic circuits containing hundreds of thousands of transistors can now be constructed on a piece of silicon crystal the size of a thumbnail. These integrated circuits, commonly called chips, enabled computers to be made smaller, cheaper and more reliable.

In 1971 a new type of chip called a microprocessor was introduced, which offered all the central processing functions of a computer on a single chip. It led to a further miniaturization of computers.

Various types of device for each of the main components of a computer system.

INPUT UNITS

joystick

light pen

mouse

graphic tablet

keyboard

MEMORY AND STORAGE UNITS

floppy disk

cassette

memory chip

CENTRAL PROCESSING UNIT

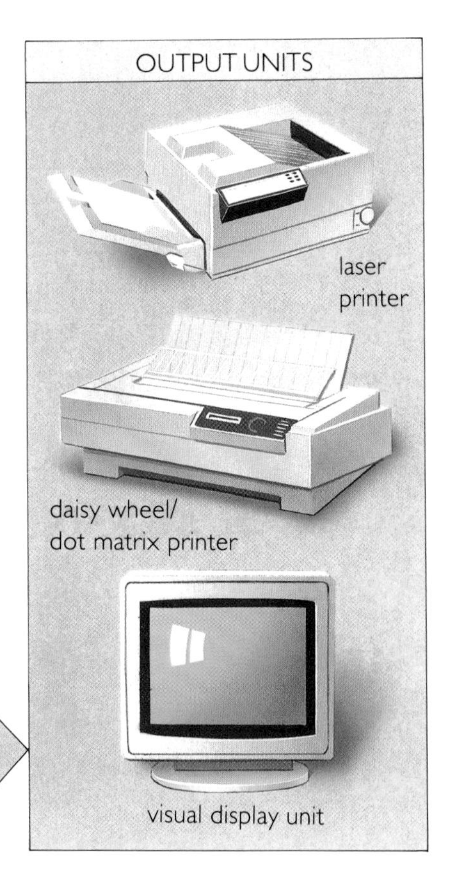

As lots of computers used the same type of microprocessor, they could all be programmed using the same 'language' of instructions. Computers no longer had to be programmed and operated by teams of specially trained people. They could now be operated by ordinary people using programs bought from software companies.

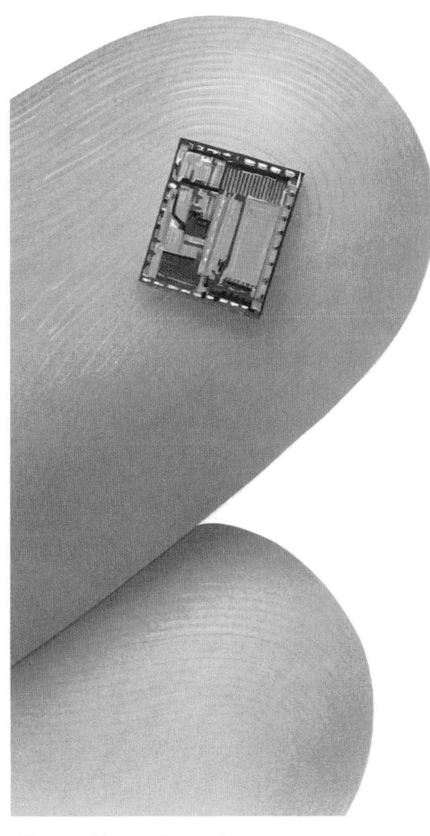

Above: *Each silicon chip contains more than 20,000 electrical components such as switches and resistors.*

SUPERCOMPUTERS

However quickly computers work, it is never fast enough for some purposes, such as weather forecasting and chip design. Some computer manufacturers specialize in designing and making the most powerful computers possible.

The Cray-2 is an example of one of these supercomputers. It has four identical central processing units (CPUs), each capable of doing 1,700 million calculations per second. The work done by a typical office desk-top computer in ten days could be done by the Cray-2 in one minute. The Cray-2 is built in a circular shape so that signals have to travel the least possible distance between any two parts of the computer.

One of the problems with cramming so much computing power into a small space is that, as the chips generate heat, the temperature inside the computer rises. If the excess heat is not carried away the computer will eventually break down. The Cray-2's 240,000 chips are housed in tanks with a cooled liquid circulating in contact with the chips.

Computer applications

All computers work by adding numbers together, but they do it incredibly quickly, making millions of calculations per second. They work so quickly that any sort of information can be converted into numbers, processed by a computer and turned back into its original or another form. For example, a photograph can be converted into a pattern of dots and each dot given a number to represent its brightness and colour. This is called digitization. Once the numbers are loaded into a computer's memory, they can be processed to change the colours in the picture, increase its contrast, improve its clarity or add extra text or symbols. The resulting pattern of numbers is then changed back into another picture. The numbers processed by the computer could equally well represent sounds (music or speech), printed text or mathematical equations.

Right: *The memory unit of a supercomputer, with tall cooling units to prevent the device overheating.*

Networks and Databases

Computer technology has improved international communications, and improved communications have in their turn led to the development of complicated computer networks. It doesn't matter to a computer whether the data it receives comes from its own keyboard or from another computer. Two computers in the same room can communicate via a connecting cable. Computers thousands of kilometres apart, perhaps in different countries, can communicate by telephone. When several computers are connected together in this way, they form a network.

A small network might consist of two or three computers in an office linked by cable so that they can exchange information and perhaps share a single printer. The largest networks link computers in different countries by satellite.

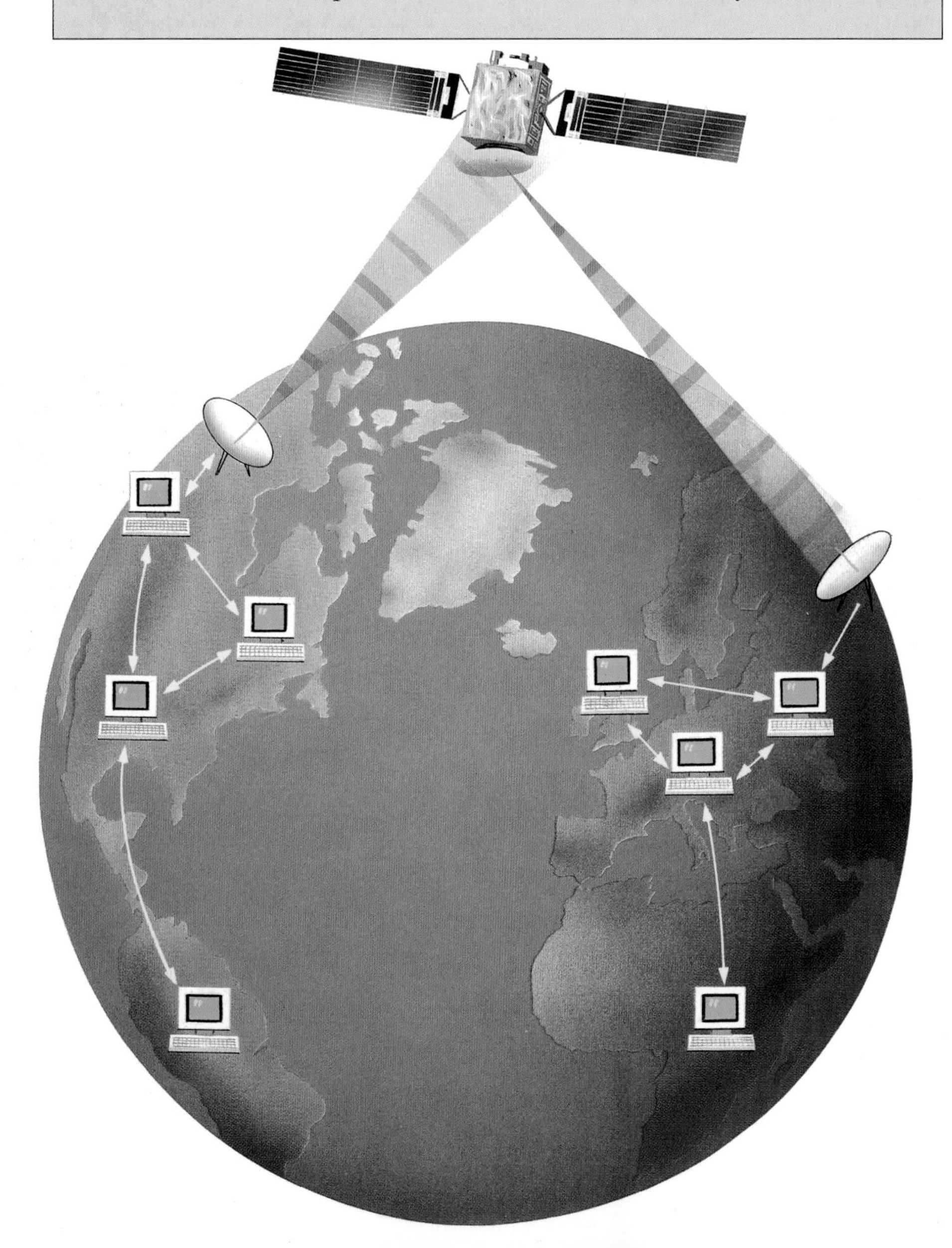

The use of networks
Some businesses rely heavily on computer networks. Financial institutions like banks now depend on computer networks to store and distribute information about the world's stock markets. In some shops, when a customer pays with a credit card, the card is 'wiped' through a slot in a card reader. Information about the card and its owner is transferred from a magnetic strip on the card to the credit card company's computer system by telephone. This checks that the card has not been reported stolen and that the owner is not spending more than his or her card allows. After these checks the correct amount is charged to the card account.

Many banks now have cash dispensers. To use one, the customer inserts a card into the machine and keys in a unique code number, a personal identification or PIN number. The information stored in the card's magnetic strip and the code number are transmitted to a central bank computer. If the two agree, the customer is allowed to go ahead and withdraw some cash.

Left: *Computer data can be transmitted worldwide via telephone communications links. These include cables and microwave radio links using satellites in fixed positions above the Earth (in geostationary orbit).*

Above: *A 'bank' of memory disc and tape units for a main frame computer. Each unit can hold the equivalent of several books of data.*

Databases

The ability of computers to communicate with each other means that information in one computer's memory can be transferred into another computer's memory, no matter how far apart they are. This feature is useful in a system called a database.

A database is a store of information in a form that a computer can handle. The information is usually stored on magnetic discs. A computer user in Britain, for example, could telephone a database in California and request information by typing questions on his or her keyboard. If the information is held in the database, it is transferred to the inquirer's computer by telephone, and it appears on his screen.

Some databases can be used by anyone with a computer and a device called a modem to link it to a telephone line. Others, such as military databases, are restricted to an authorized group of users.

PORTABLE COMPUTING

Chip manufacturers are continually finding new ways of making chips that contain more and more electronic components. The first electronic computers contained several hundred thousand components, each the size of a small light bulb, and occupied 140 sq m (1,500 sq ft) of floor area. Now, a single chip measuring 40mm by 20mm (1.5in by 0.8in) may contain just as many components, each microscopically small. A modern computer containing a few dozen chips is many times more powerful and faster than its giant ancestors. It also requires much less power.

Some computers are designed to be operated by batteries, for use by businessmen, journalists and others who sometimes work away from mains power supplies. If information stored in a computer has to be sent back to the office, the computer can be connected to an ordinary telephone with a modem. This converts the computer's data into tones (musical notes) that can be sent along a telephone line to another telephone, modem and computer almost anywhere in the world.

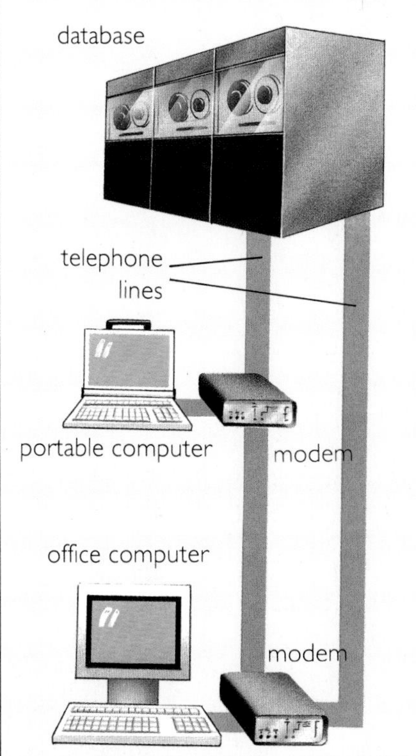

References

AI (Artificial Intelligence) The use of computers and very complex programs to simulate intelligent behaviour.

Analogue Composed of a continuously varying signal: an analogue voltage swings up and down in step with whatever it represents – a voice on a microphone cable, for example. *See also* **Digital**.

ASA *See* **ISO**.

ASCII (American Standard Code for Information Interchange) An internationally accepted way of converting characters such as letters and numbers into the 'binary' signals that a computer uses.

Babbage, Charles (1792–1871) British mathematician, who proposed building calculating machines which could be programmed. However, engineering standards were not good enough and the machine was not built.

Baird, John Logie (1888–1946) Scottish television pioneer, who demonstrated the first working television system in 1925.

Bell, Alexander Graham (1847–1922) Scottish–US inventor, who invented the telephone in Boston, Massachusetts, in 1876.

Binary A counting system based on only two numbers, zero and one.

Bug A fault in a computer program.

Cathode ray tube The main part of a television receiver, consisting of a cone-shaped glass tube. Electron guns in the neck of the tube fire electrons at the screen, at the other end of the tube.

Caxton, William (about 1422–91) The first English printer, who set up his press in Westminster in 1477.

Chip The popular name for an integrated circuit.

Clerk Maxwell, James (1831–79) Scottish physicist, who predicted the existence of electromagnetic waves.

Compact disc A disc on which music or computer data is stored as a pattern of pits in the disc's mirror-like coating. The pattern is detected by reflecting a laser beam off the disc. The pits do not reflect the beam. The CD player turns the pit pattern back into music or computer data.

Daguerreotype An early form of photograph, invented by a Frenchman, Louis Daguerre, about 1839.

Digital In computers, a pattern of electronic pulses representing data or information. Digital also means numbers, or figures, as in 'digital watch'. *See also* **Analogue**.

Floppy disc A flexible plastic disc on which computer data is stored.

Fox Talbot, William (1800–77) British inventor of the first negative-positive photographic process, called the calotype, in the 1830s.

Gutenburg, Johannes (1400–68) German printer who first used movable type about 1440.

Hacker A person who obtains unauthorized access to computer data by breaking the computer's security codes.

Hard copy Another name for computer print-out: the output of a printer connected to a computer.

Hard disc A rigid disc used to store computer data. Hard discs can store much more data than floppy discs, but they require more careful handling, avoiding contact with dust.

Hertz, Heinrich (1857–94) German physicist, who confirmed Clerk Maxwell's prediction by discovering electromagnetic (radio) waves, in 1887.

ISO (International Standards Organization) In photography, ISO followed by a number indicates the speed or sensitivity of a film. It is the same as ASA.

Microprocessor A computer's central processor unit on a single chip.

Modem A device that links a computer to a telephone so that data can be transmitted by telephone, formed from the words MOdulator-DEModulator.

Mouse A small box connected to a computer by cable. When the mouse is moved across a desk top, rollers underneath it register its direction and distance of travel. These are transmitted to the computer and a pointer on the screen moves with the mouse. By moving it around and 'clicking' switches on it, the mouse can be used to select options and move things around on the screen.

Niépce, Joseph Nicéphore (1765–1833) French pioneer of photography, who first produced a photograph on metal.

RAM (Random Access Memory) The part of the computer's memory that contains the programs and data that it is currently using. The contents of RAM disappear when the computer's power is switched off.

ROM (Read Only Memory) The part of a computer's memory where programs and data are permanently stored. Programs in ROM may control how the computer displays data or how it communicates with printers, for example.

Silicon chip The popular name for a computer chip, especially a microprocessor.

Transistor A device which controls the flow of an electric current, used as an amplifier in radios and televisions, developed in 1948.

VCR (Video Cassette Recorder) A machine for recording television programmes and images from a video camera.

Zoetrope A device which creates the illusion of moving pictures. A sequence of pictures are pasted in a strip on the inside of a drum or cylinder and, as the drum spins, the observer watches through a slit.

Index

Page references to illustrations are shown in *italic* type.